LABOR LAW AND INDUSTRIAL RELATIONS

LABOR LAW AND INDUSTRIAL RELATIONS

Marko Nikolić

SOCIETY Publishing

www.societypublishing.com

Labor Law and Industrial Relations

Marko Nikolić

Society Publishing
224 Shoreacres Road
Burlington, ON L7L 2H2
Canada
www.societypublishing.com
Email: orders@arclereducation.com

ISBN: 978-1-77469-854-9 (Hardcover)

Society Publishing publishes wide variety of books and eBooks. For more information about Society Publishing and its products, visit our website at www.societypublishing.com.

ABOUT THE AUTHOR

Marko obtained his Master's degree from the University of Belgrade - Faculty of Law in 2014. He specialized in Criminal Law, Family Law, and Environmental Law. He spent his Master's year studying international child abduction in the modern world. He was employed in the Ministry of Defense's Legal Department and was also working as a legal secretary in numerous educational institutions. His freelance engagements are including more than 40 long-term clients and he also established a consulting agency in 2021. He is the head of the sector in a company specializing in intellectual property and his focus is in trademarking. In addition to professional literature editing, he published a novel on the subject of history and mythology in 2020. Out of office his main focus are environmental and ecological issues.

TABLE OF CONTENTS

LIST OF FIGURES

LIST OF ABBREVIATIONS

ACTU	Australian Council of Trade Unions
ADR	Alternative Dispute Resolution
AI	Artificial Intelligence
ALMPs	Active Labor Market Policies
AMCU	Association of Mineworkers & Construction Union
BLS	Bureau of Labor Statistics
CBAs	Collective Bargaining Agreements
CRT	Critical Race Theory
EU	European Union
GDP	Gross Domestic Product
HDI	Human Development Index
IFAs	International Framework Agreements
ILO	International Labor Organization
IMF	International Monetary Fund
LRA	Labor Relations Act
NAFTA	North American Free Trade Agreement
NCLP	National Child Labor Project
NLRA	National Labor Relations Act
NUM	National Union of Mineworkers
RMT	Rail Maritime and Transport Union
UN	United Nations
WHO	World Health Organization

PREFACE

There is growing interest in industrial relations beyond the simplistic notions of pro and anti-trade unionism. This is a multidisciplinary subject that considers the various ways in which employers, employees, and the community negotiate and operationalize working conditions. Increasingly, there is recognition of the complexity of industrial relations where multiple actors have an interest in proceedings and could potentially undo some of the measures taken if they are not given their due consideration. The state is a major stakeholder since employment ensures stability, productivity, and income tax revenues that are necessary for a functional and stable environment. Hence, it is no longer the case that the state can adopt a hands-off approach to industrial relations.

Indeed, there are political parties and governments that are specifically formed based on fighting for the rights of workers or industrialists. However, the strict divide that was assumed four decades ago may no longer hold true. For instance, leftist governments are now aware of the difficulties that they face if they are perceived to be anti-business even as they form strong alliances with trade unions. Additionally, rightwing governments only know too well the devastating impact of industrial action if they participate in or are perceived to be treating workers with disrespect. We are also collectively questioning the power and abuses of trade union leaders. For instance, the USA has passed the so-called "right to work" measures which protect those employees who may not wish to join a trade union.

Trade unions have also changed the ways in which they engage with the government, seeing it more as a partnership than an adversarial engagement. This is based on the realization that a functional economy is necessary for people to get good paying jobs. There have been examples of economic collapse that has been precipitated by inflexible negotiations by trade union leaders. In fact, some politicians have reacted with draconian responses when it has become clear that trade unions are holding the state as hostages. The community itself has an interest in securing safe and reliable jobs as well as avoiding some of the after-effects of industrial strife.

That multiplicity of these interest groups and the intersectionality of their concerns means that industrial relations are a pertinent topic to consider currently. The book takes a broader view of industrial relations by connecting it to various facets of community life. In doing so, this book creates a collage of networks that foster productivity and harmony in communities. After all, many people spend a significant part of their lives at work. It would be foolhardy to allow that significant part of life to be spent in misery and strife. The book is not aimed at any specific discipline given the peripatetic nature of the issues being addressed. So, a historian, economist, and manager may have interest in this book.

The richness of the topic implies that this is nothing more than a starting point. There is much to consider and explore as we delve into the world of work. However, the book will raise certain key points that can be used as a basis for further exploration of this pertinent topic. Moreover, the book explicitly acknowledges the fact that what we know may be nothing more than a fraction of what is yet to be discovered. I hope you enjoy the book.

CHAPTER 1

Introduction to Industrial Relations

Contents

The opening chapter of this book introduces the notion of industrial relations. We started by defining an employment contract. This then leads to a delineation of the roles and responsibilities that emanate from such a contract with specific reference to employers and employees. The chapter considers the role and perspective of businesspeople and industrialists when an employment contract is being fashioned and delivered. Another important stakeholder that is considered in this chapter is the state or government. Strikingly, all these dynamics of industrial relations begin and end with an employment contract.

1.1. WHAT IS AN EMPLOYMENT CONTRACT

Employment contracts are a critical component of the employment relationship, and their terms can vary significantly depending on the jurisdiction in which they are created (de Luna, 2022; De Prins et al., 2020; de Vaate, 2021; Demougin et al., 2019; Desai & Randeria, 2020). In this section post, we will compare and contrast different conceptualizations of employment contracts in diverse jurisdictions to better understand how these agreements may differ from one another. Figure 1.1 highlights the key components of an employment contract.

Figure 1.1. *Components of the employment contract.*

Source: Dreamstime.

In many countries, an employment contract is considered to be a legally binding agreement between an employer and employee that outlines the rights and obligations of each party (Gasparri, 2021; Gasparri et al., 2019; Gasparri & Tassinari, 2020; Gavin, 2022; Giannakopoulos & Laliotis, 2020). Generally speaking, these agreements include details such as job duties, salary or wages, benefits packages (if applicable), termination procedures, dispute resolution processes, confidentiality clauses (if applicable), and related items. Depending on the jurisdiction in which it is created however, there may be additional provisions included within an employment contract that reflect local laws or customs.

For example, some jurisdictions require employers to provide employees with certain types of insurance coverage while others do not; similarly some countries have specific rules regarding overtime pay or vacation time that must be included in any written agreement between employer and employee (Lukacova et al., 2022; Lyddon, 2021; Lyutov, 2022; MacKenzie & Lucio, 2019; Madimutsa; Mahas-Demydas & Rudnytska, 2019). Additionally certain jurisdictions may also impose restrictions on non-compete clauses or other contractual limitations related to intellectual property rights – something that would not necessarily apply elsewhere. It is important for both employers and employees alike to familiarize themselves with local labor laws when negotiating an employment contract so as to ensure compliance with all relevant regulations.

Failure to do so could result in costly legal disputes down the line should either party feel aggrieved by any aspect of their agreement (Kolling & Schnabel, 2022; Kowalewska, 2020; Kupec et al., 2022; Lamare & Budd, 2022; Lansbury, 2021; Larsson, 2020). Furthermore, it is also worth noting that even if two parties agree upon particular terms verbally rather than through a written document – such as agreeing upon a set wage rate without signing anything – those verbal commitments still constitute legally binding obligations under most circumstances unless otherwise specified by law (e.g., minimum wage requirements). It is clear that although there are common elements shared across all forms of employment contracts regardless of jurisdiction – such as outlining job duties and compensation arrangements – there can still be significant differences based on where exactly those agreements are being made due to varying local labor laws or customs governing them accordingly.

As such both employers and employees should take care when entering into any type of contractual arrangement so as not only protect their own interests but also comply with all relevant regulations (Foster et al., 2021; Franceschini, 2020; Freedland & Dhorajiwala, 2019; Fuchs et al., 2019; Galik et al., 2022). Employment contracts are an essential part of any employment relationship, providing both employers and employees with a legally binding agreement that outlines the terms and conditions of their working arrangement. It is important to note however that not all elements of these agreements will be universal across different jurisdictions – such as minimum wage requirements or overtime pay regulations – so it is always worth taking the time to critically evaluate each component before signing anything. Figure 1.2 is an example of a basic employment contract.

EMPLOYMENT CONTRACT AGREEMENT

PARTIES

- This Employment Contract Agreement (hereinafter referred to as the **"Agreement"**) is entered into on ______________ (the **"Effective Date"**), by and between ______________________, with an address of ______________ (hereinafter referred to as the **"Employer"**), and ______________, with an address of ______________ (hereinafter referred to as the **"Employee"**) (collectively referred to as the **"Parties"**).

DUTIES AND RESPONSIBILITIES

- During the employment period, the Employee shall have the responsibility to perform the following duties:

1. ______________________________
2. ______________________________
3. ______________________________
4. ______________________________
5. ______________________________
6. ______________________________
7. ______________________________
8. ______________________________
9. ______________________________
10. ______________________________

- The Parties agree that any responsibilities provided in this Agreement may not be assigned to any other party unless both parties agree to the assignment in writing.

PAY AND COMPENSATION

Figure 1.2. *Simple employment agreement contract.*

Source: Signaturely.

At its core, an employment contract should provide details on job duties, compensation arrangements (including wages/salaries), benefits packages (if applicable) and other relevant information pertaining to the role in question (Hoffrogge, 2019; Howell, 2019, 2021; Hungler, 2022; Ilsoe & Soderqvist; Jarota, 2022; Jha & Singh, 2019). Additionally, they may also include clauses outlining disciplinary procedures for when either party fails to meet their obligations under the agreement or if there are any disputes between them which need resolving. This can help ensure that everyone involved understands what is expected from them while also providing a means by which either side can seek redress should they feel aggrieved by any aspect of their agreement.

In addition to this, many countries have specific labor laws governing certain aspects of employment contracts too – such as those relating to parental leave entitlements or health and safety standards (Smith, 2019; Solaiman; Stanev, 2019; Stanford, 2021; Stapley, 2021; Stevis, 2022; Svec et al., 2021; Tavora, 2019). Therefore, it is important for both parties involved in these agreements to familiarize themselves with local legislation prior to entering into any type of contractual arrangement. Furthermore, some jurisdictions may even require certain documents or forms be completed before work begins. Failure to do so could result in hefty fines being imposed upon either employer or employee.

It is worth noting that although most employment contracts will contain provisions allowing for termination without cause at any time (usually subject only giving reasonable notice period beforehand); there still remains legal recourse available should either party feel aggrieved by any aspect of their agreement (Nicklich & Helfen, 2019; Novitz & Andrijasevic, 2020; Nowak, 2021; Nurlinah et al., 2021; O'Keeffe & Papadopoulos, 2021). Although there are common elements shared across all forms of employment contracts regardless of jurisdiction – such as outlining job duties and compensation arrangements – there can still be significant differences based on where exactly those agreements are being made due to varying local labor laws or customs governing them accordingly (Tu et al., 2022; Velluti, 2022; Vinichenko et al., 2020; Vulkan & Larsson, 2019; Walker, 2020; Walters & Wadsworth, 2020). As such both employers and employees should take care when entering into any type of contractual arrangement so as not only protect their own interests but also comply with all relevant regulations at hand. Employment contracts are an important part of the modern working environment, providing both employers and employees with a legally binding agreement that outlines their respective rights and obligations. This is especially true in jurisdictions where labor laws are more stringent or complex than others, as it allows for greater clarity between the two parties involved when it comes to matters such as job duties, compensation arrangements, termination procedures and similar ideas.

At the same time however, there can be certain limitations associated with employment contracts depending on where they are being made – for example, some countries may not recognize certain clauses within them due to local regulations or customs governing them accordingly (Schofield-Georgeson, 2022; Schofield-Georgeson & Rawling, 2020; Schuessler et al., 2019; Schuhrke, 2019). As such it is important for both employers and employees alike to familiarize themselves with any relevant laws before entering into any contractual arrangement so as to ensure that all parties involved understand what exactly they have agreed upon and how those terms will be enforced should either side fail to comply. When it comes to different job categories, the risks, and benefits of using employment contracts can vary significantly depending on the nature of the work being done.

For instance, in a professional setting such as a law firm or accounting practice where highly specialized skills are required, an employment contract may be necessary in order to ensure that both parties understand their respective roles and responsibilities clearly (Kaine, 2020; Katsabian, 2021; Kilic, 2021; Kolling & Schnabel, 2022; Kowalewska, 2020; Kupec et al., 2022; Lamare & Budd, 2022). This is especially true if there is any potential for intellectual property rights disputes between them – having a legally binding agreement in place will help protect both sides from any potential legal issues arising out of this type of situation. Yet, when it comes to more casual jobs such as retail or hospitality positions where employees are often hired on short-term contracts with no long-term commitment involved, then an employment contract may not be necessary at all since these types of arrangements tend to be much less formal than those found in more traditional workplaces.

In addition, due to their temporary nature they also provide employers with greater flexibility when it comes to hiring and firing staff without having too many legal implications attached – something which could prove beneficial for businesses operating within certain industries or sectors where labor laws are particularly strict (Bradley & Rowland, 2021; Bray et al., 2019, 2020; Budd, 2020; Cabeza, 2019; Cam, 2021). While there can certainly be some advantages associated with using employment contracts across different job categories, it is important for both employers and employees alike to consider carefully what kind of arrangement would best suit their particular needs before entering into one so as not only ensure that everyone's rights are protected but also that any potential risks associated with doing so have been adequately addressed beforehand.

In light of this, it is clear that there are a number of reforms which could be implemented in order to make employment contracts more effective and beneficial for both parties (Bhuta, 2022; Bischoff et al., 2021; Bogoeski, 2022; Bondy, 2022; Boumans, 2022; Bourguignon & Floquet, 2019). For example, employers should consider introducing fixed-term contracts as an alternative to open-ended ones so as to provide greater job security for employees while also allowing them the flexibility they need when it comes to taking on new roles or changing jobs. Furthermore, employers should also look into providing additional benefits such as health insurance or other forms of compensation in order to ensure that their staff are adequately rewarded for their work and dedication. Finally, employers should strive towards creating a culture where communication between all parties involved is encouraged so that any potential issues can be addressed quickly and effectively before they become too serious.

By implementing these reforms, not only will businesses benefit from having better control over their labor costs but employees will also have greater peace of mind knowing that their rights are being respected and protected by the company they work for (Ritson, 2019a, b; Riva & Rizza, 2021; Roche, n.d.; Roche & Gormley, 2020; Rosetti, 2019; Roy & Dubey, 2022). Ultimately then, with careful consideration given to how best to use employment contracts within contemporary practice, both employers and employees alike can reap the rewards associated with doing so without compromising either party's interests in the process. In the next section, we will explore the roles and responsibilities of employers in the workplace.

1.2. THE ROLE AND RESPONSIBILITIES OF EMPLOYERS IN THE WORKPLACE

Employers play a critical role in the workplace, and there are several different conceptualizations of what an employer is (Mezihorak et al.; Morritt, 2022; Murphy & Turner, 2020; Nespoli, 2019; Newman et al., 2019; Nga & Nga, 2021). These include the traditional view of employers as owners or managers who provide direction to employees, as well as more modern views that emphasize collaboration between employers and employees. In this section, we will compare and contrast these two perspectives on employers in order to better understand their importance in the workplace.

The traditional view of an employer is one where they are seen as a leader or manager who provides guidance and direction to their employees (Behrens et al., 2020; Behrens & Pekarek, n.d.; Belizon, 2019; Bellace et al., 2021; Ben & Sage, 2022; Berry & McDaniel, 2022). This perspective emphasizes the hierarchical structure of organizations with clear lines of authority from top-level management down through middle management and finally to individual workers. Employers in this model have ultimate responsibility for setting goals, making decisions, providing resources, monitoring performance, and ensuring compliance with laws and regulations.

In contrast to this traditional view is a more modern approach which sees employers not just as leaders but also collaborators with their employees (Nurlinah et al., 2021; O'Keeffe & Papadopoulos, 2021; Oberfichtner et al., 2020; Opute & Koch, 2020; Ormaetxea, 2019). This perspective recognizes that successful businesses require both top-down leadership from management but also bottom-up input from workers on how best to achieve organizational objectives. Employers in this model focus less on control over employee behavior than on creating an environment where everyone can contribute ideas freely without fear of retribution or criticism for speaking up about issues they care about. They strive for open communication between all levels within the organization so that everyone feels heard and respected regardless of rank or position within it.

The employer will have different functions depending on context and need (Bedkar & Prashad, 2020; Behrens et al., 2020; Behrens & Pekarek, n.d.; Belizon, 2019; Bellace et al., 2021; Ben & Sage, 2022). These two perspectives will guide their actions towards achieving or executing those functions. Figure 1.3 is a case in point that demonstrates the role of the employer when dealing with issues of health and safety. The same principles are applicable elsewhere.

Notably, it is important for employers to recognize both perspectives when considering how best to manage their workforce effectively while still maintaining high standards for productivity and quality work output from each employee individually (Cabeza, 2019; Cam, 2021; Campolieti, 2020; Cesari et al., 2019; Chan, 2020a, b; Chantziaras et al., 2020). By understanding both sides – the need for strong leadership combined with collaborative efforts – employers can create workplaces where everyone feels valued while still achieving desired results efficiently and effectively overall. Employers have a responsibility to ensure that their employees are safe, healthy, and productive in the workplace.

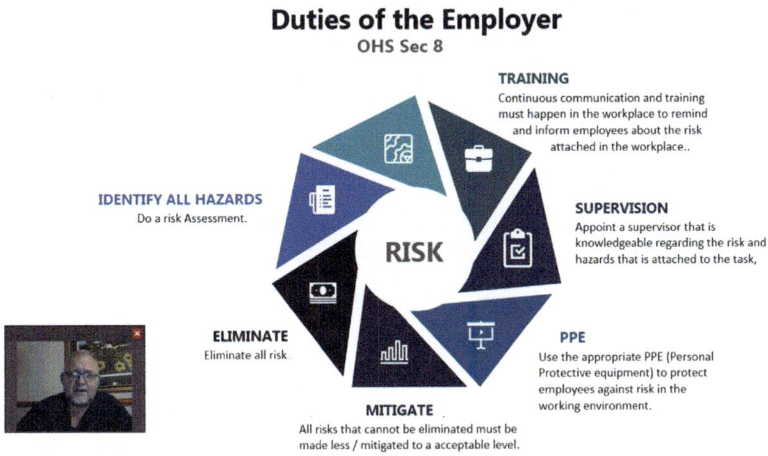

Figure 1.3. *Example of employer roles and responsibilities for health and safety.*

Source: The Safety Coach.

This includes providing adequate training and resources for workers to do their jobs well, as well as creating an environment where everyone feels respected and valued regardless of rank or position within the organization (Herrero, 2022; Hilgert, 2019; Hirsch & Mueller, 2020; Hoffrogge, 2019; Howell, 2019, 2021; Hungler, 2022). Employers should also strive to create a culture of open communication between all levels so that everyone can contribute ideas freely without fear of retribution or criticism for speaking up about issues they care about. In addition, employers must be aware of any potential legal implications when it comes to managing employee behavior in the workplace.

Employers need to understand labor laws and regulations related to wages, hours worked, overtime pay, benefits packages and other aspects of employment law in order to protect both themselves from liability as well as their employees from unfair treatment or exploitation on the job (Devinatz, 2020, 2022; Di Carlo, 2020; Diessner et al., 2022; Dobbins et al., 2020, 2021). Moreover, employers should recognize that each individual worker brings unique skill sets and perspectives which can help improve overall productivity if given proper attention by management. By fostering an atmosphere where everyone is encouraged to share ideas openly without fear of retribution or criticism, employers can create workplaces where creativity is nurtured while still achieving desired results efficiently. Overall, employers play a critical role in today's contemporary workplace by ensuring safety standards are met, understanding labor laws, promoting open communication between all levels within the organization, recognizing individual contributions from workers, and creating an environment where everyone feels respected regardless of rank or position (Wright; Wright & McLaughlin, 2021; Xie & Zhou, 2022; Yan, 2019; Yang et al.; Zbyszewska, 2021). By doing so effectively, businesses will be able set high standards for productivity while still maintaining positive morale among its workforce. Yet, the role of an employer has changed significantly over the years.

In the past, employers were primarily concerned with ensuring that their employees had a safe working environment and were paid fairly for their labor (Martin et al., 2021; McCrystal & Hardy, 2021; Mezihorak et al.; Morritt, 2022; Murphy & Turner, 2020; Nespoli, 2019). Today, however, employers are expected to do much more than just provide basic necessities for their workers. They must also be aware of current labor laws and regulations in order to protect both themselves.

Furthermore, employers should strive to create an atmosphere where all levels within the organization can communicate openly without fear of retribution or criticism (Dorrenbacher et al., 2021; Drucza, 2019; Dupuis & Greer, 2022; Edwards & Hodder, 2022; Ellem, 2021; Ellem et al., 2020). This will help foster creativity among employees while still achieving desired results efficiently. Furthermore, it is important for employers to recognize individual contributions from each worker as this can lead to increased productivity and morale throughout the workplace.

Indeed, employers should ensure that they are providing fair wages and benefits packages which reflect current market standards (Edwards & Hodder, 2022; Ellem, 2021; Ellem et al., 2020; Engblom & Lundberg, 2019; Espinosa, 2021). By doing so, businesses will be able attract top talent while also retaining existing staff members who may otherwise look elsewhere for better opportunities. Additionally, offering competitive salaries helps motivate workers by showing them that their efforts are valued by management.

Overall, it is clear that the role of an employer has evolved significantly over time (de Amorim et al., 2019; de Luna, 2022; De Prins et al., 2020; de Vaate, 2021; Demougin et al., 2019; Desai & Randeria, 2020). Employers today must not only meet safety standards but also understand labor laws in order to protect both themselves and their employees from unfair treatment or exploitation on the job. Additionally, they should strive to create open communication between all levels within the organization while recognizing individual contributions from each worker in order to increase overall productivity and morale throughout the workplace. Finally, they should offer competitive wages and benefits packages which reflect current market standards in order to attract top talent while motivating existing staff members at every level within the company. Figure 1.4 distinguishes the responsibilities of the employer from those of the employee.

EMPLOYEE

VERSUS

EMPLOYER

Visit www.PEDIAA.com

EMPLOYEE	EMPLOYER
An employee is a person who works for a company and earns a salary	An employer is a person or an organization who recruits workers to perform work and duties
Has to work for an organization or an institution	Hires the service from the employee
Should do the work for which he is hired	Should provide the compensation and other benefits along with the necessary equipment for the employees
There are various types of employees such as part-time, full-time seasonal, temporary, and leased employees	Do not have specific types
Seek job opportunities and render service	Try to develop the organization or the institution by hiring employees

Figure 1.4. *Differences between employer and employee responsibilities.*

Source: Pediaa.

By taking the steps described above effectively, businesses will be able to set high standards for productivity while still maintaining positive morale among its workforce (Martin, 2022; Martin et al., 2021; McCrystal & Hardy, 2021; Mezihorak et al.; Morritt, 2022; Murphy & Turner, 2020).

As we move into the 21st century, it is important to critically evaluate the trends that will define the role of an employer. In particular, employers must be aware of how technology and automation are changing the way work is done in order to remain competitive in their respective industries.

Additionally, they should consider how global economic shifts may affect their workforce and adjust accordingly by offering flexible working arrangements or other benefits packages which reflect current market standards (Lyddon, 2021; Lyutov, 2022; MacKenzie & Lucio, 2019; Madimutsa; Mahas-Demydas & Rudnytska, 2019; Mahmood & Banerjee, 2020). Furthermore, employers should strive to create a culture of inclusion within their organization by recognizing individual contributions from each worker while also providing opportunities for professional development and growth throughout all levels within the company. Moreover, employers should ensure that safety protocols are up-to-date with industry standards in order to protect both themselves and their employees from any potential harm on the job.

By taking these steps effectively, businesses can set high standards for productivity while still maintaining positive morale among its workforce (Lee & Tapia, 2021; Leggett, 2019; Ligthart et al., 2022; Liu, 2023; Lize et al., 2022; Lloyd & Payne, 2021; Lukacova et al., 2022). Ultimately, this will help them stay ahead of competitors as well as attract top talent who value a safe and inclusive workplace environment where everyone's efforts are valued equally regardless of background or experience level. As such, it is essential for employers today to understand these trends in order to remain successful in our ever-changing world economy. In order to do this, employers must systematically interrogate and critique the contradictions that exist within the diverse roles of employers.

This includes examining how they can balance their responsibilities as both a business leader and an employer while also considering the implications of their decisions on employee morale, productivity, and overall job satisfaction (Murphy & Turner, 2020; Nespoli, 2019; Newman et al., 2019; Nga & Nga, 2021; Ngai, 2020; Nicklich & Helfen, 2019). Additionally, it is important for them to consider how their policies may affect different groups of employees differently in terms of wages, benefits packages, working conditions, and similar ideas by taking these steps into account when making decisions about workplace policies or procedures, employers can ensure that all workers are treated fairly and equitably regardless of gender identity or race.

Furthermore, employers should strive to create a culture where everyone feels valued for their contributions while also providing opportunities for professional development and growth throughout all levels within the company (Schuessler et al., 2019; Schuhrke, 2019; Scrimger, 2020; Seghezzi; Sheldon & Thornthwaite, 2020; Smith, 2019). Moreover, employers should ensure that safety protocols are up-to-date with industry standards in order to protect both themselves and their employees from any potential harm on the job. Ultimately by understanding these trends today's businesses will be better equipped to remain competitive in our ever-changing world economy while still maintaining positive morale among its workforce.

By taking these steps effectively businesses can set high standards for productivity while still creating an inclusive environment where everyone's efforts are valued equally regardless of background or experience level – ultimately leading them towards success (Giannakopoulos & Laliotis, 2020; Giraud, 2020; Godino & Molina, 2022; Gooberman, 2022; Goods & Ellem; Goyer et al., 2022). In order to achieve this, employers must first recognize the importance of creating a workplace culture that is both equitable and inclusive. This means understanding the unique needs of each employee and providing them with the resources they need to succeed in their role. Additionally, it is important for employers to ensure that all workers are treated fairly regardless of gender identity or race – something which can be achieved through implementing policies such as equal pay for equal work and non-discrimination clauses in contracts.

Yet, businesses should also strive to create an environment where employees feel valued for their contributions while still providing opportunities for professional development and growth throughout all levels within the company (Liu, 2023; Lize et al., 2022; Lloyd & Payne, 2021; Lukacova et al., 2022; Lyddon, 2021; Lyutov, 2022; MacKenzie & Lucio, 2019). This could include offering training programs or mentorship initiatives which allow employees to gain new skill sets while also feeling supported by their employer. Furthermore, safety protocols should always be up-to-date with industry standards in order to protect both themselves and their employees from any potential harm on the job. The next section considers the other side of the coin which are the roles of the employees.

Employees are a vital part of any organization, and their roles and responsibilities have been conceptualized in various ways (O'Keeffe & Papadopoulos, 2021; Oberfichtner et al., 2020; Opute & Koch, 2020; Ormaetxea, 2019). The most common conceptualizations include the human capital theory, the resource-based view, and the job characteristics model. The human capital theory views employees as investments that can be developed to increase productivity. This approach emphasizes training and development opportunities for employees to improve their skills and knowledge base. It also encourages employers to provide incentives such as bonuses or promotions to motivate workers. While this approach is beneficial in terms of increasing employee performance, it does not take into account other factors such as job satisfaction or work-life balance which may be important considerations when evaluating an employee's overall contribution to an organization.

The resource-based view considers employees as resources that can be used strategically by organizations for competitive advantage (Schofield-Georgeson & Rawling, 2020; Schuessler et al., 2019; Schuhrke, 2019; Scrimger, 2020; Seghezzi). This perspective focuses on how individual talents can be leveraged within an organization's operations in order to gain a competitive edge over competitors. However, this approach fails to recognize the importance of team dynamics which are essential for successful collaboration between departments within an organization.

Finally, the job characteristics model looks at how certain aspects of a job affect motivation levels among employees (Thomas & Turnbull, 2021; Thornthwaite & Sheldon, 2019, 2021; Tiraboschi, 2020). This includes factors such as autonomy, task variety, feedback from supervisors and similar ideas, all of which contribute towards creating meaningful work experiences for individuals working within an organization. Although this model provides useful insights into understanding employee motivation levels better, it does not consider external influences such as organizational culture or economic conditions which could potentially impact worker morale significantly over time if left unchecked by management teams. Figure 1.5 is an example of a job description including responsibilities.

Overall, each conceptualization has its own merits, but none should be seen in isolation since they all play a role in determining how effectively organizations manage their workforce today (Flynn & Schroder, 2021; Foley & Williamson, 2021; Ford & Gillan, 2022; Ford & Ward, 2021; Forde; Forsyth, 2022). By taking into account multiple perspectives, employers will have greater insight into what motivates their staff, allowing them to create more effective strategies when it comes to managing personnel efficiently. In the public sector, employees are typically expected to adhere to a set of rules and regulations that have been established by the government. This includes following specific procedures when it comes to carrying out tasks as well as adhering to certain ethical standards. Additionally, they may also be required to take part in activities such as community outreach or volunteer work which can help promote positive relationships between citizens and their local authorities.

Job Title	Job Description	Responsibilities	Qualifications
Senior Technical Writer	ACME Documentation Services, a specialist in military documentation publication, seeks a creative but analytical problem-solver who can communicate complex design, manufacturing, and equipment operational workflows simply and effectively for maximum usability	• Interview SMEs for manufacturing and operational knowledge-gathering • Function within a project team providing services in support of technical manual and courseware development • Creation of documentationand technical illustrations utilizing CAD, Adobe Illustrator, Arbor Text Pro, XML editors, and web-based development applications • Communication with SMEs, team members, and client representatives to determine revision requirements and publication approval	• Software proficiencies described above • Familiarity with Military Documentation Standards (MIL-STD-40051 and MIL_HDBK-1222C) • Familiarity with TRADOC Regulation 350-70 for training development • Bachelor's degree or equivalent experience 5+ years of Technical Writing and/or training content development

Figure 1.5. *Example of a job role summary.*

Source: BetterUp.

The private sector is more focused on profit-making objectives and therefore places greater emphasis on efficiency and productivity from its workforce (Kowalewska, 2020; Kupec et al., 2022; Lamare & Budd, 2022; Lansbury, 2021; Larsson, 2020; Lawreniuk, 2023). Employees here are usually given more autonomy over how they carry out their duties but at the same time must remain accountable for any mistakes made during operations. Furthermore, there is often an expectation that staff will go above and beyond what is asked of them in order to ensure maximum profitability for the company.

Finally, within third sector organizations (such as charities or nonprofits) workers tend to have a much broader range of responsibilities than those found in either public or private sectors (Kupec et al., 2022; Lamare & Budd, 2022; Lansbury, 2021; Larsson, 2020; Lawreniuk, 2023; Lee & Tapia, 2021). These include not only performing day-to-day tasks but also engaging with stakeholders, fundraising initiatives, developing new strategies and similar ideas, all of which require a different set of skills compared with other types of employment opportunities. As such, these roles often come with higher levels of job satisfaction due to their ability to provide meaningful contributions towards society's development.

Overall, each type of organization has its own unique characteristics when it comes assigning roles and responsibilities among its employees (Devinatz, 2020, 2022; Di Carlo, 2020; Diessner et al., 2022; Dobbins et al., 2020, 2021). However, regardless of whether one works in the public, private or third sector there are some commonalities that should be taken into account when evaluating worker performance – namely motivation levels, accountability expectations and job satisfaction rates. By understanding these factors better, employers can create more effective strategies for managing personnel efficiently while ensuring everyone feels valued within their respective workplace environments.

At the same time, it is important to interrogate the contradictions that exist in today's employee roles (O'Keeffe & Papadopoulos, 2021; Oberfichtner et al., 2020; Opute & Koch, 2020; Ormaetxea, 2019; Ozkiziltan, 2019). On one hand, employees are expected to be highly productive and efficient while on the other they must also demonstrate a high level of creativity and innovation. This can create an environment where workers feel overwhelmed by their workload or lack motivation due to feeling undervalued for their efforts. It is therefore essential for employers to ensure that all staff members have access to adequate resources and support systems so as not to compromise job satisfaction levels.

Generally speaking, there are many complexities associated with managing personnel within any organization (Gramano & Gaudio, 2019; Grodem & Hippe, 2019; Guillaume, 2022; Guiso, 2020; Gunnigle et al., 2019). By understanding these nuances better employers can develop more effective strategies for ensuring everyone feels valued and motivated within their respective workplace environments. Furthermore, it is important to interrogate the contradictions that exist in today's employee roles so as not compromise job satisfaction levels or productivity rates. Doing this will help organizations achieve greater success in terms of both financial performance and overall morale among its workforce.

The role of an employee has changed drastically over the last 150 years (Jirjahn, 2022; Joyce et al.; Junior, 2022; Kaine, 2020; Katsabian, 2021; Kilic, 2021; Kolling & Schnabel, 2022). From manual labor to knowledge-based work, employees have had to adapt and evolve in order to remain competitive in a globalized economy. This shift has been particularly evident in countries such as the United States, where technological advancements have enabled companies to become more efficient while also requiring workers to demonstrate higher levels of creativity and innovation. As a result, employers must now consider how best they can manage their personnel so as not only ensure productivity but also job satisfaction among their staff members. Figure 1.6 highlights a case in point of knowledge and technological priorities in the modern workplace, an example of the changes in the roles of employees.

Figure 1.6. *Employee data management plan.*

Source: Shrofile.

In today's workplace environment, it is essential for employers to recognize that each individual brings unique skill sets and experiences which should be valued accordingly (Velluti, 2022; Vinichenko et al., 2020; Vulkan & Larsson, 2019; Walker, 2020; Walters & Wadsworth, 2020; Warner, 2019). For instance, some employees may excel at problem solving while others may possess strong communication abilities. However, both are equally important when it comes to achieving success within any organization. Furthermore, employers must understand that there is often a delicate balance between providing sufficient resources for staff members whilst still maintaining cost efficiency. It is almost a truism to suggest that employees need access to adequate tools and support systems so as to remain productive and efficient (da Costa & Horn, 2021; Dalla Sega, 2021; Darlington & Mustchin, 2019; Das, 2023; Das & Singh, 2021; de Amorim et al., 2019). Yet, it is equally true that employees must also demonstrate a high level of creativity and innovation. This contrast in expectations can create an environment where workers feel overwhelmed by their workload or lack motivation due to feeling undervalued for their efforts. It is therefore essential for employers to ensure that all staff members have access to adequate resources and support systems so as not compromise job satisfaction levels. Employers and organizations must also moderate their expectations so that they do not create unbearable burdens for workers.

It is clear then that managing personnel effectively requires careful consideration from both employer's side as well as from the employee's perspective (Archel et al., 2022; Ashwin et al., 2020; Avgar, 2020; Baines & Armstrong, 2019; Baines & Cunningham, 2020). Employers should strive towards creating positive working environments which promote collaboration, respect, trust, fairness, diversity, inclusion, and recognition amongst its workforce. Additionally, organizations should provide opportunities for professional development through training programs or mentorship initiatives so that everyone feels empowered with regards career progression prospects.

Finally, effective communication strategies should be implemented across all departments in order for everyone involved within the company structure to understand what is expected from them on both personal and collective levels (Vulkan & Larsson, 2019; Walker, 2020; Walters & Wadsworth, 2020; Warner, 2019; William & Cunningham, 2021). The philosophical debate surrounding the roles of employees is a complex one. On the one hand, employers have an obligation to ensure that their staff are adequately compensated for their work and provided with suitable working conditions. On the other hand, employees should be expected to take responsibility for their own performance and contribute towards achieving organizational objectives. This balance between employer's rights and employee's responsibilities can often be difficult to maintain in practice as both parties may have different expectations or interpretations of what constitutes fair treatment. Notably, it is important for employers to recognize that there is no single 'right' way when it comes to managing personnel (da Costa & Horn, 2021; Dalla Sega, 2021; Darlington & Mustchin, 2019; Das, 2023; Das & Singh, 2021; de Amorim et al., 2019). It is essential that they remain open-minded about different approaches which could potentially benefit all stakeholders involved within the organization. Furthermore, employers must strive towards creating positive working environments where everyone feels valued and respected regardless of job title or seniority level. Only then will organizations be able to foster productive relationships between its workforce which ultimately leads to increased job satisfaction levels amongst its personnel. The changing role of employees in workplaces has significant implications for both employers and employees alike. On the one hand, employers must ensure that they are providing their personnel with a safe and secure working environment which is conducive to productivity. This includes offering fair wages, reasonable working hours, job security and other benefits such as health insurance or retirement plans. Additionally, employers should strive towards creating an atmosphere where everyone feels respected regardless of their position within the organization.

At the same time, it is important for employees to understand that they have certain responsibilities when it comes to their roles in the workplace (Refslund & Arnholtz, 2022; Ritson, 2019a, b; Riva & Rizza, 2021; Roche, n.d.; Roche & Gormley, 2020). They should be expected to adhere to company policies and procedures while also taking ownership of their own performance levels by striving towards achieving organizational objectives set out by management. Furthermore, employees should be aware that there may be consequences if they fail to meet expectations or behave inappropriately at work – this could range from verbal warnings all the way up to dismissal depending on severity of misconduct. Overall, it is essential for both parties involved in any employment relationship – employer and employee – to recognize each other's rights and responsibilities so as not only maintain a healthy balance between them but also create an environment where everyone can thrive professionally (de Luna, 2022; De Prins et al., 2020; de Vaate, 2021; Demougin et al., 2019; Desai & Randeria, 2020; Devinatz, 2020). By doing so, organizations will benefit from increased job satisfaction amongst its personnel which ultimately leads to improved productivity levels across all departments. These are concerns that have informed and moderated the impact of industrialists and the business class on employee relations.

1.3. THE IMPACT OF INDUSTRIALISTS AND BUSINESSPEOPLE ON EMPLOYEE RELATIONS

Industrialists have been a source of fascination for many throughout history (Franceschini, 2020; Freedland & Dhorajiwala, 2019; Fuchs et al., 2019; Galik et al., 2022; Gall, 2021; Gardawski & Towalski, 2020). From the early days of the Industrial Revolution to modern times, industrialists have played an important role in shaping our world. As such, there are numerous conceptualizations of industrialists that have emerged over time. In this section, we will take a look at some of these different conceptualizations and offer critiques on each one.

The first concept is that of the "robber baron" – an individual who uses their wealth and power to exploit others for personal gain (Graca, 2021; Gramano & Gaudio, 2019; Grodem & Hippe, 2019; Guillaume, 2022; Guiso, 2020; Gunnigle et al., 2019). This characterization has been used to describe many prominent figures from history including John D Rockefeller and Andrew Carnegie. While it is true that these individuals did use their wealth and influence to further their own interests, they also made significant contributions to society through philanthropy and other forms of social good. Therefore, while it may be accurate to label them as robber barons in certain respects, it does not capture the full scope of their impact on society or give due credit for any positive contributions they may have made.

Another common concept is that of the "captain of industry" – an individual who uses their business acumen and entrepreneurial spirit to create jobs and spur economic growth within a region or country (Ligthart et al., 2022; Liu, 2023; Lize et al., 2022; Lloyd & Payne, 2021; Lukacova et al., 2022; Lyddon, 2021; Lyutov, 2022). This characterization has often been applied to Henry Ford or Bill Gates as examples; however, both men had questionable labor practices which could be seen as exploitative by some standards today (e.g., low wages). Additionally, while these individuals certainly created jobs in various industries during their respective eras, much like with robber barons there were likely negative externalities associated with those job creations (e.g., environmental degradation). Thus, again this concept fails to capture all aspects related to industrialism when assessing its overall impact on society at large. One of those effects is a culture of conflict and coordination in the workplace (*see* Figure 1.7).

Finally, there is the idea that industrialists can serve as agents for positive change within society by using their resources towards causes such as poverty alleviation or education reform initiatives and similar ideas (Ford & Gillan, 2022; Ford & Ward, 2021; Forde; Forsyth, 2022; Foster et al., 2021; Franceschini, 2020; Freedland & Dhorajiwala, 2019). While this view certainly holds merit given how influential wealthy individuals can be when leveraging resources towards social good projects, it should also be noted that even here there are potential pitfalls if not managed properly (e.g., conflicts-of-interests between donors/recipients). Furthermore, there remains debate about whether private sector solutions are always better than public ones when addressing societal issues.

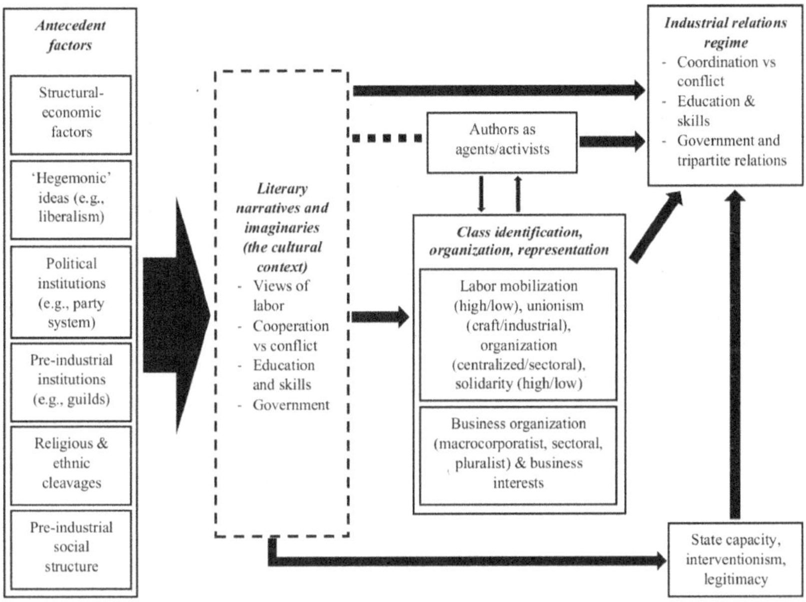

Figure 1.7. *Cultural images of labor conflict and coordination.*

Source: Cambridge University Press and Assessment.

Overall, then, while each conceptualization offers valuable insights into understanding what makes up an industrialist, none provide a complete picture nor do they necessarily reflect positively upon all aspects associated with being one (Pitteloud, 2022; Preminger & Bondy; Quinlan & Maxwell-Stewart; Radzi et al., 2022; Ramsay & Webster, 2019). It is therefore important for us all – whether we aspire towards becoming successful entrepreneurs ourselves or simply wish to understand more about how our economy works – to consider multiple perspectives before forming opinions about any particular type of entrepreneur. Doing so will help ensure we make informed decisions based on facts rather than preconceived notions which may lead us astray from reality.

The impact of industrialists on employee relations is an important topic to consider (Markey, 2020; Martin, 2022; Martin et al., 2021; McCrystal & Hardy, 2021; Mezihorak et al.; Morritt, 2022; Murphy & Turner, 2020). Industrialists are often seen as the driving force behind economic growth and development, but their influence can also have a negative effect on employees. In some cases, industrialists may be more focused on profits than providing fair wages or safe working conditions for their workers. This can lead to poor morale among employees and create a hostile work environment that affects productivity and job satisfaction.

Industrialists should strive to create positive relationships with their employees by offering competitive salaries, benefits packages, and opportunities for advancement (Hendy, 2022; Herrero, 2022; Hilgert, 2019; Hirsch & Mueller, 2020; Hoffrogge, 2019; Howell, 2019, 2021). They should also ensure that all safety regulations are followed in order to protect workers from potential hazards in the workplace. Additionally, they should provide training programs so that employees can develop new skills and stay up-to-date with industry trends. By taking these steps, industrialists will not only benefit financially but also foster better relationships with their workforce which could ultimately result in increased productivity levels across the board. In general terms, it is clear that there are both positives and negatives associated with being an industrialist (Katsabian, 2021; Kilic, 2021; Kolling & Schnabel, 2022; Kowalewska, 2020; Kupec et al., 2022; Lamare & Budd, 2022). While they do play an important role in our economy, it is essential for them to take into account how their decisions affect those around them – especially when it comes to employee relations. By creating positive working environments where everyone feels valued, industrialists can help ensure long-term success while simultaneously contributing towards social good projects within society at large.

The notion of employee relations has been redefined in recent years due to the rise of industrialists (Schofield-Georgeson & Rawling, 2020; Schuessler et al., 2019; Schuhrke, 2019; Scrimger, 2020; Seghezzi; Sheldon & Thornthwaite, 2020). Industrialists are those who own and operate large-scale businesses, often with a focus on manufacturing or production. As such, they have an immense amount of power when it comes to making decisions that affect their employees. This includes setting wages, providing benefits packages, and creating policies for workplace conduct. It is these elements that contribute towards industrial relations (*see* Figure 1.8).

In order to ensure positive relationships between employers and employees, industrialists should strive to create fair working conditions (Sanz et al., 2020; Schlachter, 2019; Schmidt & Muller, 2021; Schofield-Georgeson, 2022; Schofield-Georgeson & Rawling, 2020). This means offering competitive salaries as well as providing opportunities for advancement within the company.

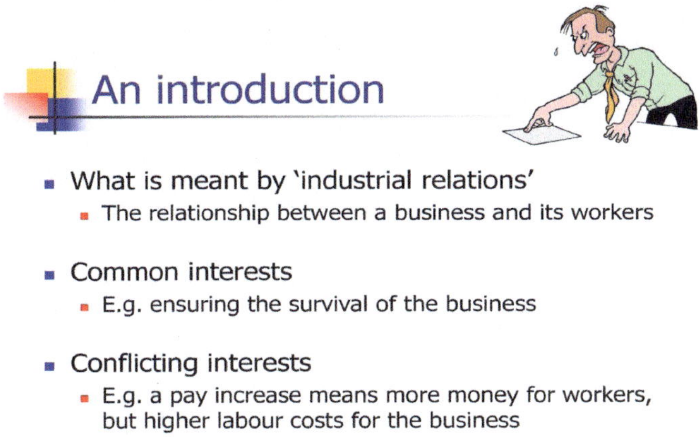

Figure 1.8. *Basic ingredients of industrial relations.*

Source: Scott Willis via SlidePlayer.

It is important for industrialists to remember that their actions have far reaching implications beyond just financial gain (Hendy, 2022; Herrero, 2022; Hilgert, 2019; Hirsch & Mueller, 2020; Hoffrogge, 2019; Howell, 2019). Their decisions can shape how people view them both inside and outside of their organization, which is why it is essential for them to take into account how their choices impact others around them – especially when it comes to employee relations. By creating positive working environments where everyone feels valued, industrialists can help ensure long-term success while simultaneously contributing towards social good projects within society at large.

From a Marxist perspective, industrialists should also be aware of the power dynamics that exist between them and their employees (Abd Razak & Mahmod, 2019, 2021; Ackers, 2020; Addison & Teixeira, 2019a, b). This is especially true when it comes to trade unionism, which can provide workers with an effective way to negotiate better wages and working conditions. By recognizing the importance of unions in protecting employee rights, industrialists can help create more equitable workplaces where everyone feels respected and valued.

Consequently, industrialists have a responsibility to ensure that they are creating positive work environments for their employees while also taking into account how their decisions impact society at large (Ashwin et al., 2020; Avgar, 2020; Baines & Armstrong, 2019; Baines & Cunningham, 2020; Bancarzewski & Hardy, 2021). By understanding the implications of trade unionism and fostering good relationships with their workforce, industrialists can not only benefit financially but also contribute towards social progress within society as a whole. It is therefore essential for them to take these considerations into account when making decisions about employee relations in order to ensure long-term success for both themselves and those around them. By doing so, industrialists can become a benevolent force in human capital development.

Industrialists have long been seen as a powerful and influential force in the world of business (Baturina et al., 2021; Beattie, 2019; Bechter et al., 2021; Bedkar & Prashad, 2020; Behrens et al., 2020; Behrens & Pekarek). However, their role is often misunderstood or overlooked when it comes to understanding how they impact human capital development. While some may view them as malevolent forces that exploit workers for their own gain, this is not necessarily true. In fact, industrialists can be an important part of creating positive work environments by recognizing the importance of employee rights and fostering good relationships with their workforce.

One way that industrialists can contribute towards human capital development is through trade unionism (Dobbins et al., 2021; Dockes, 2019; Dorigatti et al., n.d.; Dorigatti & Pedersini, 2021; Dorrenbacher et al., 2021; Drucza, 2019). Trade unions are organizations which represent employees' interests and provide them with collective bargaining power to negotiate better wages and working conditions from employers. This helps ensure that employees are treated fairly while also providing them with more job security and stability within the workplace. Industrialists who recognize the importance of trade unionism will be able to create more equitable workplaces where everyone feels respected and valued regardless of their position or background.

Another way that industrialists can foster positive work environments is by taking into account how their decisions affect society at large (Kilic, 2021; Kolling & Schnabel, 2022; Kowalewska, 2020; Kupec et al., 2022; Lamare & Budd, 2022; Lansbury, 2021). For example, if an employer decides to outsource jobs overseas instead of hiring locally, this could lead to increased unemployment rates in certain areas due to lack of available jobs. It is therefore essential for industrialists to consider these implications before making any major decisions about employment practices so as not to negatively impact local communities or economies. Despite their importance, industrialists can never completely overcome or ignore the state as a stakeholder in industrial relations.

1.4. THE STATE AS A STAKEHOLDER IN INDUSTRIAL RELATIONS

The role of the state in industrial relations has been a subject of debate for many years (Dockes, 2019; Dorigatti et al., n.d.; Dorigatti & Pedersini, 2021; Dorrenbacher et al., 2021; Drucza, 2019; Dupuis & Greer, 2022). It is widely accepted that the state plays an important role in regulating labor markets and ensuring fair wages and working conditions, but there are also those who argue that its involvement can be detrimental to both employers and employees. In this section, we will take a closer look at the pros and cons of state intervention in industrial relations.

On one hand, it is argued that government regulation helps protect workers from exploitation by employers (Howell, 2021; Hungler, 2022; Ilsoe & Soderqvist; Jarota, 2022; Jha & Singh, 2019; Jiang & Yao, 2020; Jirjahn, 2022). This includes setting minimum wage levels, providing job security through collective bargaining agreements (CBAs), enforcing health and safety standards, as well as protecting vulnerable groups such as women or ethnic minorities from discrimination. Furthermore, governments may provide financial assistance to businesses during times of economic hardship or when they need to restructure their operations due to changing market conditions.

On the other hand, some critics point out that too much government interference can lead to rigid labor markets which stifle innovation and productivity growth (Gavin, 2022; Giannakopoulos & Laliotis, 2020; Giraud, 2020; Godino & Molina, 2022; Gooberman, 2022; Goods & Ellem). They argue that excessive regulations create barriers for new entrants into the labor market while making it difficult for existing firms to adjust their workforce size according to changing demand patterns. Moreover, certain policies such as high minimum wages may reduce employment opportunities for low-skilled workers while increasing costs for businesses which could ultimately lead them towards bankruptcy or relocation abroad where labor costs are lower.

Overall, it appears clear that there is no single answer when it comes to assessing the role of the state in industrial relations; rather each situation needs careful consideration before any decisions are made regarding policy interventions by governments at all levels – local authorities included – so as not only ensure fairness between employers and employees but also promote economic growth within society more broadly speaking (Howell, 2019, 2021; Hungler, 2022; Ilsoe & Soderqvist; Jarota, 2022; Jha & Singh, 2019;

Jiang & Yao, 2020). The historiography of state interventions in industrial relations is a complex and varied one. It has been shaped by the changing economic, political, and social contexts within which it has operated over time.

In the early days of industrialization, governments tended to take a hands-off approach to labor disputes (Das, 2023; Das & Singh, 2021; de Amorim et al., 2019; de Luna, 2022; De Prins et al., 2020; de Vaate, 2021; Demougin et al., 2019). This involved allowing employers and workers to negotiate their own terms without interference from outside forces. This changed during the late 19th century when governments began intervening more actively in order to protect vulnerable workers from exploitation by powerful employers.

In the 20th century, government involvement in industrial relations increased significantly as states sought to regulate wages and working conditions through legislation such as minimum wage laws or CBAs between unions and employers (Behrens & Pekarek, n.d.; Belizon, 2019; Bellace et al., 2021; Ben & Sage, 2022; Berry & McDaniel, 2022; Bhuta, 2022). This trend continued into the 21st century with many countries introducing new regulations aimed at protecting employees' rights while also promoting economic growth through measures such as tax incentives for businesses that create jobs or invest in research and development activities. The government was always an important factor in industrial relations (*see* Figure 1.9).

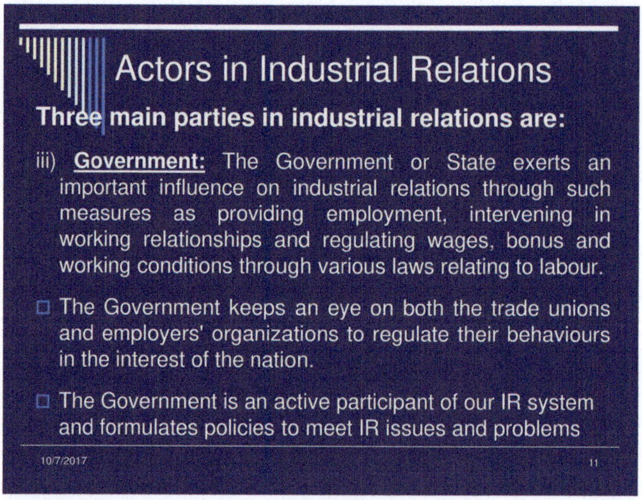

Figure 1.9. *Actors in industrial relations.*

Source: Imogene Mitchell via SlidePlayer.

At present there is much debate about how far governments should go when it comes to regulating labor markets (Lee & Tapia, 2021; Leggett, 2019; Ligthart et al., 2022; Liu, 2023; Lize et al., 2022; Lloyd & Payne, 2021). Some argue that intervention is necessary in order to ensure fairness between employers and employees (*see* Figure 1.10) while others point out that too much regulation can stifle economic growth and innovation. As such, it is important to examine the constraints and facilitators for the state as a stakeholder in industrial relations.

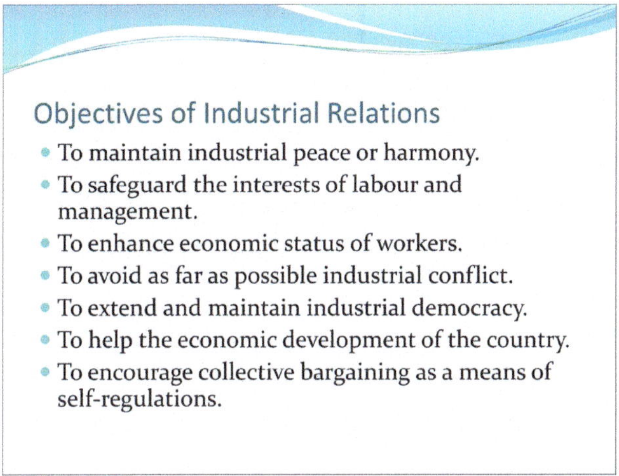

Figure 1.10. *Objectives of industrial relations.*

Source: Della Matthews.

The first constraint on government involvement in industrial relations is its limited resources (Dobbins et al., 2020, 2021; Dockes, 2019; Dorigatti et al., n.d.; Dorigatti & Pedersini, 2021; Dorrenbacher et al., 2021). Governments are often unable to devote sufficient funds or personnel to effectively monitor labor markets or enforce regulations. This means that even if laws are passed, they may not be adequately enforced due to lack of capacity. Additionally, governments may face political pressure from powerful employers who oppose certain regulations or CBAs which could limit their ability to intervene in labor disputes.

On the other hand, there are also several factors which facilitate government involvement in industrial relations (Goyer et al., 2022; Graca, 2021; Gramano & Gaudio, 2019; Grodem & Hippe, 2019; Guillaume, 2022; Guiso, 2020). Firstly, public opinion can play an important role; when citizens become aware of unfair practices by employers, they often demand action from their elected representatives which can lead to new legislation being introduced or existing laws being strengthened. Secondly, international organizations such as the International Labor Organization (ILO) provide guidance on best practice for states when it comes to regulating labor markets and protecting workers' rights. Finally, some countries have established independent bodies tasked with monitoring compliance with labor standards; these agencies can help ensure that employers comply with relevant laws and regulations without interference from outside forces.

While there are both constraints and facilitators for the state as a stakeholder in industrial relations, ultimately it is up to each individual country how far they choose to go when it comes to regulating labor markets (Gooberman, 2022; Goods & Ellem; Goyer et al., 2022; Graca, 2021; Gramano & Gaudio, 2019; Grodem & Hippe, 2019). It is therefore essential that governments take into account all available evidence before making decisions about how best to protect employees' rights while also promoting economic growth through measures such as tax incentives for businesses that create jobs or invest in research and development activities. By doing so, they can ensure that their citizens are able to benefit from the economic opportunities available in a globalized world.

The political economy of state participation in industrial relations is an important and complex issue (MacKenzie & Lucio, 2019; Madimutsa; Mahas-Demydas & Rudnytska, 2019; Mahmood & Banerjee, 2020; Mailand, 2019). It involves understanding how governments interact with employers, workers, and other stakeholders when it comes to regulating labor markets. On one hand, states have the power to set minimum wages, establish CBAs between unions and employers, or pass laws protecting workers' rights. On the other hand, there are several constraints on what states can do due to international trade agreements or domestic politics.

First of all, many countries have signed up to free trade agreements which limit their ability to impose tariffs or quotas on imported goods (Cam, 2021; Campolieti, 2020; Cesari et al., 2019; Chan, 2020a, b; Chantziaras et al., 2020; Chen et al., n.d.). This means that governments cannot use protectionist measures as a way of supporting local industries. Similarly, some countries may be reluctant to introduce new regulations for fear of damaging business confidence or discouraging foreign investment. This could lead them towards adopting more lenient policies than would otherwise be desirable in order to maintain economic stability and growth. At the same time, there are also facilitators for state involvement in industrial relations

(Gunther & Hopner, 2023; Haipeter, 2020; Hakansta et al., n.d.; Hamberger, 2020; Harvey & Turnbull, 2020). For example, certain international treaties such as those relating to human rights provide legal frameworks which governments must adhere to if they wish not only to protect employees but also demonstrate commitment towards upholding these standards both domestically and abroad. In addition, regional organizations like the European Union (EU) offer support through initiatives designed specifically aimed at improving working conditions across member states – something which has been further strengthened by the introduction of the European Pillar of Social Rights.

The tension between capitalism and state control over industrial relations policy is a complex one (Ngai, 2020; Nicklich & Helfen, 2019; Novitz & Andrijasevic, 2020; Nowak, 2021; Nurlinah et al., 2021; O'Keeffe & Papadopoulos, 2021). On the one hand, there are clear drawbacks to government intervention in this area – particularly when it comes to international trade. However, on the other hand, there are also benefits which can be derived from such involvement – not least in terms of providing legal protection for employees and promoting social justice across borders. Ultimately, it is up to individual countries to decide how best they wish to balance these two competing interests.

While capitalism has been an effective driver of economic growth and development, its inherent contradictions with state control over industrial relations policy must be acknowledged if we are to ensure that workers' rights remain protected both domestically and internationally (Eustace, 2021; Fang et al., 2021; Fergus & Godfrey, 2021; Flynn & Schroder, 2021; Foley & Williamson, 2021). It is only through careful consideration of both sides that governments will be able to strike a balance between protecting their citizens whilst simultaneously encouraging business confidence and foreign investment. In the coming years, it is likely that we will see a shift in the patterns of state engagement with trade unions and non-unionized workers.

As governments become increasingly aware of their responsibilities to protect employees' rights, they are likely to take a more active role in regulating industrial relations policy (Fergus & Godfrey, 2021; Flynn & Schroder, 2021; Foley & Williamson, 2021; Ford & Gillan, 2022; Ford & Ward, 2021). This could include introducing legislation which requires employers to recognize CBAs or providing incentives for companies who adhere to certain standards when dealing with labor disputes. Additionally, states may also seek to strengthen existing international treaties on labor rights – such as those outlined by the ILO.

Ultimately, it is important that governments remain cognizant of both sides of this debate if they wish to ensure that workers' rights are respected while simultaneously encouraging economic growth and development (Gunnigle et al., 2019; Gunther & Hopner, 2023; Haipeter, 2020; Hakansta et al., n.d.; Hamberger, 2020; Harvey & Turnbull, 2020). By charting future trends in the patterns of state engagement with trade unions and non-unionized workers, governments can ensure that their citizens receive adequate protection whilst still allowing businesses enough freedom to thrive within an ever-changing global economy. This is a delicate balance between fairness for workers and not discouraging business.

CHAPTER 1 SUMMARY

As we have introduced industrial relations, it becomes clear that this is a multi-faceted and complex phenomenon that goes beyond simplistic interest. The employment contract opens a relationship between the employer and employer. However, the relationship also elicits outside and additional interests such as the state or government. Besides, the business community also has an interest in ensuring good industrial relations. A legal context, as explored in the next chapter, sets out the rules that control the conduct of these interactions.

CHAPTER 2

Setting the Legal Context for Industrial Relations

Contents

The second chapter focuses on the legal context that can be conducive or detrimental to the conduct of industrial relations. Social concerns are a key component of this equation since both employers and employees are members of society. We will explore the politics of trade unionism and their impact on industrial relations. The chapter will explain some of the legal frameworks that are considered when developing and harnessing industrial relations. In doing so, the chapter makes an economic argument for this phenomenon. We will also explore how social dialog is an instrumentality and outcome of communication during industrial relations. Such elements emanate from the concerns of society regarding the relationships that exist between employers and employees.

2.1. SOCIAL CONCERNS ABOUT WORKING CONDITIONS

The working conditions of employees are a major social concern (Teipen & Mehl, 2021; Tesser & Serapioni, 2021; Thomas & Turnbull, 2021; Thornthwaite & Sheldon, 2019, 2021). Poor working conditions can lead to physical and mental health issues, as well as decreased productivity and morale. It is important for employers to ensure that their workers have safe, healthy, and comfortable work environments in order to maximize the potential of their workforce.

One key issue related to working conditions is safety (Schlachter, 2019; Schmidt & Muller, 2021; Schofield-Georgeson, 2022; Schofield-Georgeson & Rawling, 2020). Employers must provide adequate safety measures such as protective equipment, proper training on how to use it correctly, and regular maintenance checks on machinery or tools used by employees. Additionally, employers should be aware of any hazardous materials present in the workplace and take steps to reduce exposure risks for workers.

Another key issue is ergonomics – ensuring that workspaces are designed with comfort in mind so that employees do not experience fatigue or discomfort while performing tasks throughout the day (Ritson, 2019b; Riva & Rizza, 2021; Roche, n.d.; Roche & Gormley, 2020; Rosetti, 2019; Roy & Dubey, 2022; Roy, 2022). This includes providing adjustable chairs or desks so that each employee can customize their workspace according to their individual needs. Another way is making sure there is enough space between workstations; using non-slip flooring; providing adequate lighting; and ensuring good air quality through ventilation systems or other means.

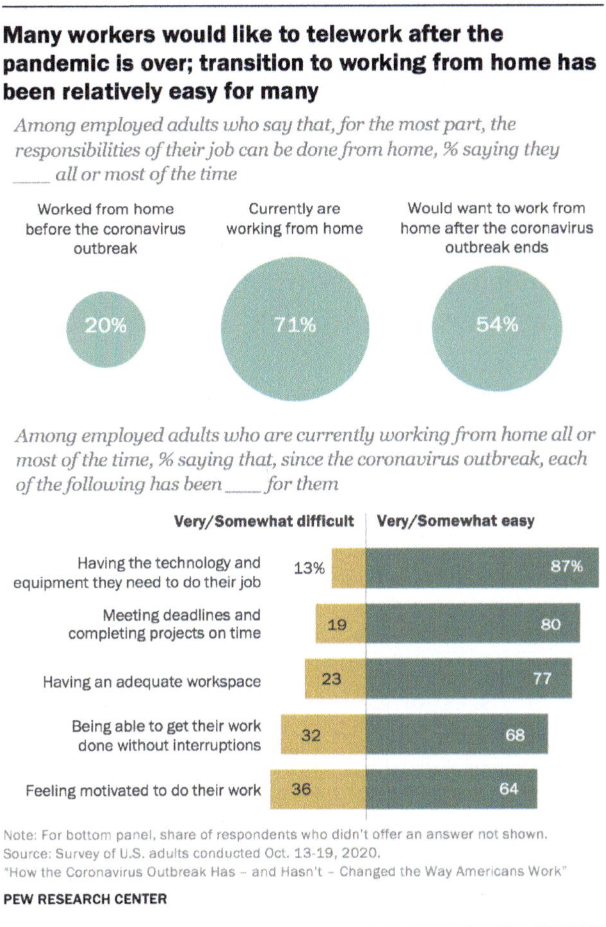

Figure 2.1. *Impact of the coronavirus on the American workplace.*

Source: Pew Research Center.

Finally, employers should also consider psychological factors when designing workplaces – creating an environment where employees feel respected and valued will help foster a positive atmosphere which can improve morale among staff members (Colas-Neila & Fargas, 2019; Collins et al., 2020; Cooke et al., 2019; Croucher & Okland, 2021; D'Art, 2020; da Costa & Horn, 2021). This could include offering flexible hours or remote work options if possible. It also involves encouraging open communication between management and staff members. Then, recognizing achievements with rewards such as bonuses or promotions. Another intervention is implementing policies against discrimination based on gender identity/

expression, race/ethnicity, and similar ideas, promoting diversity within teams and similar ideas. Some of these considerations may be adjusted when the work ecology changes. Figure 2.1 is an example of such a change when working from home became commonplace during the COVID-19 pandemic.

Overall, it is essential for employers to prioritize worker wellbeing when designing workplaces – this will not only benefit individuals but also create a more productive workforce overall (Thornthwaite & Sheldon, 2019, 2021; Tiraboschi, 2020; Tomassetti, 2021; Trif & Szabo). By taking into account these key social concerns about working conditions they can ensure they are creating an environment where everyone feels safe, comfortable, and respected at all times. The quality of working conditions is determined by a variety of social factors. These include physical elements such as the layout and design of the workplace, ergonomics, safety measures, and access to amenities like restrooms or break rooms; but also, psychological aspects such as job satisfaction, work-life balance, and respect for employees' rights. All these components are essential in creating an environment where workers can thrive.

When it comes to physical elements, employers should ensure that their workplaces meet all relevant health and safety regulations – this includes providing adequate lighting levels; ensuring floors are slip-resistant; installing appropriate fire protection systems and similar ideas (William & Cunningham, 2021; Williamson et al., 2019; Wright; Wright & McLaughlin, 2021; Xie & Zhou, 2022). They should also consider ergonomic principles when designing workspaces – making sure desks/chairs are adjustable so they can be tailored to individual needs; providing sufficient space between furniture items; using anti-glare screens on computers and similar ideas. Additionally, employers should provide access to basic amenities such as bathrooms, drinking water facilities, and if necessary, air conditioning or other means.

In terms of psychological factors, employers need to make sure they create an atmosphere which encourages employee engagement and motivation (Cooke et al., 2019; Croucher & Okland, 2021; D'Art, 2020; da Costa & Horn, 2021; Dalla Sega, 2021; Darlington & Mustchin, 2019). This could involve offering competitive salaries/benefits packages; implementing flexible hours or remote work options if possible; encouraging open communication between management and staff members; recognizing achievements with rewards such as bonuses or promotions; implementing policies against discrimination based on gender identity/expression, race/

ethnicity, and similar ideas; promoting diversity within teams and similar ideas. The multiplicity of interventions is meant to ensure fairness and good morale.

It is clear that there are many social determinants which influence the quality of working conditions in any given workplace (Tu et al., 2022; Velluti, 2022; Vinichenko et al., 2020; Vulkan & Larsson, 2019; Walker, 2020). Employers must take into account both physical elements (such as health and safety regulations) and psychological factors (such as job satisfaction) when designing their workplaces in order to ensure everyone feels safe, comfortable, and respected at all times. By doing so they will not only benefit individuals but also create a more productive workforce overall. Theories of social stratification can be used to critique the differentials, inequalities, and inequities of working patterns in the world.

Social stratification is a system by which society ranks categories of people in a hierarchy based on their access to resources such as wealth, power, and prestige (Kowalewska, 2020; Kupec et al., 2022; Lamare & Budd, 2022; Lansbury, 2021; Larsson, 2020; Lawreniuk, 2023). This theory helps us understand how certain groups are more likely than others to experience poverty or lack access to quality education and healthcare services. It also explains why some individuals have greater opportunities for career advancement than others due to their race/ethnicity, gender identity/ expression and similar ideas. Although the industrial revolution helped to socially uplift some people (*see* Figure 2.2), it also created new inequalities and inequities.

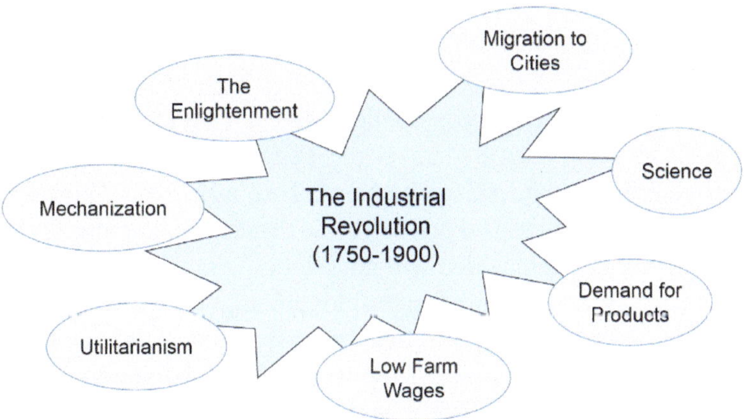

Figure 2.2. *Effects of the industrial revolution of 1750–1900.*

Source: SPH – Boston University.

When it comes to the workplace, social stratification can lead to disparities between employees with regards to wages, benefits packages, working hours and similar ideas (Bhuta, 2022; Bischoff et al., 2021; Bogoeski, 2022; Bondy, 2022; Boumans, 2022; Bourguignon & Floquet, 2019). For example, women may receive lower salaries than men for doing the same job; racial minorities may not be given equal opportunities for promotion; disabled workers may face discrimination when applying for jobs. All these factors contribute towards creating an unequal playing field where certain individuals are disadvantaged simply because of who they are rather than what they can do.

In order to combat this issue employers must ensure that all staff members are treated fairly regardless of gender identity/expression, race/ethnicity, and similar ideas (Radzi et al., 2022; Ramsay & Webster, 2019; Ravn & Oyum, 2020; Razak et al., 2022; Refslund & Arnholtz, 2022). They should strive towards creating an inclusive environment where everyone feels valued and respected. By taking these steps employers will not only help reduce inequality but also foster a sense of belonging amongst their workforce – something which is essential for any successful business (De Prins et al., 2020; de Vaate, 2021; Demougin et al., 2019; Desai & Randeria, 2020; Devinatz, 2020, 2022). However, it is important to consider the cost-benefit analysis of such social investments. On one hand, employers may have to incur additional costs in order to implement these measures – for example, they may need to invest in training and development programs or provide better salaries/benefits packages. On the other hand, there are numerous benefits associated with improving working conditions across the world – increased productivity; improved morale; reduced turnover rates and similar ideas.

Ultimately, it is up to employers themselves to decide whether investing in social initiatives is worth their while (Tavora, 2019; Teipen & Mehl, 2021; Tesser & Serapioni, 2021; Thomas & Turnbull, 2021; Thornthwaite & Sheldon, 2019). However, if done correctly these investments can lead to a more equitable workplace which will benefit both employees and businesses alike. Therefore, it is essential that employers take into account all aspects of this cost-benefit analysis before making any decisions about how best to improve working conditions across the world. Despite the potential benefits of improving working conditions across the world, there are still some ideological arguments against such initiatives (Schuhrke, 2019; Scrimger, 2020; Seghezzi; Sheldon & Thornthwaite, 2020; Smith, 2019; Solaiman; Stanev, 2019). For example, some people argue that these measures will lead to a decrease in competition and thus reduce economic growth. Others believe that employers should not be responsible for providing social welfare services as this is the role of government. Finally, there are those who feel that any attempts to improve working conditions will only serve to increase costs for businesses without necessarily leading to any tangible improvements in employee wellbeing or productivity levels.

Ultimately, it is important to consider all sides of the argument before making any decisions about how best to improve working conditions across the world (Bray et al., 2019, 2020; Budd, 2020; Cabeza, 2019; Cam, 2021; Campolieti, 2020; Cesari et al., 2019). While it may be true that certain investments could lead to increased costs for businesses, it is also possible that these same investments could result in improved morale amongst staff members; reduced turnover rates; and ultimately higher profits. The contradictions have led to debates which led to the emergence of the politics of trade unionism.

2.2. THE POLITICS OF TRADE UNIONISM

Trade unionism is a form of collective bargaining that has been used for centuries to protect the rights and interests of workers (Barklamb, 2021; Barry & Wilkinson, 2022; Baturina et al., 2021; Beattie, 2019; Bechter et al., 2021; Bedkar & Prashad, 2020). It is an important part of labor history, as it has helped shape the way we think about labor relations today. In this section, we will analyze the politics of trade unionism and how it affects our society.

The first thing to understand about trade unions is that they are organizations formed by workers in order to negotiate better wages, working conditions, and other benefits with employers (Walker, 2020; Walters & Wadsworth, 2020; Warner, 2019; William & Cunningham, 2021; Williamson et al., 2019). Trade unions have traditionally been associated with left-wing politics due to their focus on protecting worker's rights from exploitation by employers. This association has led some people to view trade unions as being anti-capitalist or even socialist in nature. However, this is not necessarily true; while many trade unions do advocate for progressive policies such as higher minimum wages or stronger workplace safety regulations, there are also those who support more conservative economic policies such as lower taxes or deregulation of certain industries.

In addition to its political implications, trade unionism can also be seen as a tool for social change and empowerment among marginalized groups within society (Darlington & Mustchin, 2019; Das, 2023; Das & Singh, 2021; de Amorim et al., 2019; de Luna, 2022; De Prins et al., 2020). For example, women have often faced discrimination in the workplace due to gender bias; however, through collective bargaining power provided by trade unions they can fight back against these injustices and gain greater equality in terms of pay and job opportunities compared to men. Similarly, minority groups may use their collective strength through organized labor movements in order to challenge racism or other forms of discrimination within their workplaces or communities at large.

Yet, it should be noted that while there are certainly political implications associated with trade unionism – both positive and negative – ultimately its primary purpose is simply providing workers with a voice when negotiating with employers over wages and working conditions so that everyone involved can benefit from fair treatment under the law regardless of race or gender identity (Jha & Singh, 2019; Jiang & Yao, 2020; Jirjahn, 2022; Joyce et al.; Junior, 2022; Kaine, 2020; Katsabian, 2021; Kilic, 2021). By understanding how these dynamics work together we can ensure that all members of society receive equal protection under the law no matter what their background may be. There are many reasons why workers may decide to join a trade union (*see* Figure 2.3) and getting protection is an underlying theme in all of them.

Table I: Reasons for Joining Trade Unions

Reason for joining trade union	Worker (500)	Manager (60)	TU Leader (40)	Total (600)	Per-cent	Rank Preference		
						Worker	Manager	TU Leader
Safeguard against victimization	30	10	5	45	8	4	3	4
Protect & promote workers interest	120	20	16	156	26	2	1	1
Decent remuneration	280	6	9	295	49	1	5	2
Establishing legitimate rights	60	9	7	76	13	3	4	3
Resolve industrial grievances	10	15	3	28	5	5	2	5
Total	500	60	40	600	100			

(Source: Field Survey)

Figure 2.3. *Example of diverse reasons for joining a trade union.*

Source: Rajesh & Manoj (2014).

Overall, analyzing the politics behind trade unionism helps us understand why it remains an important part of modern labor relations today (Civinskas

& Dvorak, 2019; Clayton, 2021; Clibborn, 2019, 2020, 2021; Colas-Neila & Fargas, 2019). Through understanding its role in empowering marginalized groups, advocating for progressive policies, and providing workers with a voice during negotiations; we can see why it continues to play an integral role in shaping our economy. As long as people continue fighting for fairness within our workplaces then hopefully this type of collective action will remain strong into future generations.

Political theory can be used to critique trade unionism in the 21st century (Campolieti, 2020; Cesari et al., 2019; Chan, 2020a, b; Chantziaras et al., 2020; Chen et al., n.d., 2023). Trade unions have been around for centuries, and while they are often associated with labor movements of the past, their relevance today is just as important. By understanding how political theories such as Marxism, liberalism, and anarchism shape our current economic landscape we can better understand why trade unions remain a vital part of modern labor relations.

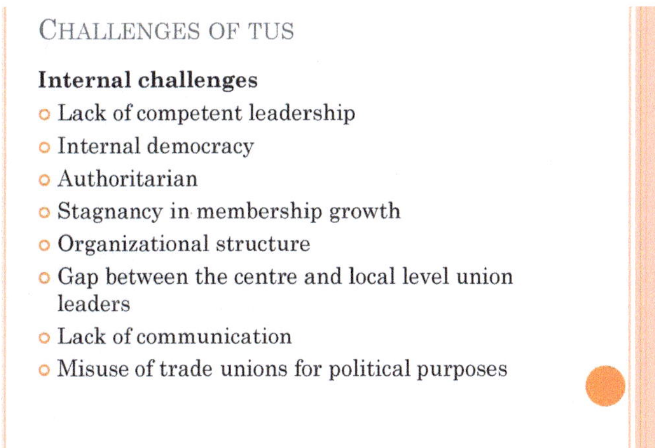

Figure 2.4. *Examples of the internal challenges faced by a major trade union.*

Source: Rose Greer.

Marxist theory views trade unionism as an essential tool for workers to gain power over employers by collectively bargaining for higher wages and improved working conditions (Joyce et al.; Junior, 2022; Kaine, 2020; Katsabian, 2021; Kilic, 2021; Kolling & Schnabel, 2022; Kowalewska, 2020). This type of collective action allows workers to challenge oppressive systems that keep them from achieving economic justice within society. Liberal theorists also view trade unionism positively, believing it helps create a more equitable distribution of wealth among all members of society regardless of race or gender identity. Anarchists on the other hand see it as a way to disrupt traditional hierarchies so that everyone has equal access to resources without relying on government intervention. These contrasting theories can explain some of the challenges that trade unions face today (*see* Figure 2.4 for an example).

In addition, trade unions provide marginalized groups with an opportunity to advocate for progressive policies that benefit all members of society (Mezihorak et al.; Morritt, 2022; Murphy & Turner, 2020; Nespoli, 2019; Newman et al., 2019; Nga & Nga, 2021). For example, many organizations focus on advocating for fair pay laws which help ensure women receive equal pay compared to men in similar positions. They also work towards eliminating discrimination based on race or sexual orientation within workplaces, so everyone receives fair treatment under the law regardless of their background.

Despite any preconceived notions associated with trade unionism, there are still some contradictions that exist within the movement (Howell, 2021; Hungler, 2022; Ilsoe & Soderqvist; Jarota, 2022; Jha & Singh, 2019; Jiang & Yao, 2020). For instance, while unions may advocate for progressive policies and economic justice, they can also be seen as a tool of corporate power in certain cases. This is because many organizations have been known to negotiate contracts that favor employers over workers in terms of wages and benefits. Additionally, some unions have been accused of being too focused on protecting their own interests rather than those of all members within society.

Furthermore, due to the changing nature of workspaces, specializations, and industries, traditional forms of trade unionism may not always be effective (Stevis, 2022; Svec et al., 2021; Tavora, 2019; Teipen & Mehl, 2021; Tesser & Serapioni, 2021; Thomas & Turnbull, 2021). As technology advances and more people become specialized in different fields, it becomes increasingly difficult for one organization to represent everyone's interests. In addition, since most workplaces now operate on a global scale, it is hard for any single union to effectively organize workers across multiple countries or regions.

While trade unionism has historically provided marginalized groups with an opportunity to challenge oppressive systems and advocate for progressive policies that benefit all members of society regardless of race or gender identity, there are still some contradictions associated with the movement today (Diessner et al., 2022; Dobbins et al., 2020, 2021; Dockes,

2019; Dorigatti et al., n.d.; Dorigatti & Pedersini, 2021). From negotiating contracts that favor employers over workers to its inability to effectively organize workers across multiple countries or regions due to technological advancements and specialization trends – these issues must be addressed if we want trade unions to continue advocating for economic justice within our societies. Ultimately, it is up to us as individuals and members of society to decide whether or not trade unionism is a force for good based on our own normative values and ethics.

In the end, we must remember that trade unions are only one part of a larger movement towards economic justice in our societies (Lukacova et al., 2022; Lyddon, 2021; Lyutov, 2022; MacKenzie & Lucio, 2019; Madimutsa; Mahas-Demydas & Rudnytska, 2019). We must continue to work together with other organizations and activists in order to ensure that everyone has access to fair wages, safe working conditions, and equal opportunities regardless of their race or gender identity. Only then can we truly say that trade unionism is a force for good within our societies.

The success of trade unions in some countries and their failure in others is a complex issue that requires further exploration (Schmidt & Muller, 2021; Schofield-Georgeson, 2022; Schofield-Georgeson & Rawling, 2020; Schuessler et al., 2019). It is clear, however, that the decline of union membership has had an impact on workers' rights and economic justice around the world. In order to ensure that trade unions continue to be a force for good within our societies, we must address the issues mentioned above as well as other challenges facing organized labor today. Only then can we hope to see a resurgence of trade unionism across all countries and regions.

At the same time, it is important to understand why some societies, politicians, and opinion-leaders oppose mass trade unionization (Svec et al., 2021; Tavora, 2019; Teipen & Mehl, 2021; Tesser & Serapioni, 2021; Thomas & Turnbull, 2021; Thornthwaite & Sheldon, 2019). In many cases, these opponents are motivated by a desire to maintain their own power or privilege. They may fear that organized labor will challenge their authority or disrupt existing economic systems. Additionally, they may be concerned about the potential for unions to become too powerful and threaten the stability of society as a whole. Finally, there is often an ideological opposition to trade unions based on conservatism.

Ultimately, we must recognize that trade unionism can be a force for good in our societies if it is properly regulated and supported by governments and other stakeholders (Morritt, 2022; Murphy & Turner, 2020; Nespoli, 2019;

Newman et al., 2019; Nga & Nga, 2021; Ngai, 2020; Nicklich & Helfen, 2019). We must also ensure that workers' rights are respected and protected so that everyone has access to fair wages and safe working conditions regardless of their race or gender identity. By doing this we can help create more equitable societies where all people have access to economic justice and opportunity. The law is part of this process.

2.3. DEVELOPING A LEGAL FRAMEWORK OF INDUSTRIAL RELATIONS

Industrial relations are an important part of any business, and developing a legal framework to ensure that these relationships remain healthy is essential (Foley & Williamson, 2021; Ford & Gillan, 2022; Ford & Ward, 2021; Forde; Forsyth, 2022; Foster et al., 2021). A well-crafted industrial relations policy can help protect both employers and employees from potential disputes or misunderstandings. It also helps create a safe working environment for all parties involved.

The first step in creating an effective industrial relations policy is to understand the relevant laws and regulations governing employment in your jurisdiction (Stapley, 2021; Stevis, 2022; Svec et al., 2021; Tavora, 2019; Teipen & Mehl, 2021; Tesser & Serapioni, 2021). This includes understanding the rights of workers, such as minimum wage requirements, overtime pay rules, vacation entitlements, health, and safety standards, and similar ideas. Once you have a clear understanding of the applicable laws and regulations, you can begin drafting your own policies that will be tailored to meet the needs of your organization.

When crafting an industrial relations policy, it is important to consider how it will affect both employers and employees alike (Roy, 2022; Roychowdhury, 2019; Rubery et al.; Sakharuk, 2021; Sanchez-Mosquera, 2022; Sanz et al., 2020). For example, if you plan on introducing new disciplinary procedures or performance management systems then make sure they are fair for everyone involved – this could include providing training opportunities for staff, so they understand their rights under the new system before it is implemented. Additionally, consider how collective bargaining agreements (CBAs) may impact your policies; if there are existing union contracts in place then make sure they are taken into account when formulating your own rules around wages or other benefits provided by the company.

It is also important to remember that while having a strong legal framework is beneficial for protecting both employers and employees alike; communication between all parties should still be encouraged at every stage of the development process (Ellem, 2021; Ellem et al., 2020; Engblom & Lundberg, 2019; Espinosa, 2021; Eustace, 2021; Fang et al., 2021). This ensures everyone understands what is expected from them within their role within the organization as well as helping build trust between employer/employee relationships which ultimately leads to better productivity levels overall. Figure 2.5 is an example of an industrial relations framework on a national level beyond company policies. Nevertheless, company policy remains an important starting point for the development of these legal frameworks.

Figure 2.5. *Legal framework for industrial relations in Uganda.*

Source: Farida Sanjaya.

Finally, once you have developed an effective industrial relations policy do not forget about regularly reviewing it – changes in legislation or industry trends may mean certain aspects need updating over time so keep up with any developments that could potentially affect your business operations (Forde; Forsyth, 2022; Foster et al., 2021; Franceschini, 2020; Freedland & Dhorajiwala, 2019; Fuchs et al., 2019). Doing so will help ensure continued success for years to come. One of the important aids for this process is trade union law and related regulations. Trade union law has been around for centuries, and its evolution over time and across the globe is an interesting one. In Europe, trade unions have existed since the Middle Ages, when guilds were formed to protect workers' rights. These guilds eventually evolved into modern-day labor unions in the 19th century.

In North America, trade unionism began with the formation of craft unions in Canada during the early 1800s (Hungler, 2022; Ilsoe & Soderqvist; Jarota, 2022; Jha & Singh, 2019; Jiang & Yao, 2020; Jirjahn, 2022; Joyce et al.). The first major labor organization was established in 1866 by a group of printers who called themselves "The Knights of Labor" – this organization would later become one of the most influential labor organizations in history. In Australia, trade unionism dates back to 1856 when stonemasons formed their own association to fight for better wages and working conditions. This led to other trades forming similar associations which ultimately resulted in what we now know as today's Australian Council of Trade Unions (ACTU).

In Asia, Japan was one of the earliest countries to adopt trade union laws with its Industrial Disputes Act being passed in 1947 – this act provided protection for workers against unfair dismissal or discrimination based on race/gender and similar ideas, while also allowing them collective bargaining rights if they so desired. Similarly South Korea adopted its own version known as "the Basic Law on Labor Relations" which came into effect from 1988 onwards providing similar protections as those found within Japanese legislation but also introducing additional measures such as minimum wage regulations too. These different hotspots of trade union history all demonstrate its importance of social, political, and economic development.

Understanding these histories can be important for crafting your own framework for human resources (Quinlan & Maxwell-Stewart; Radzi et al., 2022; Ramsay & Webster, 2019; Ravn & Oyum, 2020; Razak et al., 2022). Finally, it should be noted that while there are many similarities between different countries' approaches towards labor relations there are still some differences depending upon where you look – so make sure you do your research before formulating any policies or procedures related specifically to your business operations. Doing so will help ensure compliance with local laws whilst also protecting both employers and employees alike from potential disputes down line.

The development of trade union law across the world has been a long and complex process, with different countries taking their own approach to protecting workers' rights (Demougin et al., 2019; Desai & Randeria, 2020;

Devinatz, 2020, 2022; Di Carlo, 2020; Diessner et al., 2022). While there are some commonalities between these approaches, there are also divergent patterns that can be observed depending on where you look. Collective bargaining is an important component of these developments (*see* Figure 2.6).

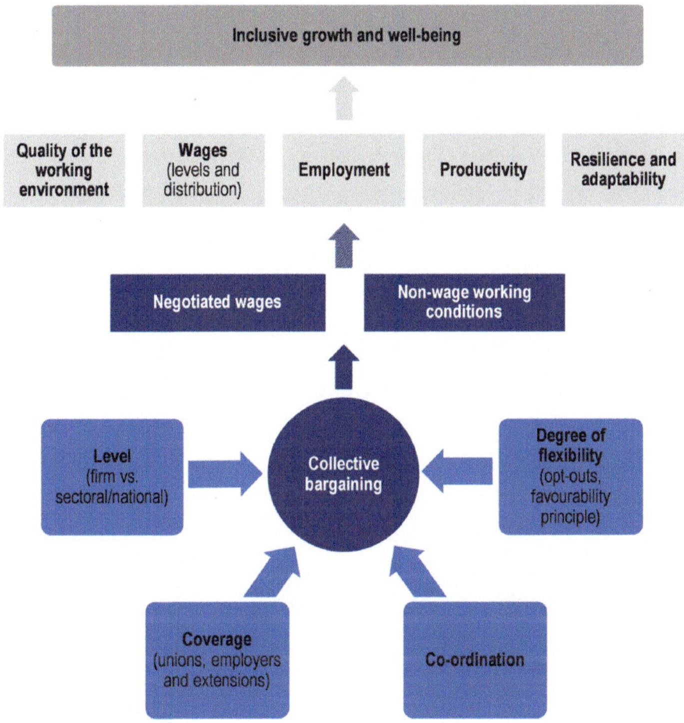

Figure 2.6. *The role of collective bargaining systems for labor market performance.*

Source: OECD iLibrary.

In Europe for example, many countries have adopted legislation similar to the European Union's (EU) Charter of Fundamental Rights which provides protection against discrimination in employment as well as collective bargaining rights for employees (Bray et al., 2020; Budd, 2020; Cabeza, 2019; Cam, 2021; Campolieti, 2020; Cesari et al., 2019; Chan, 2020a, b). This is particularly true in Germany where its Works Constitution Act (Betriebsverfassungsgesetz) was passed in 1952 – this act provided a framework for employee representation within companies while also allowing them certain legal protections such as those related to dismissal or working hours and similar ideas. Similarly, France has its Labor Code which came into effect from 1945 onwards providing similar protections but also introducing additional measures such as minimum wage regulations too.

Moving away from Europe we find that other countries have taken their own approach towards labor relations (Gramano & Gaudio, 2019; Grodem & Hippe, 2019; Guillaume, 2022; Guiso, 2020; Gunnigle et al., 2019; Gunther & Hopner, 2023). Japan being one example that is uniquely relevant to other industrialized nations who claim the liberal democracy mantra. In other parts of Asia, we see much the same pattern emerging – China having introduced its Labor Law back in 1994 which provides protection against unfair dismissal and discrimination whilst also allowing collective bargaining if desired by either party involved. India too has followed suit here with its own raft of legislation and policy amendments.

The United States meanwhile has had various pieces of legislation over time including the National Labor Relations Act (NLRA) passed back in 1935 – this act provided basic rights for employees when it comes to forming unions and engaging in collective bargaining activities amongst other things (Trif & Szabo; Truyols, 2019; Tu et al., 2022; Velluti, 2022; Vinichenko et al., 2020; Vulkan & Larsson, 2019; Walker, 2020). This is despite the move towards capitalism and the political polarization that has often characterized perceptions of trade unions in the USA. Some politicians have posited a so-called "third way" in which the traditional divisions between the left and right are blurred in favor of consensus.

While there may be differences between how different countries approach labor relations, they all share some common elements at least when it comes to protecting workers' rights and ensuring fair treatment within workplaces (Sanchez-Mosquera, 2022; Sanz et al., 2020; Schlachter, 2019; Schmidt & Muller, 2021; Schofield-Georgeson, 2022). It is therefore important for employers everywhere to familiarize themselves with local laws so they can ensure compliance and protect both themselves and their employees alike from potential disputes. The development of trade union law across the world has been a long and complex process, with different countries taking their own approach to protecting workers' rights. Despite this, there are some commonalities that can be seen in many countries' laws. For example, most nations have adopted legislation which provides protection for employees against unfair dismissal or discrimination based on race/gender and similar ideas, while also allowing them collective bargaining rights if they so desire.

In Europe, the EU has implemented several directives over the years which provide a framework for labor relations within its member states –

such as those related to working time, health, and safety regulations (Larsson, 2020; Lawreniuk, 2023; Lee & Tapia, 2021; Leggett, 2019; Ligthart et al., 2022; Liu, 2023; Lize et al., 2022). Similarly in North America, the United States and Canada have both adopted legislation which provides protection for workers' rights. However, there are still some areas where trade union law is lacking in certain parts of the world. For example, in many developing countries such as India or China, labor laws are often weak or non-existent – leaving workers vulnerable to exploitation by employers who may not be held accountable for their actions. This can lead to a lack of job security and poor working conditions for those employed in these countries.

In addition to this, even when trade union laws do exist, they may not always be enforced effectively due to a lack of resources or political will from governments (Solaiman; Stanev, 2019; Stanford, 2021; Stapley, 2021; Stevis, 2022; Svec et al., 2021; Tavora, 2019; Teipen & Mehl, 2021). This means that employees may find themselves unable to access justice if they feel their rights have been violated by an employer – leading them into further hardship and insecurity. While progress has been made in terms of protecting workers' rights across the globe through various pieces of legislation and regulations – there is still much work left to do before all employees everywhere can enjoy fair treatment within their workplaces. It is therefore essential that governments continue investing resources into strengthening existing laws and introducing new ones where necessary so that everyone can benefit from improved working conditions as well as job security.

Within North America, the United States and Canada have both adopted legislation which provides protection for workers' rights (Adewumi, 2021; Agarwal et al., 2020; Ahuja, 2020; Amosse et al., 2019; Archel et al., 2022; Ashwin et al., 2020). This is consistent with their credentials as leading liberal democracies. Nevertheless, there are other parts of the world that have been considerably less successful in embedding a trade union movement. Some of these countries lack structure while others simply lack political will. Then there are the risks of trade unionism which include industrial strife. Risk-averse politicians have therefore kept away from trade union issues.

Some jurisdictions do not have sufficient protections for workers (Ackers, 2020; Addison & Teixeira, 2019a, b; Adewumi, 2021; Agarwal et al., 2020; Ahuja, 2020). Even when trade union laws do exist, they may not always be enforced effectively due to a lack of resources or political will from governments. This means that employees may find themselves unable to access justice if they feel their rights have been violated by an employer – leading them into further hardship and insecurity. Moreover, some politicians perceive trade unionists as a threat to their power and influence. This impasse is not helped by trade unionists who are overly militant in their approaches.

Moving further east we find Japan leading the way when it comes to labor relations legislation in the Asia Pacific region (Mahmood & Banerjee, 2020; Mailand, 2019; Markey, 2020; Martin, 2022; Martin et al., 2021; McCrystal & Hardy, 2021). Australia is another country that has taken steps towards protecting worker's rights by introducing its Fair Work Act 2009 – this act covers everything from wages and conditions through to dispute resolution procedures. Despite differences between individual countries' approaches towards labor relations there are still some common threads running throughout all these different pieces of legislation – namely providing protection for employees whilst also allowing them collective bargaining powers if desired. This shows just how important it is for businesses operating internationally to ensure compliance with local laws wherever possible in order to avoid any potential disputes down line. Moreover, the economic impact of industrial relations makes them a high priority for any government.

2.4. THE IMPACT OF INDUSTRIAL RELATIONS ON THE ECONOMY

Industrial relations play a critical role in the economic development of any nation (Amosse et al., 2019; Archel et al., 2022; Ashwin et al., 2020; Avgar, 2020; Baines & Armstrong, 2019; Baines & Cunningham, 2020). It is an important factor that affects the productivity, efficiency, and profitability of businesses. Industrial relations refer to the relationship between employers, employees, and trade unions in a workplace setting. This relationship can have both positive and negative impacts on the economy as a whole.

The most obvious impact of industrial relations on the economy is job creation or destruction (Hirsch & Mueller, 2020; Hoffrogge, 2019; Howell, 2019, 2021; Hungler, 2022; Ilsoe & Soderqvist; Jarota, 2022). When there are good working relationships between employers and employees, it encourages investment which leads to more jobs being created for people who need them. On the other hand, when there are poor working conditions or unfair labor practices, it can lead to job losses due to strikes or lockouts by workers protesting against their employer's actions.

Another way industrial relations affect economic growth is through wage levels and CBAs (Jarota, 2022; Jha & Singh, 2019; Jiang & Yao, 2020; Jirjahn, 2022; Joyce et al.; Junior, 2022; Kaine, 2020; Katsabian, 2021). CBAs are negotiated between employers and trade unions representing workers in order to set wages at fair levels that reflect current market conditions while also providing benefits such as health insurance coverage or vacation time off work for employees. Higher wages mean increased spending power for consumers which helps stimulate economic activity while lower wages may reduce consumer spending leading to slower growth rates overall.

Finally, industrial relations also influence business costs such as production costs associated with labor-management disputes over issues like overtime pay or safety regulations compliance requirements imposed by government agencies like OSHA (Occupational Safety & Health Administration) (Peruzzo et al.; Pitteloud, 2022; Preminger & Bondy; Quinlan & Maxwell-Stewart; Radzi et al., 2022; Ramsay & Webster, 2019). These disputes often result in higher production costs due to delays caused by negotiations over these matters which can ultimately hurt businesses' bottom lines if not resolved quickly enough resulting in reduced profits for companies operating within certain industries affected by these types of disputes. It is clear that industrial relations have far reaching implications on economies around the world from job creation/destruction rates all the way down to individual business operations costs.

These dynamics are associated with labor-management disputes over various issues related directly back into this field of study itself (Ravn & Oyum, 2020; Razak et al., 2022; Refslund & Arnholtz, 2022; Ritson, 2019a, b; Riva & Rizza, 2021). This has the effect of making it one worth paying close attention to in our ever-changing globalized world today. When it comes to industrial relations, there are two main perspectives: economic development and social development. The economic development perspective focuses on the impact of industrial relations on a country's economy. This includes job creation/destruction rates, wages, productivity levels, and other factors that affect a nation's overall economic performance. On the other hand, the social development perspective looks at how industrial relations can improve working conditions for employees as well as their quality of life in general by providing better wages and benefits packages or improved safety regulations compliance requirements imposed by government agencies like OSHA. As Figure 2.7 shows, globalization is another dynamic to consider in these analyzes.

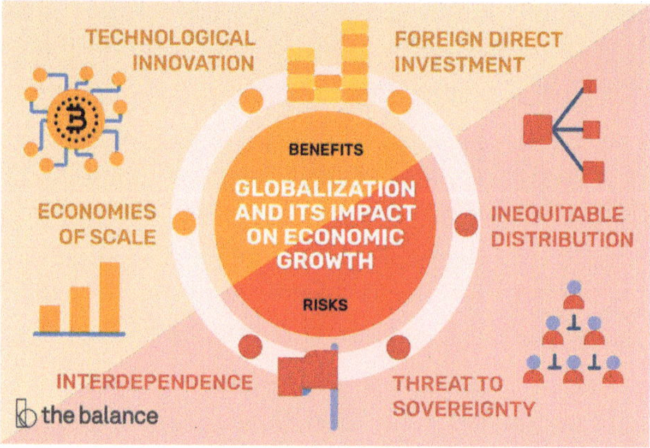

Figure 2.7. *Impact of globalization on economic growth.*

Source: The Balance.

The economic development perspective is primarily concerned with increasing efficiency within an industry while also creating jobs which will ultimately lead to increased GDP growth for a given country over time (Gasparri, 2021; Gasparri et al., 2019; Gasparri & Tassinari, 2020; Gavin, 2022; Giannakopoulos & Laliotis, 2020). This approach often involves reducing labor costs through automation or outsourcing certain tasks to cheaper labor markets abroad in order to maximize profits for businesses operating within this sector of the economy. Additionally, this approach may involve introducing new technologies into production processes in order to increase output levels while simultaneously decreasing input costs associated with labor-management disputes over various issues related directly back into this area of policy and practice.

In contrast, the social development perspective takes a more holistic view when looking at industrial relations focusing not only on improving efficiency but also taking into account employee welfare such as providing better wages and benefits packages or improved safety regulations compliance requirements imposed by government agencies (Baines & Armstrong, 2019; Baines & Cunningham, 2020; Bancarzewski & Hardy, 2021; Barklamb, 2021; Barry & Wilkinson, 2022). This approach seeks to create an environment where workers feel valued and respected leading them to be more productive thus resulting in higher output levels from businesses operating within certain industries affected by these types of disputes. Additionally, this type of approach may help reduce turnover rates due to improved morale among employees who feel they are being treated fairly leading them to stay longer with their current employers rather than seeking out alternative employment opportunities elsewhere, potentially saving companies money in terms of recruitment fees associated with hiring new personnel.

Both approaches have their merits when it comes to managing industrial relations effectively (Boumans, 2022; Bourguignon & Floquet, 2019; Bradley & Rowland, 2021; Bray et al., 2019, 2020). However, depending upon what goals you wish to achieve (whether it is maximizing profits through increased efficiency or creating an environment where workers feel valued and respected) either one could be suitable depending upon your particular situation so make sure you do your research before deciding which path is best suited for your business operations. It is also worth considering whether there is a good fit between your organizational goals and the requirements of the context within which you operate your business. A case in point are the imperatives of industrialization (*see* Figure 2.8).

PATTERNS OF CHANGE: Industrialization

Effects of Industrialization	
Size of Cities	• Growth of factories, bringing job seekers to cities • Urban areas doubling, tripling, or quadrupling in size • Factories developing near sources of energy • Many new industrial cities specializing in certain industries
Living Conditions	• No sanitary codes or building controls • Lack of adequate housing, education, and police protection • Lack of running water and indoor plumbing • Frequent epidemics sweeping through slums • Eventually, better housing, healthier diets, and cheaper clothing
Working Conditions	• Industrialization creating new jobs for workers • Workers trying to keep pace with machines • Factories dirty and unsanitary • Workers running dangerous machines for long hours in unsafe conditions • Harsh and severe factory discipline • Eventually, higher wages, shorter hours, and better working conditions
Emerging Social Classes	• Growing middle class of factory owners, shippers, and merchants • Upper class of landowners and aristocrats resentful of rich middle class • Lower middle class of factory overseers and skilled workers • Workers overworked and underpaid • In general, a rising standard of living, with some groups excluded

Figure 2.8. *Patterns of change in industrialization.*

Source: Insights IAS.

The economic development perspective emphasizes the importance of creating an environment conducive to business growth by providing incentives such as tax breaks or subsidies for businesses operating within certain industries while also ensuring that workers receive fair wages and benefits so they can continue contributing positively towards their respective economies (Haipeter, 2020; Hakansta et al., n.d.; Hamberger, 2020; Harvey & Turnbull, 2020; Hendy, 2022; Herrero, 2022; Hilgert, 2019). This approach is often seen in countries with strong labor unions where CBAs are negotiated between employers and employees in order to ensure both sides get what they want out of any given situation without sacrificing too much from either side. The social development perspective seeks to protect workers from exploitation while also promoting better labor-management relationships which ultimately leads to increased job satisfaction among employees resulting in higher morale throughout entire organizations leading up to even further positive impacts on their respective economies.

One of the more interesting dynamics is the relationship between industrial relations and human development (Junior, 2022; Kaine, 2020; Katsabian, 2021; Kilic, 2021; Kolling & Schnabel, 2022; Kowalewska, 2020; Kupec et al., 2022). The human development index (HDI) is a measure of the average achievements in a country in three basic dimensions of human development: health, education, and living standards. It is used to compare countries across the globe based on their histories, current status, and future prospects for social-economic development. Countries with higher HDIs tend to have better industrial relations policies and practices than those with lower HDIs due to their greater ability to invest in labor-management initiatives such as CBAs or safety regulations compliance requirements.

These correlations are demonstrated empirically in existing research (Fuchs et al., 2019; Galik et al., 2022; Gall, 2021; Gardawski & Towalski, 2020; Gasparri, 2021; Gasparri et al., 2019). For example, countries like Norway which has an HDI score of 0.944 are known for having strong labor unions that negotiate CBAs between employers and employees while also providing workers with improved working conditions such as safety regulations and compliance requirements. Contrastingly, countries like India (which has an HDI score of 0.647) still lack adequate protection for its workers from exploitation despite recent efforts by the government to improve labor laws and regulations throughout the country.

It is clear that there is a correlation between the HDI of a country and its industrial relations policies and practices (Giraud, 2020; Godino & Molina, 2022; Gooberman, 2022; Goods & Ellem; Goyer et al., 2022; Graca, 2021). Countries with higher HDIs tend to have better industrial relations policies and practices than those with lower HDIs due to their greater ability to invest in labor-management initiatives such as CBAs or safety regulations compliance requirements. This ultimately leads to even further positive impacts on their respective economies.

A comparative case study analysis of industrial relations in Nordic countries versus Sub-Saharan African countries provides a unique insight into the differences between these two regions (Lawreniuk, 2023; Lee & Tapia, 2021; Leggett, 2019; Ligthart et al., 2022; Liu, 2023; Lize et al., 2022; Lloyd & Payne, 2021). In general, Nordic countries have higher HDI scores than those found in Sub-Saharan Africa, and this is reflected in their respective labor laws and regulations. For example, Finland has an HDI score of 0.890 which is significantly higher than that of Nigeria (0.521). This difference can be seen through the various labor policies implemented by each country such as CBAs or safety regulations compliance requirements.

In comparison to Nordic countries, many Sub-Saharan African nations lack adequate protection for their workers from exploitation despite recent efforts by the government to improve labor laws and regulations throughout the region (Gasparri & Tassinari, 2020; Gavin, 2022; Giannakopoulos & Laliotis, 2020; Giraud, 2020; Godino & Molina, 2022). This can be attributed to lower levels of HDI scores which are indicative of poorer economic conditions within these nations compared to those found in more developed parts of the world such as Europe or North America. As a result, employers often take advantage of lax enforcement mechanisms when it comes to workplace rights violations leading up even further negative impacts on their respective economies.

It is important for governments around the world to recognize that investing in better industrial relations policies and practices will ultimately lead up to even further positive impacts on their respective economies (Dorigatti & Pedersini, 2021; Dorrenbacher et al., 2021; Drucza, 2019; Dupuis & Greer, 2022; Edwards & Hodder, 2022). By doing so, they can ensure that workers are provided with improved working conditions such as safety regulations and compliance requirements while also providing them with fair wages through CBAs between employers and employees. Ultimately, this will help create a more equitable society where everyone benefits from increased economic growth.

The findings of this comparative case study suggest that there is a direct correlation between the HDI of a country and its industrial relations policies and practices (Gall, 2021; Gardawski & Towalski, 2020; Gasparri, 2021; Gasparri et al., 2019; Gasparri & Tassinari, 2020; Gavin, 2022). Countries with higher HDIs tend to have better industrial relations policies and practices than those with lower HDIs. This differential can be partially explained by the greater ability of advanced nations to invest in labor-management initiatives such as CBAs or safety regulations compliance requirements, hence positively impacting on their respective economies. Therefore, it is important for governments around the world to prioritize investing in improving working conditions for all citizens regardless of where they live so that everyone can benefit from improved economic growth opportunities. One of the instrumentalities for this goal is social dialog.

2.5. DEVELOPING A SOCIAL DIALOG FOR INDUSTRIAL RELATIONS AND COMMUNICATION

In today's ever-evolving business landscape, it is essential for companies to develop a social dialog between their employees and management (Ellem et al., 2020; Engblom & Lundberg, 2019; Espinosa, 2021; Eustace, 2021; Fang et al., 2021; Fergus & Godfrey, 2021). This dialog should be used to foster better industrial relations and communication within the workplace. The development of a social dialog can help create an environment where both parties feel comfortable expressing their opinions and ideas in order to reach mutually beneficial outcomes. It also helps build trust between employers and employees, which is key for successful collaboration.

One way to start developing this type of relationship is by creating open forums or discussion groups that allow workers to voice their concerns without fear of retribution from management (Lyutov, 2022; MacKenzie & Lucio, 2019; Madimutsa; Mahas-Demydas & Rudnytska, 2019; Mahmood & Banerjee, 2020). These forums should be moderated by someone who understands the needs of both sides, such as a human resource professional or union representative. Additionally, these discussions should focus on topics related to job satisfaction, safety protocols, wages/benefits packages, and similar ideas, so that all stakeholders have an opportunity to provide input into decisions that affect them directly.

Another important aspect of fostering good industrial relations is providing regular feedback sessions with supervisors or managers about employee performance and progress towards goals set out at the beginning of each year or project cycle (Nowak, 2021; Nurlinah et al., 2021; O'Keeffe & Papadopoulos, 2021; Oberfichtner et al., 2020; Opute & Koch, 2020). This allows employees to understand how they are being evaluated while giving them an opportunity to ask questions about any areas where they may need additional support or guidance from management in order achieve success in their roles. Finally, it is important for companies to recognize the importance of listening when engaging in conversations with staff members regarding workplace issues; this will ensure everyone feels heard and respected during negotiations over changes within the organization.

By taking these steps towards building strong relationships through effective communication channels, businesses can create positive working environments where everyone feels valued and appreciated for their contributions – ultimately leading toward greater productivity (Dupuis & Greer, 2022; Edwards & Hodder, 2022; Ellem, 2021; Ellem et al., 2020; Engblom & Lundberg, 2019). Social dialog is an important tool for advancing positive industrial relations, but it also has its limitations. For example, while conversations between employees and management can be beneficial in terms of understanding each other's perspectives and finding common ground on issues, they may not always lead to a resolution that satisfies both parties. Additionally, social dialog can be difficult to facilitate when there are large numbers of people involved or if the topics being discussed are complex or sensitive in nature. As Figure 2.9 shows, the lack of good communication can become a major barrier to positive industrial relations.

MAJOR HURDLES TO IMPROVE INDUSTRIAL RELATIONS CLIMATE IN NEPAL

- Lack of transparency
- Low concern for social dialogue at work place
- Trade Union affiliation to political parties
- Lack of good understanding of IRs values and standards among employers
- Existing problems like power outage, inconsistent industrial, policies, global market competition, political instability etc.

Figure 2.9. *Barriers to relations in Nepal.*

Source: Ethan Warren.

In addition to these potential drawbacks, it is important to remember that social dialog should never replace formal processes such as CBAs or grievance procedures; rather, it should supplement them by providing an additional avenue for communication between employers and employees (Hilgert, 2019; Hirsch & Mueller, 2020; Hoffrogge, 2019; Howell, 2019, 2021; Hungler, 2022; Ilsoe & Soderqvist; Jarota, 2022). Ultimately, the success of any workplace relationship depends on mutual respect and trust –

something which must be cultivated through regular interactions over time. Overall, social dialog is a valuable tool for promoting positive industrial relations within organizations.

Nevertheless, businesses must recognize its merits as well as its limitations in order to ensure successful outcomes from their efforts (Barry & Wilkinson, 2022; Baturina et al., 2021; Beattie, 2019; Bechter et al., 2021; Bedkar & Prashad, 2020; Behrens et al., 2020). By taking into account all aspects of communication – including listening carefully to employee concerns – companies can create strong relationships with their staff members that will benefit everyone involved. In today's ever-evolving business landscape, it is essential for companies to develop a social dialog between their employees and management. This dialog should be used to foster better industrial relations and communication within the workplace.

As Figure 2.10 shows, this is a multidisciplinary endeavor that calls for inclusivity (Ozkiziltan, 2019, 2020; Peetz, 2021; Peetz et al., 2020; Peruzzo et al.; Pitteloud, 2022; Preminger & Bondy). For example, some cultures may place a greater emphasis on respect for authority figures than others; this could lead to misunderstandings if managers do not take the time to explain why certain decisions have been made or what expectations they have for staff members. Similarly, cultural norms around communication styles can also affect how conversations between management and employees unfold – something which should be taken into consideration when setting up feedback sessions or other forms of dialog within the organization.

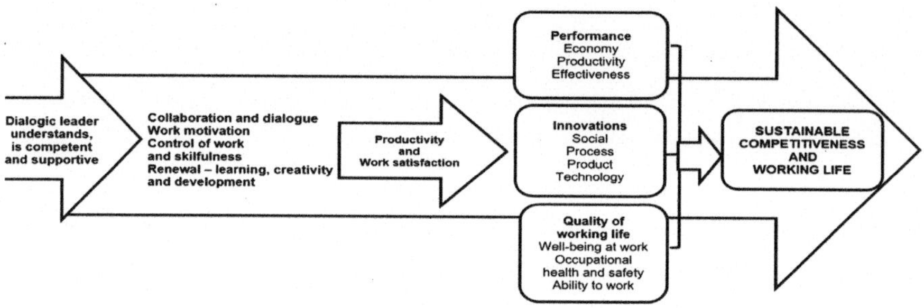

Figure 2.10. *The multidisciplinary framework of dialogic leadership and development.*

Source: Syvänen & Loppela (2022).

Ultimately, conducting a cultural relativism critique of social dialog in industrial relations is essential for creating positive working environments where everyone feels respected and valued regardless of their background or culture (Truyols, 2019; Tu et al., 2022; Velluti, 2022; Vinichenko et al., 2020; Vulkan & Larsson, 2019; Walker, 2020; Walters & Wadsworth, 2020). By taking the time to understand different perspectives on workplace issues, businesses can ensure that all parties involved are heard during negotiations over changes within the organization. However, it is important to note that communication can only go so far in diffusing industrial strife.

While dialog between management and employees is essential for creating a positive working environment, there are certain limitations which must be taken into consideration when attempting to resolve conflicts within the workplace (Tiraboschi, 2020; Tomassetti, 2021; Trif & Szabo; Truyols, 2019; Tu et al., 2022; Velluti, 2022; Vinichenko et al., 2020).

In addition, language barriers can also impede effective communication in industrial relations contexts (Collins et al., 2020; Cooke et al., 2019; Croucher & Okland, 2021; D'Art, 2020; da Costa & Horn, 2021; Dalla Sega, 2021). If workers come from different countries with varying levels of English proficiency (or any other language used by the company), then it is likely that misunderstandings will arise due to miscommunication or misinterpretation of instructions given by supervisors or colleagues. This could lead to further conflict as well as decreased productivity overall – something which businesses should strive to avoid at all costs.

Finally, power dynamics play an important role in determining how successful negotiations over changes within an organization will be (Abd Razak & Mahmood, 2019; Ackers, 2020; Addison & Teixeira, 2019a, b; Adewumi, 2021). If one party holds more power than another (e.g., employers vs employees), then it is likely that their interests will prevail regardless of whether they are actually beneficial for everyone involved in the dispute resolution process – thus making it difficult for both sides to reach a mutually satisfactory agreement without outside intervention such as mediation services provided by labor unions or government agencies like OSHA (Occupational Safety & Health Administration).

CHAPTER 2 SUMMARY

This chapter has explored the setting and legal context for industrial relations. At the center of this context are social concerns about working conditions. These concerns have led to the emergence and subsequent politicization of the trade union movement. By developing a legal framework for industrial relations, there is scope for better stabilization of the economy and the avoidance of industrial strife. The chapter argues that social dialog and complex communication networks are necessary for the fostering of good industrial relations. The latter is a term that will be explored in more detail within the next chapter.

CHAPTER 3

The Conceptualization of Industrial Relations

Contents

The third chapter in this book further conceptualizes industrial relations to add to the ideas that were introduced in the first two chapters. We will summarize the history of global and local industrial relations. In doing so, this chapter introduces some dispute resolution mechanisms such as communication, arbitration, and negotiation. Moreover, the chapter highlights the kind of strife and violence that can erupt if these techniques are not strategically deployed in time. We start this exploration with a historical review of industrial relations.

3.1. A BRIEF HISTORY OF INDUSTRIAL RELATIONS

Industrial relations are an important part of the global economy, and understanding their origins can help us better understand how they have evolved over time (Budd, 2020; Cabeza, 2019; Cam, 2021; Campolieti, 2020; Cesari et al., 2019; Chan, 2020a, b; Chantziaras et al., 2020). Industrial relations refer to the relationship between employers, employees, and labor unions in a workplace setting. This includes collective bargaining agreements (CBAs), wages, and benefits negotiations, dispute resolution processes, and other aspects of employment law. The history of industrial relations dates back to the 19th century when workers began organizing into trade unions in order to protect their rights as laborers.

The first major union was formed in England in 1824 by skilled artisans who sought better working conditions for themselves and others like them. This movement spread across Europe during this period with similar organizations forming throughout France, Germany, Italy, Spain, and other countries on the continent (Newman et al., 2019; Nga & Nga, 2021; Ngai, 2020; Nicklich & Helfen, 2019; Novitz & Andrijasevic, 2020; Nowak, 2021). In North America during this same period there were also efforts to organize labor movements, but these were largely unsuccessful due to strong opposition from business owners who feared that such organizations would threaten their profits or power within society. It was not until after World War I that organized labor began gaining traction in North America with large-scale strikes taking place throughout Canada and the United States during this time period.

Today industrial relations remain an integral part of many economies around the world as governments seek ways to ensure fair treatment for both employers and employees while promoting economic growth at the same time (Roche, n.d.; Roche & Gormley, 2020; Rosetti, 2019; Roy & Dubey, 2022; Roy, 2022; Roychowdhury, 2019). In some countries such as Japan there is a long tradition of cooperation between management and labor which has helped create one of the most successful economies on earth while elsewhere more adversarial approaches still exist where disputes often end up being resolved through court proceedings or government intervention rather than through negotiation between parties involved directly involved in a conflict situation. Figure 3.1 summarizes a comparative analysis of industrial relations across selected countries.

Table 3 – Key Aspects of the National Industrial Relations System in each Country

	Union Density and organisation	Statutory support for Employee Representation	Coverage and Level of Collective Bargaining
Germany	Density at 30% Unions organised mainly by sectors with unions covering multiple occupations within firms	Two forms of 'co-determination': workplace-based Works Councils and employee representation on Supervisory Boards. The coverage of each has fallen recently	Coverage at 80% Industry-based bargaining being still the dominant form, though some rise in firm-based collective agreements in the last few years
Spain	Density at 15% Two main union groups – one communist, the other more moderate socialist. A third smaller (anarchist) confederation exists	Workers committees (comite de empresas) are empowered to reach collective agreements with management. Unions are highly influential on the committees	Coverage at 75% Industry-based bargaining formally the key level, but considerable variation in practice between regions and firms
UK	Density at 30% Unions organised traditionally by craft / occupation – more recently, mergers have created larger general unions	Mainly through the Employment Relations Act (2000) which stipulates provisions for ballots on recognition. Some additional rights through European Directives	Coverage at 40% Collapse of multi-employer bargaining in last 20 years means that firm and plant bargaining are now the principal levels
US	Density at 14% History of 'business unionism' in which firms represent workers' narrow economic interests	Tortuous procedure for gaining legal support for union recognition; employers traditionally hostile to organising campaigns and courts offer little sympathy for unions	Coverage at 20??% Collapse of 'pattern bargaining means that where bargaining exists it is almost always at the level of the individual workplace

Figure 3.1. *Key aspects of national industrial relations systems in selected countries.*

Source: Edwards et al. (2004).

No matter what approach is taken however it is clear that industrial relations will continue playing an important role globally for years to come as businesses strive towards creating equitable workplaces where everyone can benefit from mutual respect regardless of background or position within a company hierarchy (Behrens et al., 2020; Behrens & Pekarek, n.d.; Belizon, 2019; Bellace et al., 2021; Ben & Sage, 2022; Berry & McDaniel, 2022). Understanding its origins helps us appreciate just how far we have come since those early days when workers first started fighting for their rights all those centuries ago. The differential approaches to industrial relations across nations can be explained by a variety of factors.

Firstly, the history and culture of each nation plays an important role in determining how labor-management relationships are structured (Fang et al., 2021; Fergus & Godfrey, 2021; Flynn & Schroder, 2021; Foley & Williamson, 2021; Ford & Gillan, 2022). For example, countries with strong trade union movements such as the United Kingdom or Germany tend to have more adversarial systems while those without such organizations like Japan or South Korea often favor cooperative models. Secondly, economic conditions also play a part in shaping these dynamics as countries with higher levels of unemployment may find it difficult to maintain harmonious working environments due to increased competition for jobs. Finally, government policies can also influence how employers and employees interact with one another – for instance, some governments may provide incentives for businesses that adopt certain practices which could lead them towards adopting more collaborative approaches rather than confrontational ones.

Overall, there is no single answer when it comes to explaining why different nations take varying approaches towards industrial relations but understanding the various factors at play helps us appreciate just how complex this issue really is (Mahas-Demydas & Rudnytska, 2019; Mahmood & Banerjee, 2020; Mailand, 2019; Markey, 2020; Martin, 2022). By taking into account historical context, cultural norms, economic realities, and governmental regulations we can gain insight into why certain strategies work better than others in specific contexts and hopefully use this knowledge to create fairer workplaces around the world where everyone benefits from mutual respect regardless of their background or position within a company hierarchy. Differentiated industrial relations across regions can have a significant impact on the way businesses operate and how employees are treated.

It is important to understand the various factors that contribute to this phenomenon in order to ensure that workers' rights are respected, and employers are able to remain competitive in an increasingly globalized economy (Sheldon & Thornthwaite, 2020; Smith, 2019; Solaiman; Stanev, 2019; Stanford, 2021; Stapley, 2021; Stevis, 2022). Historical context, cultural norms, economic realities, and governmental regulations all play a role in shaping industrial relations policies and practices around the world. By taking these into account we can gain insight into why certain strategies work better than others in specific contexts and hopefully use this knowledge to create fairer workplaces where everyone benefits from mutual respect regardless of their background or position within a company hierarchy. Figure 3.2 is an illustration of how different countries can adopt different approaches to industrial relations to address contextual diversities.

Figure 1

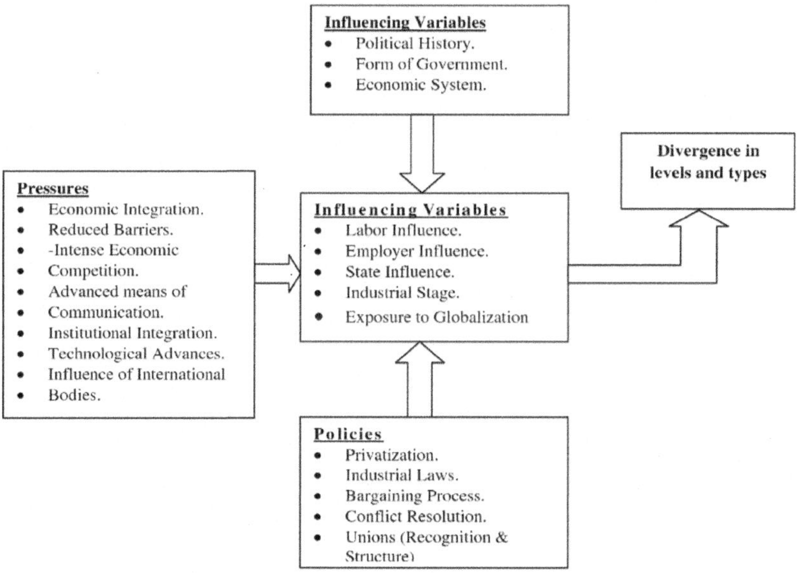

Figure 3.2. *Key dynamics in the industrial relations of India, China, and South Korea.*

Source: Ali (2005).

The implications of differentiated industrial relations across regions for policy makers, employers, employees, unions, and other stakeholders cannot be overstated (Sanchez-Mosquera, 2022; Sanz et al., 2020; Schlachter, 2019; Schmidt & Muller, 2021; Schofield-Georgeson, 2022). For policy makers it is essential that they take into account regional differences when formulating laws related to labor standards as well as incentives for businesses which promote more collaborative approaches towards employee-employer relationships rather than confrontational ones. Employers must also be aware of local customs when dealing with staff so as not to inadvertently cause offense or create disharmonious working environments due to increased competition for jobs. Finally, governments should consider providing incentives for businesses that adopt certain practices which could lead them towards adopting more collaborative approaches rather than confrontational ones.

By understanding the various factors at play when it comes to differentiated industrial relations across regions, we can gain insight into why certain strategies work better than others in specific contexts – ultimately leading us towards creating fairer workplaces around the world (Guiso, 2020; Gunnigle et al., 2019; Gunther & Hopner, 2023; Haipeter, 2020; Hakansta et al., n.d.; Hamberger, 2020). This will help ensure that workers' rights are respected while allowing employers to remain competitive in an increasingly globalized economy. Transnational or cross-culturally consistent industrial relations are essential for the success of any business. It is important to recognize that different countries have different laws and regulations when it comes to labor rights, which can lead to a variety of approaches being taken by employers in order to remain compliant with local legislation.

This means that businesses must be aware of the various cultural nuances at play when dealing with employees from other countries so as not to create an environment where workers feel disrespected or undervalued due to their background (Desai & Randeria, 2020; Devinatz, 2020, 2022; Di Carlo, 2020; Diessner et al., 2022; Dobbins et al., 2020). In addition, companies should strive towards creating employee-employer relationships rather than confrontational ones.

By taking these steps we can ensure that transnational and cross-cultural industrial relations become increasingly rationalized and justified regardless of hierarchical considerations (Bellace et al., 2021; Ben & Sage, 2022; Berry & McDaniel, 2022; Bhuta, 2022; Bischoff et al., 2021; Bogoeski, 2022). Industrial relations theory can help explain the differences between national, regional, continental, and global industrial relations. It is important to note that these differences are not only due to cultural or economic factors but also due to the different legal frameworks in place across countries.

As a case in point, some countries may have more stringent labor laws than others which could lead to a greater emphasis on collective bargaining and unionization in those countries compared with other nations where such regulations are less strict (Gardawski & Towalski, 2020; Gasparri, 2021; Gasparri et al., 2019; Gasparri & Tassinari, 2020; Gavin, 2022; Giannakopoulos & Laliotis, 2020). Additionally, certain regions may be more prone towards adopting particular approaches when it comes to dealing with employees – for instance, some areas may favor paternalistic relationships while others prefer a more collaborative approach. Furthermore, there are often disparities between how workers from different backgrounds are treated within companies – particularly when it comes to wages and job security.

This is especially true of migrant workers who often find themselves at a disadvantage as they lack local knowledge or contacts which could help them secure better employment opportunities or higher salaries (Refslund & Arnholtz, 2022; Ritson, 2019a, b; Riva & Rizza, 2021; Roche, n.d.; Roche & Gormley, 2020). As such, employers should strive towards creating equal opportunities for all their staff regardless of their background so as not to create an environment where certain groups feel devalued due to their background. In conclusion, understanding the various theories behind industrial relations can help us understand why there exist differences between national, regional, continental, and global approaches when it comes to managing employee-employer relationships. By taking into account both cultural and economic factors we can ensure that workplaces become increasingly fair around the world while allowing businesses to achieve competitiveness in dynamic economies. One of the instrumentalities that might be utilized is conflict resolution.

3.2. CONFLICT RESOLUTION TECHNIQUES IN INDUSTRIAL RELATIONS

Conflict resolution is an important part of industrial relations (Riva & Rizza, 2021; Roche, n.d.; Roche & Gormley, 2020; Rosetti, 2019; Roy & Dubey, 2022; Roy, 2022; Roychowdhury, 2019). It involves the process of resolving disputes between employers and employees, or between different groups within a workplace. Conflict can arise from a variety of sources, including differences in opinion, misunderstandings, and disagreements over working conditions or wages. In order to ensure that conflicts are resolved quickly and effectively, it is important for employers to have effective conflict resolution techniques in place. One common technique used in conflict resolution is mediation (Rubery et al.; Sakharuk, 2021; Sanchez-Mosquera,

2022; Sanz et al., 2020; Schlachter, 2019; Schmidt & Muller, 2021). This involves bringing together both parties involved in the dispute with a neutral third party who will help them come to an agreement on how best to resolve their issues. Mediation allows both sides to express their views without fear of retribution or judgment from either side, which can be beneficial when trying to reach a mutually agreeable solution.

Another popular technique used by many companies is arbitration (Mahmood & Banerjee, 2020; Mailand, 2019; Markey, 2020; Martin, 2022; Martin et al., 2021; McCrystal & Hardy, 2021). This involves having an independent arbitrator review the facts surrounding the dispute and make a binding decision based on what they believe would be fair for all parties involved. Arbitration can often provide quicker results than other methods as it does not require lengthy negotiations between both sides before reaching an agreement.

Finally, some organizations may choose to use negotiation as their primary method for resolving conflicts among employees or management teams (Thornthwaite & Sheldon, 2021; Tiraboschi, 2020; Tomassetti, 2021; Trif & Szabo; Truyols, 2019; Tu et al., 2022). Negotiation requires both sides to work together towards finding solutions that are acceptable for everyone involved while also taking into account any potential legal implications that could arise from certain decisions being made during negotiations such as changes in employment contracts or wage increases/decreases and similar ideas. Negotiations should always take place with respect and understanding so that all parties feel comfortable expressing their opinions without fear of repercussions later down the line if things do not go according to plan initially. Figure 3.3 highlights the key skills necessary for conflict resolution.

No matter which approaches you decide upon when dealing with workplace conflicts, it is essential that you remain open-minded throughout the process (Cesari et al., 2019; Chan, 2020a, b; Chantziaras et al., 2020; Chen et al., n.d., 2023; Cillo & Pradella, 2019). By doing this, you will be able to create better relationships amongst your staff members, improve morale, increase productivity levels, reduce stress levels amongst workers, and ultimately lead your organization towards success. With these tips in mind, you will be well equipped to handle any future disputes efficiently and effectively.

From a Marxist perspective, conflict resolution in industrial relations is an important tool for maintaining the power of the capitalist class (Peetz, 2021; Peetz et al., 2020; Peruzzo et al.; Pitteloud, 2022; Preminger & Bondy;

Quinlan & Maxwell-Stewart). Conflict resolution can be used to maintain control over workers and their wages by creating a system where employers have more leverage than employees. This allows employers to dictate terms and conditions that are beneficial to them while leaving workers with little or no bargaining power. Furthermore, it also serves as a way for capitalists to keep wages low and profits high by preventing unions from gaining too much influence in negotiations.

Figure 3.3. *Examples of key conflict resolution skills.*

Source: The Balance.

Marxists argue that this type of conflict resolution does not lead to true justice or equality between employer and employee but instead reinforces existing inequalities within society (Madimutsa; Mahas-Demydas & Rudnytska, 2019; Mahmood & Banerjee, 2020; Mailand, 2019; Markey, 2020). They believe that any form of negotiation should take into account both sides' interests rather than just those of the employer, so that all parties involved can benefit from the outcome equally. Additionally, Marxists suggest that collective bargaining should be encouraged as it gives workers more power when negotiating with employers which could potentially lead to better working conditions and higher wages for employees.

It is clear that there are many different approaches one can take when dealing with workplace conflicts (Clibborn, 2020, 2021; Colas-Neila & Fargas, 2019; Collins et al., 2020; Cooke et al., 2019; Croucher & Okland, 2021). However, if you want your organization to succeed then it is essential you remain open-minded throughout the process. By doing this, you will be able to create better relationships amongst your staff members, improve morale, increase productivity levels, reduce stress levels amongst workers, and ultimately lead your organization towards success. From a Marxist perspective however, conflict resolution in industrial relations must take into account both sides' interests rather than just those of the employer so as not to reinforce existing inequalities within society.

Only then will we see true justice being served. Conflict resolution in industrial relations is an important topic that has been studied by many theorists over the years (Warner, 2019; William & Cunningham, 2021; Williamson et al., 2019; Wright; Wright & McLaughlin, 2021; Xie & Zhou, 2022). It is essential for organizations to understand how to effectively manage workplace conflicts so as not to disrupt productivity and morale levels amongst their staff members. Different theories have been proposed on how best to resolve these issues, ranging from traditional approaches such as negotiation and mediation, through to more modern methods like collective bargaining and arbitration.

Traditional approaches such as negotiation and mediation involve both parties coming together with a mediator present in order to discuss the issue at hand (Berry & McDaniel, 2022; Bhuta, 2022; Bischoff et al., 2021; Bogoeski, 2022; Bondy, 2022; Boumans, 2022; Bourguignon & Floquet, 2019). This approach allows each side of the conflict to express their views openly without fear of judgment or retribution. The aim here is for both sides of the dispute to come up with a mutually beneficial solution which can be agreed upon by all involved. This can form part of the corporate strategies for conflict resolution (*see* Figure 3.4).

Figure 3.4. *Strategies and techniques for managing conflict.*

Source: Tyonote.

More modern methods such as collective bargaining are often seen as being more effective than traditional approaches due its ability to provide workers with greater power when negotiating terms with employers (Galik et al., 2022; Gall, 2021; Gardawski & Towalski, 2020; Gasparri, 2021; Gasparri et al., 2019; Gasparri & Tassinari, 2020). Collective bargaining involves representatives from both sides meeting together in order to negotiate better working conditions, wages, and other benefits for employees. This method has become increasingly popular amongst unions who believe it gives them more leverage when dealing with employers.

Marxists also suggest that collective bargaining should be encouraged within industrial relations because it helps reduce inequality between workers and employers (Avgar, 2020; Baines & Armstrong, 2019; Baines & Cunningham, 2020; Bancarzewski & Hardy, 2021; Barklamb, 2021). By allowing workers more power during negotiations, Marxists argue that this will lead towards fairer outcomes where both employer and employee can benefit equally from any agreement reached. Furthermore, they believe this could potentially lead towards better working conditions, higher wages, and improved job security for employees – something which would ultimately benefit society overall.

In contrast, some argue that collective bargaining is not always the best approach to resolving conflicts between employers and employees (Scrimger, 2020; Seghezzi; Sheldon & Thornthwaite, 2020; Smith, 2019; Solaiman; Stanev, 2019; Stanford, 2021). For example, it can be difficult for workers to negotiate effectively when they lack knowledge or experience in this area. Additionally, there may be a power imbalance which makes it harder for workers to get their voices heard during negotiations. This could lead towards unfair outcomes where employers are able to take advantage of their position and impose unfavorable terms on employees.

Another alternative approach is mediation – a process whereby an independent third party helps both sides reach an agreement without having any vested interest in the outcome (Guillaume, 2022; Guiso, 2020; Gunnigle et al., 2019; Gunther & Hopner, 2023; Haipeter, 2020; Hakansta et al., n.d.; Hamberger, 2020). Mediation has been used successfully in many different contexts including labor disputes, family law matters, and even international conflicts. It allows both parties involved to express their views openly and honestly while also providing them with guidance from someone who understands the situation better than either side does alone. Furthermore, mediators often have access to resources which can help facilitate more productive conversations between all parties involved. Ultimately, there is no one-size-fits-all solution when it comes to conflict resolution within industrial relations (Chan, 2020a, b; Chantziaras et al., 2020; Chen et al., n.d., 2023; Cillo & Pradella, 2019; Civinskas & Dvorak, 2019). Different approaches will work better depending on the context and culture of each particular workplace. However, by understanding how culturally influenced philosophies such as collective bargaining and mediation can help resolve disputes between employers and employees, we can ensure that everyone's interests are taken into account before any decisions are made.

As we move into the 21st century, it is likely that conflict resolution within industrial relations will become increasingly complex (Edwards & Hodder, 2022; Ellem, 2021; Ellem et al., 2020; Engblom & Lundberg, 2019; Espinosa, 2021; Eustace, 2021). With advances in technology and globalization, employers, and employees are more connected than ever before. This means that disputes can arise quickly and spread rapidly across different countries or industries. As such, it is important for both parties to be aware of the potential risks associated with these types of conflicts so they can take steps to prevent them from escalating further.

In addition to this, there has been a growing trend towards using alternative dispute resolution (ADR) methods such as mediation or arbitration when dealing with labor disputes (Ford & Gillan, 2022; Ford & Ward, 2021; Forde; Forsyth, 2022; Foster et al., 2021; Franceschini, 2020). Communication will be an asset in these processes.

3.3. COMMUNICATION AS A KEY INGREDIENT OF INDUSTRIAL RELATIONS

The history of communications in industrial relations is a long and complex one (Eustace, 2021; Fang et al., 2021; Fergus & Godfrey, 2021; Flynn & Schroder, 2021; Foley & Williamson, 2021). From the earliest days of labor unions to modern day collective bargaining, communication has been an integral part of how workers and employers interact. In this section, we will explore the evolution of communication in industrial relations over time. Figure 3.5 highlights some forms of basic communication that are a good starting point for industrial relations.

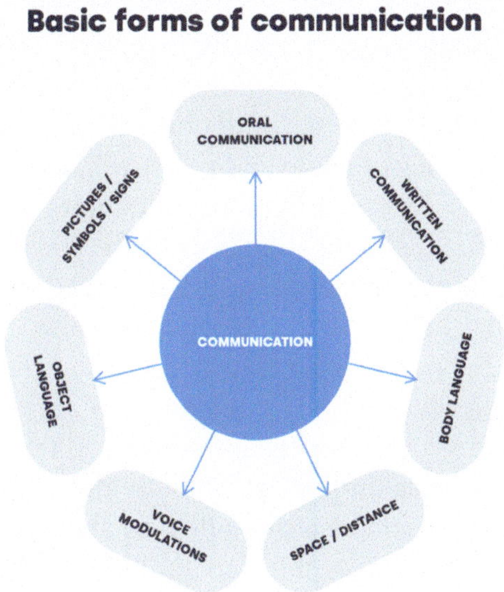

Figure 3.5. *The basic forms of communication.*

Source: CloudTalk.

In the early 19th century, labor unions began to form as a way for workers to protect their rights and interests against powerful employers (Novitz & Andrijasevic, 2020; Nowak, 2021; Nurlinah et al., 2021; O'Keeffe & Papadopoulos, 2021; Oberfichtner et al., 2020). At first, these organizations were largely informal networks that relied on word-of-mouth communication between members. As union membership grew, however, more formal methods of communication became necessary. This included newsletters and pamphlets distributed by union organizers as well as meetings held at local halls or other public spaces where members could discuss issues affecting them collectively.

As technology advanced throughout the 20th century so too did methods of communicating within industrial relations contexts (Roy & Dubey, 2022; Roy, 2022; Roychowdhury, 2019; Rubery et al.; Sakharuk, 2021; Sanchez-Mosquera, 2022). The invention of radio allowed for mass broadcasts about labor disputes while television provided another platform for disseminating information about strikes or negotiations between management and employees' representatives. With the advent of computers came even more sophisticated ways to communicate with each other such as email listservs which enabled people from all around the world to share ideas quickly and easily without having to physically meet up in person every time there was something important, they wanted to discuss or debate about workplace matters.

Today, digital technologies have revolutionized how we communicate with each other when it comes to industrial relations topics like wages, working conditions or job security concerns among other things (Razak et al., 2022; Refslund & Arnholtz, 2022; Ritson, 2019a, b; Riva & Rizza, 2021; Roche, n.d.; Roche & Gormley, 2020). Social media platforms like Twitter allow us not only to send messages but also engage in real-time conversations with our peers who may be located anywhere across the globe – making it easier than ever before for workers' voices to be heard no matter where they are based geographically speaking. Additionally, online forums provide yet another avenue through which individuals can connect with one another on various labor related topics allowing them access resources that would otherwise remain inaccessible due traditional means.

Overall, it is clear that advances in technology have had a profound impact on how we communicate within industrial relations contexts today compared to what was available just a few decades ago (Drucza, 2019; Dupuis & Greer, 2022; Edwards & Hodder, 2022; Ellem, 2021; Ellem et al., 2020; Engblom & Lundberg, 2019). By providing new tools for dialog, collaboration, education, and advocacy these advancements have helped empower both sides involved (employers and employees) ensuring better outcomes overall when it comes to negotiating terms and conditions under which work takes place. In the past, communication between employers and employees was largely limited to face-to-face meetings or written correspondence.

This type of dialog is still used today but it has been supplemented by a variety of other models that have emerged as technology has advanced (Addison & Teixeira, 2019a, b; Adewumi, 2021; Agarwal et al., 2020; Ahuja, 2020; Amosse et al., 2019). For instance, video conferencing allows for remote negotiations while email and text messaging provide quick ways to send messages back and forth without having to wait days or weeks for responses like before. Furthermore, social media platforms such as Facebook and Twitter are increasingly being utilized in industrial relations contexts allowing workers from all over the world to connect with one another and share their experiences – something which would not be possible through traditional means alone. Similarly, online forums offer yet another way individuals can engage each other on various labor related topics providing access to resources that may otherwise remain inaccessible due geographical constraints and similar ideas. Figure 3.6 highlights the potency of communication in industrial relations.

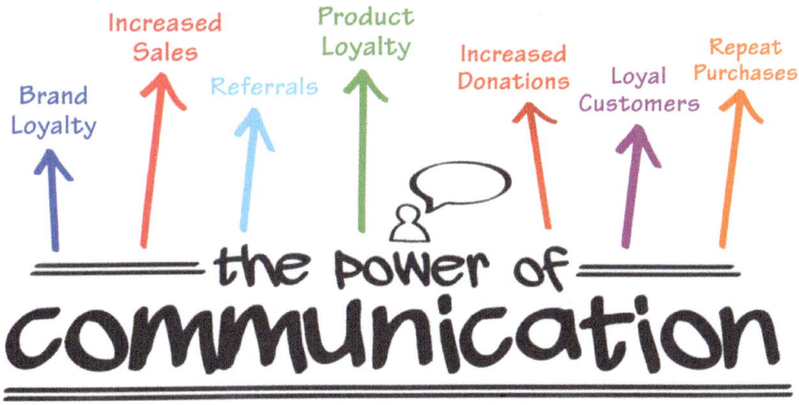

Figure 3.6. *The potency of communication.*

Source: Arshi Singla via Linked-In.

In order to do this, it is essential that we understand how communication theories and models can be applied in industrial relations contexts (Stanford, 2021; Stapley, 2021; Stevis, 2022; Svec et al., 2021; Tavora, 2019; Teipen & Mehl, 2021; Tesser & Serapioni, 2021). By doing so, we can better identify the most effective ways of engaging with one another as well as develop strategies for resolving conflicts when they arise. For example, the use of game theory has been found to be particularly useful in helping employers and employees come up with mutually beneficial solutions during negotiations. Similarly, social exchange theory provides a framework for understanding how people interact within an organization based on their perceived costs and benefits associated with any given situation.

Finally, it is important to note that technology also plays an important role in facilitating communication between parties involved in industrial relations contexts today (Campolieti, 2020; Cesari et al., 2019; Chan, 2020a, b; Chantziaras et al., 2020; Chen et al., n.d., 2023). This includes things like video conferencing which allows individuals from different parts of the world connect virtually without having travel long distances or spend large amounts money on airfare and similar ideas, online discussion boards which provide a platform for workers discuss various topics related labor rights and similar ideas, and even virtual reality simulations which allow participants experience what it is like to work under certain conditions before actually committing themselves anything concretely. All these tools have helped make dialog more efficient while at same time providing access to resources that may otherwise remain inaccessible due geographical constraints and similar ideas.

Overall, by applying communication theories and models appropriately within industrial relations contexts today we can ensure better outcomes overall when it comes to negotiating terms and conditions under which work takes place – something which will benefit both sides involved (employers and employees). Additionally, advances in technology have provided us with new tools for dialog collaboration education advocacy allowing us to take full advantage of them and ensuring everyone gets a fair deal out of the process no matter where they are located geographically speaking or what language they speak natively.

It is clear that understanding how to apply these concepts effectively will go a long way towards improving our ability to communicate effectively within such settings, ultimately leading to improved results all around (Ahuja, 2020; Amosse et al., 2019; Archel et al., 2022; Ashwin et al., 2020; Avgar, 2020; Baines & Armstrong, 2019). The relationship between communication strategies and industrial relations is an important one. Communication strategies are essential for successful negotiations, as they provide a platform for both parties to express their needs and interests in order to reach a mutually beneficial agreement. Furthermore, effective communication can help build trust between the two sides, which is key when it comes to long-term relationships.

In order to understand how communication strategies can be used effectively within industrial relations contexts today, we must first look at the various theories and models that exist (McCrystal & Hardy, 2021; Mezihorak et al.; Morritt, 2022; Murphy & Turner, 2020; Nespoli, 2019; Newman et al., 2019). For example, there are theories such as game theory which focus on understanding how different players interact with each other in order to achieve their desired outcomes; or negotiation theory which looks at how people negotiate with each other in order to come up with solutions that benefit all involved parties. Additionally, there are also models such as the "win-win" model which focuses on finding common ground between two sides so that everyone gets something out of the deal – this type of approach has been found particularly useful when it comes to resolving conflicts within organizations or industries where multiple stakeholders need to be taken into account. Communication theory is an important tool for understanding how people interact and communicate with each other (Roche & Gormley, 2020; Rosetti, 2019; Roy & Dubey, 2022; Roy, 2022; Roychowdhury, 2019; Rubery et al.; Sakharuk, 2021). It can be used to help us understand the dynamics of global and local industrial relations, as well as providing a framework for resolving conflicts between stakeholders. Communication theories provide insight into how messages are sent, received, interpreted, and responded to in different contexts. This knowledge can then be applied to improve communication within organizations or industries where multiple stakeholders need to be taken into account.

One example of a communication theory that has been found particularly useful when it comes to resolving conflicts within organizations or industries is the Johari Window Model (Abd Razak & Mahmod, 2019, 2021; Ackers, 2020; Addison & Teixeira, 2019a). This model was developed by psychologists Joseph Luft and Harry Ingham in 1955 and provides a way of looking at interpersonal relationships from four perspectives: open self (what we know about ourselves), blind self (what others know about us, but we do not), hidden self (what we know about ourselves, but others do not) and unknown self (unknown by both parties). By using this model, it becomes easier to identify areas where misunderstandings may occur due to lack of information or miscommunication between parties involved in negotiations over terms and conditions.

Another example is the Transactional Analysis Theory developed by Eric Berne in 1964 which looks at interactions between two people based on their roles such as parent-child or adult-adult and similar ideas (Opute & Koch, 2020; Ormaetxea, 2019; Ozkiziltan, 2019, 2020; Peetz, 2021; Peetz et al., 2020). This theory helps us better understand why certain behaviors might arise during negotiations so that they can be addressed more effectively leading towards improved outcomes overall for all those involved. It is clear that understanding how to apply these concepts effectively will go a long way towards improving our ability to communicate effectively within such settings, ultimately leading to improved results all around. With this knowledge now available there really should not be any excuse not to make use of its potential to ensure the best possible outcome in every situation regardless of the size, scope, or complexity of the issue being discussed or negotiated upon. Arbitrators consider these dynamics when facilitating industrial relations.

3.4. THE ROLE OF ARBITRATORS IN INDUSTRIAL RELATIONS

Arbitration is a form of dispute resolution that has been used in industrial relations for centuries (Ormaetxea, 2019; Ozkiziltan, 2019, 2020; Peetz, 2021; Peetz et al., 2020; Peruzzo et al.; Pitteloud, 2022). It involves the use of an impartial third party to resolve disputes between employers and employees, or between unions and employers. This section will provide a detailed global history of arbitration in industrial relations, from its origins to its current state.

The earliest recorded instance of arbitration dates back to ancient Greece, where it was used as a means of settling disputes among citizens (Preminger & Bondy; Quinlan & Maxwell-Stewart; Radzi et al., 2022; Ramsay & Webster, 2019; Ravn & Oyum, 2020). In the Middle Ages, it was adopted by merchants as a way to settle commercial disputes without resorting to litigation. By the 19th century, arbitration had become widely accepted as an effective method for resolving labor-management conflicts in Europe and North America. Throughout these changes, the role of the state was important (*see* Figure 3.7).

In 1872, Britain passed the Trade Disputes Act which allowed workers' organizations (unions) to take collective action against their employers if they felt their rights were being violated. The act also provided for voluntary arbitration when negotiations failed; this marked the first time that governments officially recognized and endorsed arbitration as an ADR mechanism in industrial relations matters. In 1919, following World War I, international efforts began with the formation of the International Labor Organization (ILO).

The ILO sought to promote social justice through international standards on labor rights and working conditions (Rosetti, 2019; Roy & Dubey, 2022; Roy, 2022; Roychowdhury, 2019; Rubery et al.; Sakharuk, 2021; Sanchez-Mosquera, 2022). One such standard was compulsory binding arbitration for all labor-management disputes involving public services or essential industries like mining or transportation. This set off a wave of legislation across many countries mandating compulsory binding arbitration when negotiations fail between unions and employers over wages or other terms related to employment contracts – known today as "collective bargaining agreements" (CBAs).

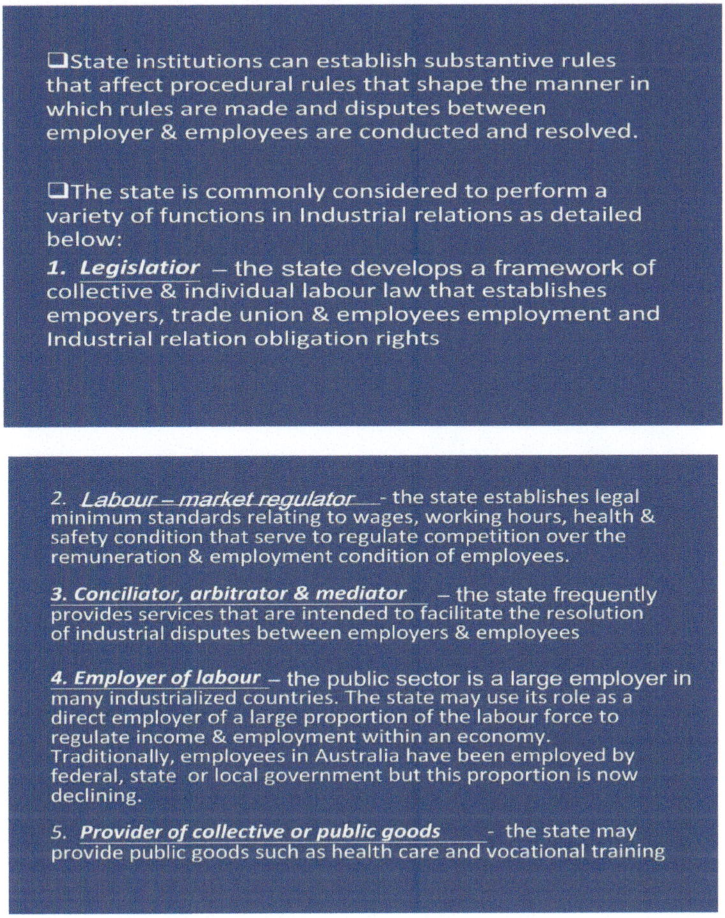

Figure 3.7. *The role of the state in industrial relations.*

Source: "Jaden" (2012) via Slide Serve.

Today, most industrialized nations have laws requiring mandatory mediation before any strike can be called by either side during collective bargaining negotiations (Walters & Wadsworth, 2020; Warner, 2019; William & Cunningham, 2021; Williamson et al., 2019). Some countries even require both sides to agree on an arbitrator before any negotiation can begin at all. Additionally, many countries have established specialized courts dedicated solely towards hearing cases related specifically to labor law issues such as unfair dismissal claims or discrimination complaints brought forth by employees against their employers.

We can see how far we have come since ancient times when it comes down to using alternative methods like arbitration instead of traditional court proceedings within Industrial Relations contexts around the world – making sure that both parties are heard fairly and justly while avoiding costly legal fees or lengthy delays associated with going through court systems (Bancarzewski & Hardy, 2021; Barklamb, 2021; Barry & Wilkinson, 2022; Baturina et al., 2021; Beattie, 2019). We hope this section has given your insight into how important arbitration is globally and why it should continue being utilized moving forward so everyone involved gets fair treatment regardless of what country they live in.

	Collective dispute settlement	Extension of collective agreements	Wage-setting (private)	Wage-setting (public)
Spain 1990s–2007	Bipartite agreements on extra-judicial conflict resolution enhance autonomous resolution	Statutory extension	Statutory minimum wage Increasing autonomy (bipartite agreements)	Extension of collective bargaining conditional on state budget
Spain 2007–2012	Unilateral changes enable a greater role for arbitration	No change	Unilateral approval of opting-out from higher level wage increases and changes in wages by the employer	Unilateral imposition of pay cuts and freezes
Portugal 1990s–2007	Conflict resolution mostly through the judicial channel	Statutory extension but social partners retain the initiative	Indirect state intervention in wage bargaining; sporadic direct intervention	Increasing autonomy; recognition of collective bargaining
Portugal 2007–2012	Little change: system still predominantly based on arbitration	Limits on the extension of collective agreements	No significant change	Unilateral imposition of pay cuts and freezes
Greece 1990s–2007	Increasing autonomy (arbitration and mediation extended)	Statutory extension possible on initiative of Ministry of Labour	Indirect state intervention in wage bargaining; sporadic direct intervention	Pay determined by government after consultation with trade unions
Greece 2007–2012	Compulsory arbitration is likely to become more important	Limits on the extension of collective agreements on the agenda, but not yet approved	Companies allowed to deviate from terms established at higher levels	Unilateral imposition of pay cuts and freezes

Figure 3.8. *Historical review of differentiated trade union mechanism in selected countries.*

Source. Molina (2014).

Today, most industrialized nations have some form of legal framework governing labor-management relations that includes provisions for mandatory binding arbitration when negotiations fail (Godino & Molina, 2022; Gooberman, 2022; Goods & Ellem; Goyer et al., 2022; Graca, 2021; Gramano & Gaudio, 2019). In addition, international organizations such as ILO have developed guidelines on how best practices should be applied during these proceedings. For example, ILO recommends that all parties involved should be given equal opportunity to present evidence before an independent tribunal, while ensuring fairness throughout proceedings. Figure 3.8 contextualizes these relationships in trade unionism.

Overall, since its inception centuries ago, arbitration has evolved into one of the most important tools available today for resolving workplace conflicts peacefully without resorting to costly litigation procedures (Agarwal et al., 2020; Ahuja, 2020; Amosse et al., 2019; Archel et al., 2022; Ashwin et al., 2020; Avgar, 2020). Its widespread acceptance across different cultures demonstrates just how effective this process can be when properly implemented according to established standards set out by international bodies like ILO. With continued improvements made over time, there is no doubt that this practice will remain relevant well into future generations too.

When it comes to industrial relations, arbitration is a widely accepted form of dispute resolution (Tesser & Serapioni, 2021; Thomas & Turnbull, 2021; Thornthwaite & Sheldon, 2019, 2021). This process involves the appointment of an independent third party (arbitrator) who will listen to both sides and make a decision based on evidence presented by each side. The arbitrator's decision is legally binding and can be enforced in court if necessary.

Arbitration has been used for centuries as a way to resolve disputes between employers and employees, but its use varies greatly from country to country (Belizon, 2019; Bellace et al., 2021; Ben & Sage, 2022; Berry & McDaniel, 2022; Bhuta, 2022; Bischoff et al., 2021). In some countries, such as the United States, arbitration is mandatory when negotiations fail. This means that all parties involved must agree to submit their case before an arbitrator or else face potential legal action. On the other hand, in countries like India, arbitration is voluntary and only takes place when both parties agree upon it beforehand.

In addition, different countries have adopted different approaches towards how they handle these proceedings (Roychowdhury, 2019; Rubery et al.; Sakharuk, 2021; Sanchez-Mosquera, 2022; Sanz et al., 2020; Schlachter,

2019). For example, in China, labor disputes are handled through collective bargaining rather than individual cases being brought before an arbitrator. Similarly, Japan has developed its own system known as "conciliation" which allows for mediation between two parties prior to any formal hearing taking place.

While there may be differences in how various nations approach industrial relations issues through arbitration procedures, one thing remains clear: this practice continues to play an important role across many cultures today (Nga & Nga, 2021; Ngai, 2020; Nicklich & Helfen, 2019; Novitz & Andrijasevic, 2020; Nowak, 2021; Nurlinah et al., 2021). By providing a fair platform for resolving workplace conflicts without resorting to costly litigation processes or lengthy court battles, this method of dispute resolution helps ensure that everyone involved gets their day in court. The arbitrator's decision is usually binding and cannot be appealed in court.

Arbitration has been used for centuries as a way to resolve disputes between employers and employees, but its use varies greatly from country to country (Seghezzi; Sheldon & Thornthwaite, 2020; Smith, 2019; Solaiman; Stanev, 2019; Stanford, 2021; Stapley, 2021). In some countries, such as the United States, arbitration provisions are included in CBAs or labor contracts. These provisions allow either party to initiate arbitration proceedings if negotiations fail. On the other hand, many European countries have adopted more formalized systems that require mandatory binding arbitration when negotiations fail.

In India, there are two main types of industrial relations: voluntary negotiation and compulsory conciliation (D'Art, 2020; da Costa & Horn, 2021; Dalla Sega, 2021; Darlington & Mustchin, 2019; Das, 2023; Das & Singh, 2021). Voluntary negotiation occurs when both parties agree upon terms without any external intervention, while compulsory conciliation requires government involvement through appointed mediators or arbitrators. While this system does not provide for mandatory binding arbitration like in Europe, it still provides workers with protection against unfair treatment by their employers.

China has recently implemented new regulations regarding labor disputes which include provisions for mediation and arbitration depending on the severity of the case at hand (Ashwin et al., 2020; Avgar, 2020; Baines & Armstrong, 2019; Baines & Cunningham, 2020; Bancarzewski & Hardy, 2021). Unlike other countries mentioned above however, Chinese law does not provide for mandatory binding arbitration unless specifically requested by one or both parties involved in the dispute. This means that even though mediation may take place first before resorting to litigation procedures, ultimately it is up to those involved whether they wish to pursue further legal action or accept whatever outcome was reached through mediation/ arbitration processes instead.

Overall then we can see just how different approaches towards resolving workplace conflicts vary across different parts of the world – from voluntary negotiation systems found in US and India; to more formalized ones requiring mandatory binding arbitration like those seen in Europe and China, respectively (Ilsoe & Soderqvist; Jarota, 2022; Jha & Singh, 2019; Jiang & Yao, 2020; Jirjahn, 2022; Joyce et al.; Junior, 2022). It goes without saying then that understanding local laws governing industrial relations within your own jurisdiction is essential if you want to ensure fair outcomes during any potential future disputes too. This chapter will close by exploring an example of industrial strife as a consequence of the failure to successfully implement industrial relations.

3.5. EXAMPLE OF INDUSTRIAL STRIFE AND VIOLENCE

Industrial strife is a term used to describe the conflict between employers and employees, often resulting in violence (Croucher & Okland, 2021; D'Art, 2020; da Costa & Horn, 2021; Dalla Sega, 2021; Darlington & Mustchin, 2019). This type of conflict has been around for centuries, but its conceptualization has changed over time. In this section, we will explore different ways that industrial strife has been understood throughout history.

In the early 19th century, industrial strife was seen as an inevitable consequence of capitalism and class struggle (Peetz et al., 2020; Peruzzo et al.; Pitteloud, 2022; Preminger & Bondy; Quinlan & Maxwell-Stewart; Radzi et al., 2022). The working classes were viewed as having little power or agency in their own lives; instead, they were subject to the whims of their employers who had all the economic power. As such, workers resorted to strikes and other forms of protest in order to make their voices heard and demand better wages and working conditions from their bosses. Figure 3.9 is an example of a history of industrial strife in the USA as marked by key events.

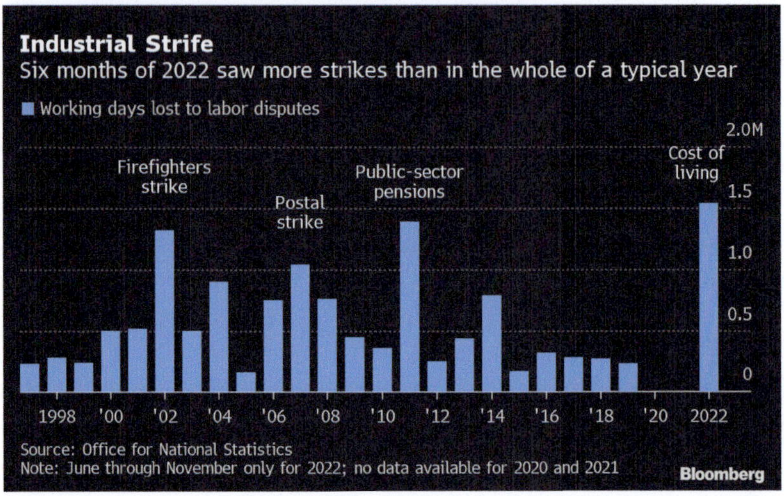

Figure 3.9. *Industrial strife in 1998–2022.*

Source: Bloomberg.

By the late 19th century, however, there was a shift towards viewing industrial strife as something more than just a result of capitalist exploitation (Beattie, 2019; Bechter et al., 2021; Bedkar & Prashad, 2020; Behrens et al., 2020; Behrens & Pekarek, n.d.; Belizon, 2019). It began to be seen as an expression of collective action by workers against oppressive systems that denied them basic rights like fair pay or safe working conditions. This new understanding led to increased support for labor unions which sought to protect worker's rights through collective bargaining with employers on behalf of all members within a particular industry or trade union organization.

The 20th century saw further changes in how industrial strife was perceived by society at large (Cillo & Pradella, 2019; Civinskas & Dvorak, 2019; Clayton, 2021; Clibborn, 2019, 2020, 2021). With advances in technology came greater automation which meant fewer jobs available for manual laborers while those who remained employed faced increasingly precarious work situations due to outsourcing and downsizing practices adopted by many companies during this period. As such, it became increasingly difficult for workers' demands for better wages or improved safety standards at workplaces could not be met without significant resistance from management. Consequently, violent protests became commonplace among disgruntled employees seeking justice.

Finally, today's conceptualizations have shifted yet again with some scholars arguing that modern day industrial strife should no longer be viewed solely through an economic lens but rather one that takes into account social issues such as gender inequality, racism, xenophobia, and similar ideas, which can also contribute significantly towards creating hostile environments where violence may erupt (Bechter et al., 2021; Bedkar & Prashad, 2020; Behrens et al., 2020; Behrens & Pekarek, n.d.; Belizon, 2019; Bellace et al., 2021). Overall, it is clear that our understanding of what constitutes 'industrial strife' has evolved considerably over time – from being simply a product of capitalist exploitation during the early 19th century; to being seen as an expression collective action against oppressive systems during late 19th century; and finally, today where it encompasses both economic concerns along with broader social issues.

Understanding these changing conceptualizations is essential if we are ever going to achieve lasting peace between employers and employees (Addison & Teixeira, 2019b; Adewumi, 2021; Agarwal et al., 2020; Ahuja, 2020; Amosse et al., 2019; Archel et al., 2022). The history of industrial strife is a long and complex one, with its roots stretching back to the early 19th century when workers began to organize themselves in order to fight for better wages and working conditions. This period saw the emergence of labor unions which sought to protect their members from exploitation by employers. As these organizations grew in strength, so too did the level of violence associated with them – strikes became commonplace as disgruntled employees sought justice through direct action.

In response, governments around the world began introducing legislation aimed at curbing such activities (Bradley & Rowland, 2021; Bray et al., 2019, 2020; Budd, 2020; Cabeza, 2019; Cam, 2021; Campolieti, 2020). In Britain for example, The Trade Union Act 1871 was passed which made it illegal for unions to use force or intimidation against employers or other workers. Similarly, in America during this time laws were introduced that prohibited collective bargaining and outlawed certain types of strikes.

By late 19th century however, our understanding of what constituted 'industrial strife' had shifted somewhat; with some scholars arguing that it should no longer be viewed solely through an economic lens but rather one that takes into account social issues such as gender inequality, racism, and similar ideas, which can also contribute significantly towards creating hostile environments where violence may erupt (Freedland & Dhorajiwala, 2019; Fuchs et al., 2019; Galik et al., 2022; Gall, 2021; Gardawski & Towalski, 2020). This shift in thinking led to a new wave of activism amongst workers who now sought not only better pay and working conditions but also greater recognition for their rights as citizens. This period saw the rise of mass protests across Europe and North America demanding equal rights regardless of race or gender along with improved safety standards on factory floors and similar ideas, all culminating in various landmark pieces legislation being passed throughout much 20th century (e.g., The Equal Pay Act, 1970).

At present, tests have become commonplace among disgruntled employees seeking justice – whether they are protesting unfair dismissal or inadequate compensation packages – while governments continue to introduce measures designed to ensure fair treatment of both sides involved in any dispute (Giraud, 2020; Godino & Molina, 2022; Gooberman, 2022; Goods & Ellem; Goyer et al., 2022; Graca, 2021; Gramano & Gaudio, 2019). Figure 3.10 illustrates that industrialized countries like the UK are facing industrial strife in the post-COVID-19 era. Moreover, modern-day industrial strife has come to encompass broader social issues such those mentioned above; thus, making it essential we understand changing conceptualizations if ever want to achieve lasting peace between employers and employees.

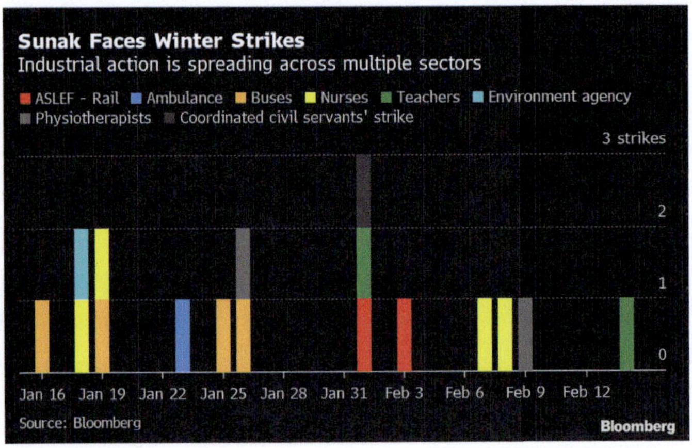

Figure 3.10. *Increase in strike action in the UK 2022–2023.*

Source: Bloomberg.

In this regard, there are two main theoretical perspectives which have been used to explain the causes of violent industrial strife (Oberfichtner et al., 2020; Opute & Koch, 2020; Ormaetxea, 2019; Ozkiziltan, 2019, 2020; Peetz, 2021). The first is Marxist theory, which suggests that class struggle between capitalists (employers) workers (employees) lies at the heart of any conflict. According to Marxists, employers will always seek to maximize their profits while minimizing costs; thus, leading them to exploit employees by paying low wages and providing poor working conditions. This in turn leads workers to become increasingly dissatisfied with their situation eventually resulting in mass protests or strikes as they attempt to gain better pay and improved rights.

The second perspective is known as pluralist theory, which argues that power within an organization should be shared among different groups rather than concentrated in one particular group such as management or shareholders (Lize et al., 2022; Lloyd & Payne, 2021; Lukacova et al., 2022; Lyddon, 2021; Lyutov, 2022; MacKenzie & Lucio, 2019). Pluralists believe that when all stakeholders involved are given an opportunity to voice their opinions then it can lead to more harmonious relationships between employers and employees – ultimately reducing chances of industrial strife occurring in the future. Furthermore, they argue that if governments introduce policies to ensure fair treatment of both sides, then this could also help prevent disputes from escalating into violence or other forms of unrest.

Overall, it is clear that understanding changing conceptualizations surrounding industrial strife is essential if we ever want to achieve lasting peace between employers and employees (Williamson et al., 2019; Wright; Wright & McLaughlin, 2021; Xie & Zhou, 2022; Yan, 2019; Yang et al.; Zbyszewska, 2021). By looking at both Marxist and pluralist theories we can gain greater insight into why these conflicts occur and how best address them going forward – ensuring everyone involved is treated fairly regardless of race, gender, and similar ideas. This is done so no one is left feeling disenfranchised or powerless again in future. In order to prevent, mitigate, and respond to violent industrial strife, it is important for employers and employees alike to understand the changing conceptualizations of industrial strife.

Marxist theories suggest that these conflicts arise due to a power imbalance between management and workers, with the former having more control over resources than the latter (Sakharuk, 2021; Sanchez-Mosquera, 2022; Sanz et al., 2020; Schlachter, 2019; Schmidt & Muller, 2021; Schofield-Georgeson, 2022). This can lead to feelings of disenfranchisement among workers which in turn can result in violence or other forms of unrest. On the other hand, pluralist theories argue that power should be shared among different groups rather than concentrated on one particular group such as management or shareholders. Pluralists believe that when all stakeholders involved are given an opportunity to voice their opinions then it can lead to more harmonious relationships between employers and employees.

Furthermore, they argue that if governments introduce policies to ensure fair treatment for both sides, then this could also help prevent disputes from escalating into violence or other forms of unrest.

It is also essential for organizations dealing with industrial strife issues to have clear strategies to address them quickly and effectively before they escalate out of control (Chen et al., 2023; Cillo & Pradella, 2019; Civinskas & Dvorak, 2019; Clayton, 2021; Clibborn, 2019, 2020). For example, companies may want to consider implementing mediation processes where representatives from each side come together to discuss grievances find mutually beneficial solutions without resorting physical force intimidation tactics and similar ideas, while government agencies need develop comprehensive plans handle any potential outbreaks civil disobedience so they able act swiftly appropriately when needed. Finally, businesses must ensure their staff members are aware of rights responsibilities under relevant laws and regulations – including those related labor unions CBAs – so everyone knows what to expect during negotiations times conflict resolution too.

Overall, it is clear that understanding changing conceptualizations surrounding industrial strife is essential if we ever want to achieve lasting peace in organizations and institutions (Quinlan & Maxwell-Stewart; Radzi et al., 2022; Ramsay & Webster, 2019; Ravn & Oyum, 2020; Razak et al., 2022). By looking at both Marxist and pluralist theories we can gain greater insight into why these conflicts occur and how best address them going forward – ensuring everyone involved is treated fairly regardless of race, gender, and similar issues, so no one is left feeling disenfranchised or powerless again in future. With proper prevention strategies put in place along with effective mitigation responses available when needed there is no reason why workplace disputes cannot be resolved peacefully without resorting violence every time.

CHAPTER 3 SUMMARY

This chapter has conceptualized industrial relations. It started with a historical view of how industrial relations emerged as a key concern and the rules that accompany them. The chapter introduced some of the instrumentalities of industrial relations such as conflict resolution, communication, and arbitration. At the same time, the chapter demonstrated the risk of violence and strife if these relations are not sufficiently addressed in policy and practice. The latter issue of practice is explored further in the next chapter.

CHAPTER 4

The Practice of Industrial Relations

Contents

The fourth chapter in this book explores the practice of industrial relations. For example, the chapter highlights the links between democratic governance, productivity, efficiency, and good industrial relations. We review a case study of multinational corporations as key stakeholders in policy and practice. This leads to a discussion of international law and its impact on domestic industrial relations. The chapter closes with a case study of migrant workers and how industrial relations may impact on them because of their socially excluded status. Of course, the outcomes for all workers and employers in terms of industrial relations are strongly influenced by the level of democratization and good governance in nations.

4.1. DEMOCRATIC GOVERNANCE AND INDUSTRIAL RELATIONS

Democratic governance is a system whereby public policies and decisions are determined by the majority of citizens in a given society (Gunther & Hopner, 2023; Haipeter, 2020; Hakansta et al., n.d.; Hamberger, 2020; Harvey & Turnbull, 2020; Hendy, 2022). This differs from industrial relations which refers to the ways employers, employees' representatives, unions, or governments interact with one another within an employment setting. Democratic governance allows individuals to have their input into how laws and regulations should work for them in order to ensure fairness across all parties involved.

In recent years, there has been an increased focus on the impact of democratic governance on industrial relations (Hamberger, 2020; Harvey & Turnbull, 2020; Hendy, 2022; Herrero, 2022; Hilgert, 2019; Hirsch & Mueller, 2020). This section will explore some key research papers, models, theories, and practice knowledge that have helped to shape our understanding of this important topic. First off is a paper by Dr. David Bercuson titled "T*he Impact of Democratic Governance on Industrial Relations*" which examines how different forms of democracy can affect labor-management relationships in various countries around the world. The paper looks at both direct and indirect effects such as changes in union membership rates or collective bargaining agreements (CBAs) due to democratization processes. It also explores how these impacts may be moderated by other factors such as economic conditions or government policies. Figure 4.1 highlights the points of commonality between industrial relations and democratic governance.

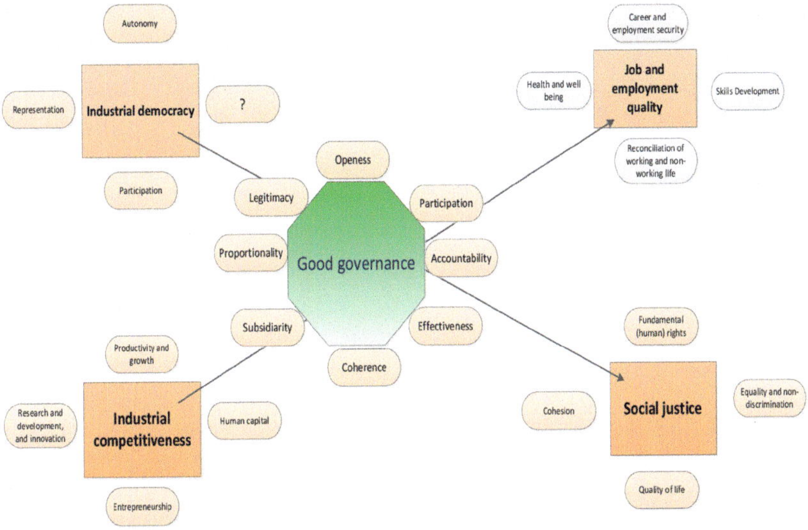

Figure 4.1. *Mapping the dimensions of industrial relations and good governance.*

Source: Welz et al. (2014).

Next up is a model developed by Professor John Dunlop called the "*Industrial Relations System Model*" which provides a framework for analyzing labor-management interactions within any given country. This is based on its political system, legal environment, social structure, and economic context (Hakansta et al., n.d.; Hamberger, 2020; Harvey & Turnbull, 2020; Hendy, 2022; Herrero, 2022; Hilgert, 2019; Hirsch & Mueller, 2020). At its best, the model helps us understand why certain types of democracies are more likely to produce better outcomes for workers than others when it comes to wages and working conditions.

Finally, we come to two influential theories: pluralist theory (which argues that power should be shared among multiple stakeholders) and neo-corporatist theory (which suggests that employers should cooperate with unions) (Chantziaras et al., 2020; Chen et al., n.d., 2023; Cillo & Pradella, 2019; Civinskas & Dvorak, 2019; Clayton, 2021). Both provide useful insights into how different systems of democratic governance can influence industrial relations practices in different ways depending upon their particular contexts – something which practitioners need to take into account when making decisions about workplace issues like pay negotiations or dispute resolution procedures. Democratic governance does indeed play an important role in shaping industrial relations dynamics across many countries worldwide – something which needs further exploration if we are going truly to understand its full implications for workers everywhere (Thornthwaite & Sheldon, 2019, 2021; Tiraboschi, 2020; Tomassetti, 2021; Trif & Szabo). Researchers have found that democratic governance has a significant impact on industrial relations. Democratic governments are more likely to promote collective bargaining and other forms of worker representation in order to ensure fair wages and working conditions for employees. Additionally, they tend to be more open to dialog between employers and workers when it comes to resolving disputes or negotiating terms of employment.

This can lead to better outcomes for both parties as well as improved labor-management relations overall (Nespoli, 2019; Newman et al., 2019; Nga & Nga, 2021; Ngai, 2020; Nicklich & Helfen, 2019; Novitz & Andrijasevic, 2020). Furthermore, democratic governments often provide greater legal protections for workers than those provided by authoritarian regimes, which helps create a safer work environment where employees feel secure in their rights and duties. Ultimately, the presence of strong democratic institutions is essential for ensuring healthy industrial relations within any society. The role of democratic governance in industrial relations has been a subject of debate for many years. While some argue that it is essential to ensure fair and equitable working conditions, others contend that it can lead to an inefficient use of resources and impede economic growth (Mailand, 2019; Markey, 2020; Martin, 2022; Martin et al., 2021; McCrystal & Hardy, 2021; Mezihorak et al.; Morritt, 2022). It is pertinent that we examine the theoretical arguments surrounding democratic governance in industrial relations from both sides of the debate. These theories bear in mind the good governance procedures that are set internationally (*see* Figure 4.2).

Indicator	**EC**	**OECD**	**World Bank**	**UN**	**Mandelkern Group**
Openness	X	X		X	X
Participation	X		X	X	
Accountability	X	X	X	X	X
Effectiveness	X	X	X	X	
Coherence	X				
Proportionality	X				X
Subsidiarity	X				X

Figure 4.2. *Evaluating good governance among world institutions.*

Source: Welz et al. (2014).

At its core, democratic governance is based on the principle that workers should have a say in how their workplace operates (Chen et al., n.d., 2023; Cillo & Pradella, 2019; Civinskas & Dvorak, 2019; Clayton, 2021; Clibborn, 2019). This includes having input into decisions such as wages, hours worked, job security and other aspects related to employment rights. Proponents of this approach argue that by giving employees more control over their work environment they are more likely to be satisfied with their jobs and motivated to perform better. Furthermore, they suggest that allowing workers greater autonomy leads to increased productivity which ultimately benefits employers as well as employees themselves.

On the other hand, opponents point out several potential drawbacks associated with democratic governance in industrial relations (Engblom & Lundberg, 2019; Espinosa, 2021; Eustace, 2021; Fang et al., 2021; Fergus & Godfrey, 2021; Flynn & Schroder, 2021). Firstly, they claim that it can lead to an inefficient allocation of resources due to decision-making processes being bogged down by bureaucracy or disagreements between different stakeholders involved in negotiations. Secondly, there is also concern about whether or not workers are adequately informed about their rights under such systems which could result in them making uninformed decisions or being taken advantage of by employers who may be able to exploit loopholes within these systems for their own benefit at the expense of employees' welfare. Finally, critics also worry about whether or not democracy itself is suitable for managing complex workplaces where multiple interests need balancing simultaneously without sacrificing efficiency or quality standards set by management teams responsible for overseeing operations on behalf of shareholders and customers.

While there are certainly merits associated with introducing elements of democracy into workplace settings through CBAs, etc., one must consider all angles before deciding if this approach would be beneficial overall given its potential drawbacks outlined above (Bischoff et al., 2021; Bogoeski, 2022; Bondy, 2022; Boumans, 2022; Bourguignon & Floquet, 2019; Bradley & Rowland, 2021). Ultimately though only time will tell if such measures prove successful when implemented correctly but until then we must remain open minded when discussing these issues so as not make any hasty judgments either way regarding what works best for everyone involved in modern day industrial relations scenarios today. One of the emerging debates today concerns the best way of ensuring productivity even as promoting effective industrial relations.

4.2. PRODUCTIVITY AND EFFICIENCY AS KEY CONCERNS OF THE INDUSTRIALISTS

Productivity is a key factor in the success of any large industry (Addison & Teixeira, 2019b; Adewumi, 2021; Agarwal et al., 2020; Ahuja, 2020; Amosse et al., 2019; Archel et al., 2022). It has been studied extensively by academics, and there are numerous theories, models, case studies, and debates surrounding it. In this section post we will critically evaluate the interests of industrialists in promoting productivity. The most obvious benefit to increased productivity for an industrialist is that it leads to higher profits. This can be achieved through cost savings from improved efficiency or increased output with fewer resources. Additionally, greater productivity can lead to better customer service as well as improved employee morale due to less stress on workers and more job satisfaction from completing tasks quickly and efficiently.

Nevertheless, there are also some potential drawbacks associated with increasing productivity too quickly or without proper planning (Goods & Ellem; Goyer et al., 2022; Graca, 2021; Gramano & Gaudio, 2019; Grodem & Hippe, 2019; Guillaume, 2022). For example, if production increases faster than demand then companies may find themselves overproducing goods which could result in losses due to unsold inventory or price reductions needed to move excess stock off shelves. Furthermore, if employees feel they are being pushed too hard then their morale may suffer leading them to become disengaged at work which could further reduce overall performance levels within the company. Figure 4.3 is a quality and productivity framework that is typically of the ones used in industry.

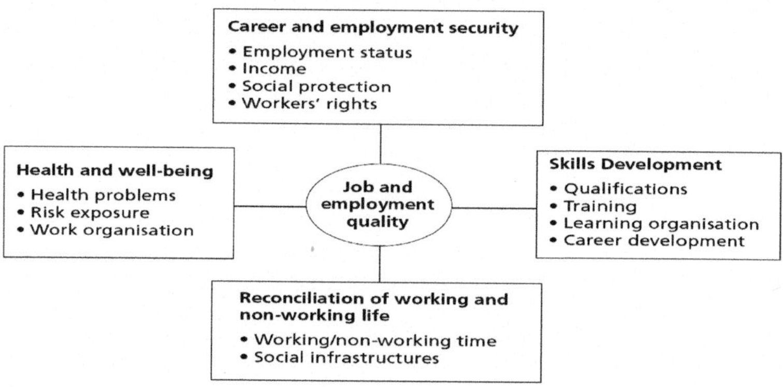

Figure 4.3. *Quality framework of work and employment.*

Source: Welz et al. (2014).

Despite these potential risks though, many industrialists still see great value in pursuing higher levels of productivity as long as they do so responsibly and strategically plan for growth accordingly (Tomassetti, 2021; Trif & Szabo; Truyols, 2019; Tu et al., 2022; Velluti, 2022; Vinichenko et al., 2020; Vulkan & Larsson, 2019). One way this can be done is by investing in technology such as automation systems which allow businesses to increase output while reducing labor costs at the same time – something that has become increasingly popular among larger corporations recently due its ability to improve both efficiency and profitability simultaneously when implemented correctly. Additionally, training programs designed specifically for improving worker skill sets have also proven effective at boosting performance levels across entire organizations.

Overall, it is clear that there are both benefits and drawbacks associated with increasing productivity within big industries (Das & Singh, 2021; de Amorim et al., 2019; de Luna, 2022; De Prins et al., 2020; de Vaate, 2021; Demougin et al., 2019). However, when done properly, investments into new technologies combined with targeted training initiatives can help ensure that any gains made outweigh any potential losses incurred along the way. As such, it is no surprise why many industrialists continue striving towards ever-higher levels of performance despite all the challenges involved. Indeed, productivity is an implicit requirement of good industrial relations (*see* Figure 4.4).

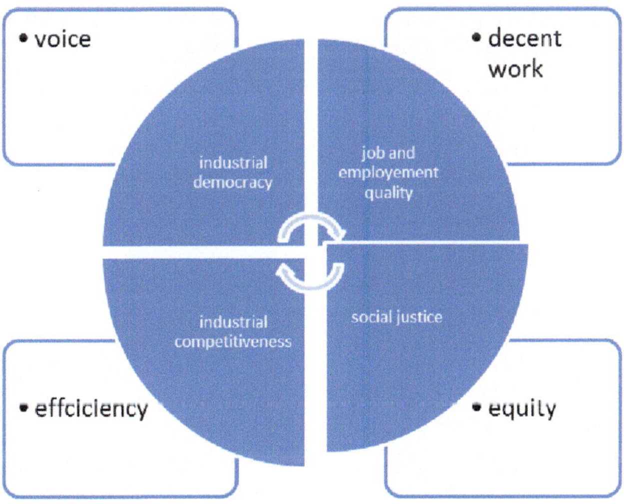

Figure 4.4. *Key requirements of effective industrial relations.*

Source: Welz et al. (2014).

Productivity is a key factor in determining the economic performance of any nation (Vinichenko et al., 2020; Vulkan & Larsson, 2019; Walker, 2020; Walters & Wadsworth, 2020; Warner, 2019). It is defined as the ratio between output and input, which measures how efficiently resources are used to produce goods and services. Productivity has been widely studied by economists for decades, with various arguments being put forward about its contribution to economic performance. In this section, we will critically evaluate these arguments using vivid contemporary examples.

One argument suggests that productivity growth leads to higher wages and improved living standards for workers (Cillo & Pradella, 2019; Civinskas & Dvorak, 2019; Clayton, 2021; Clibborn, 2019, 2020, 2021). This can be seen in countries such as China where rapid increases in productivity have led to significant improvements in average incomes over the past two decades. Similarly, research conducted by the International Labor Organization (ILO) found that increased labor productivity was associated with higher real wages across all sectors of employment worldwide.

Another argument states that productivity growth helps reduce unemployment levels by creating more jobs through increased demand for goods and services produced at lower costs due to greater efficiency gains from technological advances or better management practices (Harvey & Turnbull, 2020; Hendy, 2022; Herrero, 2022; Hilgert, 2019; Hirsch & Mueller, 2020; Hoffrogge, 2019). This has been demonstrated recently during the COVID-19 pandemic when many businesses adopted digital technologies such as remote working tools or automation systems which enabled them to remain operational despite lockdowns imposed on their physical premises – thus helping preserve jobs while increasing overall efficiency levels within those organizations.

Finally, it is argued that high levels of productivity lead to an increase in GDP per capita since more value can be generated from fewer inputs – resulting in greater wealth creation opportunities for individuals and nations alike (Bondy, 2022; Boumans, 2022; Bourguignon & Floquet, 2019; Bradley & Rowland, 2021; Bray et al., 2019, 2020). For example, Singapore's impressive GDP per capita figures are largely attributed to its highly productive workforce which consistently ranks among the top 10 globally according to World Bank data. The implication is that nations have an interest in ensuring high productivity to support their economic goals.

Overall, then, there is strong evidence suggesting that productivity plays a major role in driving economic performance both domestically and internationally – leading not only towards higher wages but also reduced unemployment rates alongside increased GDP per capita figures (Devinatz, 2022; Di Carlo, 2020; Diessner et al., 2022; Dobbins et al., 2020, 2021; Dockes, 2019). To ensure continued success however, governments must continue investing heavily into research and development initiatives aimed at improving existing processes while introducing new ones so as to keep up with ever changing global trends. Only then will they be able to stand out amongst their peers on an international stage.

In conclusion, it is clear that productivity contributes significantly towards economic performance – providing tangible benefits both now and into future generations if managed correctly (Bourguignon & Floquet, 2019; Bradley & Rowland, 2021; Bray et al., 2019, 2020; Budd, 2020; Cabeza, 2019). Therefore, policy makers should strive towards creating an environment conducive towards innovation and creativity so as to maximize potential returns from investments made into this area whilst simultaneously ensuring equitable distribution of wealth throughout society. With careful planning and execution, nations around the world could soon reap rewards associated with having one most productive workforce's planet earth. Multinational corporations have become an important aspect of this equation.

4.3. HOW MULTINATIONAL CORPORATIONS CONDUCT INDUSTRIAL RELATIONS?

Industrial relations among multinational corporations have become increasingly complex in recent years (Rosetti, 2019; Roy & Dubey, 2022; Roy, 2022; Roychowdhury, 2019; Rubery et al.; Sakharuk, 2021). With the rise of globalization, companies are now operating across multiple countries and cultures, making it difficult to maintain harmonious working relationships between employers and employees. This section will critically evaluate various arguments surrounding industrial relations among multinational corporations using vivid contemporary examples.

Recent academic studies have highlighted the importance of understanding cultural differences when managing international labor relations (Ozkiziltan, 2020; Peetz, 2021; Peetz et al., 2020; Peruzzo et al.; Pitteloud, 2022; Preminger & Bondy; Quinlan & Maxwell-Stewart). For example, a study conducted by researchers at Harvard Business School found that different countries had varying levels of acceptance for certain management practices such as performance-based pay or flexible work arrangements. The authors concluded that "managers must be aware of local norms and expectations when attempting to implement new policies" (HBS, 2020). This highlights the need for managers to consider cultural nuances when dealing with international labor issues. This is particularly important as globalization becomes more widespread and embedded (*see* Figure 4.5).

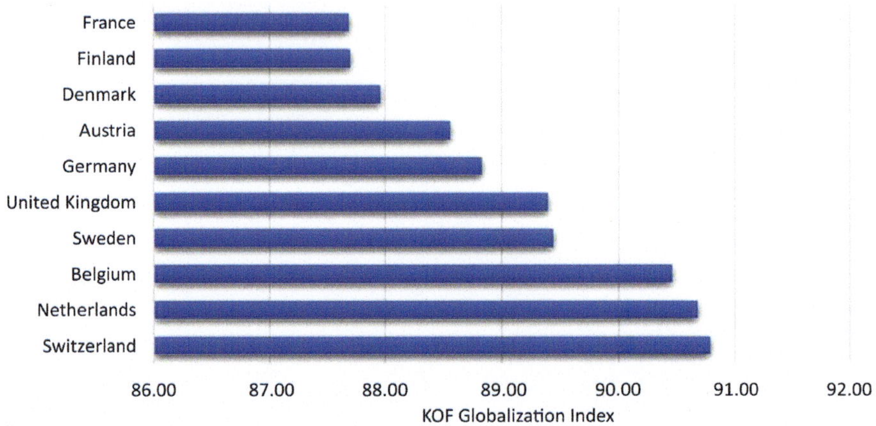

Figure 4.5. *KOF globalization index for selected European countries.*

Source: Kyove et al. (2021).

Theories such as Hofstede's Cultural Dimensions Theory can also provide useful insights into how different cultures view workplace dynamics and power structures (Hofstede, 1980). According to this theory, there are six dimensions which influence how people interact in a given culture: individualism vs collectivism; power distance; uncertainty avoidance; masculinity vs femininity; long-term orientation vs short-term orientation; and indulgence vs restraint (de Vaate, 2021; Demougin et al., 2019; Desai & Randeria, 2020; Devinatz, 2020, 2022; Di Carlo, 2020). By taking these factors into consideration, managers can better understand their workforce's attitudes towards authority figures and develop strategies accordingly.

Case studies can also offer valuable insight into effective approaches for managing industrial relations among multinationals (Clibborn, 2021; Colas-Neila & Fargas, 2019; Collins et al., 2020; Cooke et al., 2019; Croucher & Okland, 2021). For instance, a case study conducted by researchers at Stanford University examined how Apple Inc., one of the world's largest technology companies, managed its global workforce (Stanford, 2018). The authors found that Apple had implemented several initiatives designed to foster collaboration between its teams located around the world including regular video conferences between team members from different countries as well as cross-cultural training programs aimed at helping employees better understand each other's perspectives on business matters (Stanford, 2018). These findings demonstrate how important it is for multinationals to invest in initiatives which promote mutual understanding amongst their staff if they wish to achieve successful outcomes from their operations abroad. Another variable that multinational corporations must consider is the internationalization of business (*see* Figure 4.6) across borders and jurisdictions.

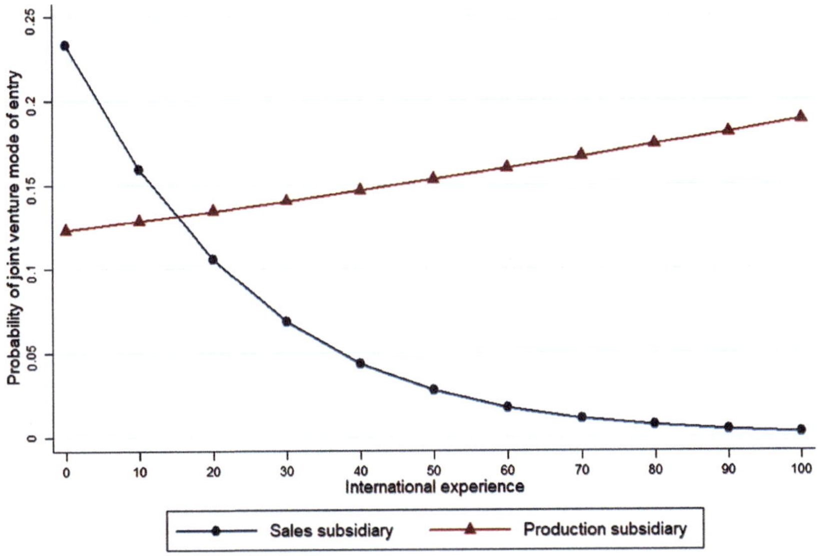

Figure 4.6. *Moderating role of international experience on the relationship between subsidiary type and entry mode decision.*

Source: Ko (2019).

In addition to theoretical models and case studies, debates about industrial relations among multinationals often focus on merits versus demerits associated with particular approaches or strategies used by firms operating internationally (Jiang & Yao, 2020; Jirjahn, 2022; Joyce et al.; Junior, 2022; Kaine, 2020; Katsabian, 2021; Kilic, 2021; Kolling & Schnabel, 2022). On one hand, proponents argue that adopting an open approach towards employee engagement allows firms greater flexibility in responding quickly to changing market conditions while simultaneously promoting trust within teams. On the other hand, critics contend that too much openness may lead workers feeling overwhelmed due lack of clear boundaries or guidelines.

It is therefore essential for organizations to ensure they strike a balance between providing sufficient autonomy without compromising structure and necessary efficient functioning.

Despite these differing opinions, there appears to be an emerging consensus point regarding the role communication plays fostering a positive working environment across borders (Bogoeski, 2022; Bondy, 2022; Boumans, 2022; Bourguignon & Floquet, 2019; Bradley & Rowland, 2021; Bray et al., 2019). Studies suggest strong emphasis placed on developing effective channels dialog helps build bridges and minimize potential conflicts arising out of misunderstandings related language barriers and cultural differences. Furthermore, research indicates having senior leadership actively involved in the process communicating company values mission statement is key in ensuring all stakeholders feel valued and respected regardless nationality origin.

Finally, philosophical discussions abound concerning ethical implications engaging foreign workers particularly those employed under precarious contractual arrangements such zero-hour contracts piece rate wages, etc. (Dalla Sega, 2021; Darlington & Mustchin, 2019; Das, 2023; Das & Singh, 2021; de Amorim et al., 2019; de Luna, 2022). While some commentators believe exploiting vulnerable populations is unethical and immoral, others present a counter argument stating individuals should freely choose the type of employment that best suits them given circumstances. Hence, it is important to consider the economic climate prevailing during a specific time period.

This question remains a hotly debated topic in today's society (Clibborn, 2019, 2020, 2021; Colas-Neila & Fargas, 2019; Collins et al., 2020; Cooke et al., 2019). There are no easy answers bearing in mind any prospects for industrial harmonization which remain uncertain. Yet, there are hopeful signs of progress being made in the area of human rights protection. Managing industrial relations among multinational corporations requires careful consideration of both theoretical models as well as practical solutions based on real-world examples.

Companies must be mindful of cultural differences when implementing policies while also investing in initiatives which promote mutual understanding amongst staff members located around the globe if they wish to achieve successful outcomes from their operations abroad (Clayton, 2021; Clibborn, 2019, 2020, 2021; Colas-Neila & Fargas, 2019; Collins et al., 2020). Ultimately though it is up to senior leadership teams within organizations themselves to make sure the right decisions are taken to ensure fair treatment for all parties involved in any corporate activity. Reference to international law is often an important consideration for multinational corporations as well as domestic businesses.

4.4. INTERNATIONAL LAW AND DOMESTIC INDUSTRIAL RELATIONS

The relationship between international law and domestic industrial relations has been a subject of debate for many years (Lamare & Budd, 2022; Lansbury, 2021; Larsson, 2020; Lawreniuk, 2023; Lee & Tapia, 2021; Leggett, 2019; Ligthart et al., 2022). This section will provide an overview of the various arguments surrounding this issue, with particular focus on contemporary examples. It will also reference important academic studies, highlight relevant theories and limitations, evaluate descriptive and explanatory models, summarize existing case studies and implications, discuss emerging debates and philosophical arguments before summarizing the topic in conclusion.

International law is often seen as having a significant impact on domestic industrial relations due to its ability to shape labor standards across countries (Espinosa, 2021; Eustace, 2021; Fang et al., 2021; Fergus & Godfrey, 2021; Flynn & Schroder, 2021; Foley & Williamson, 2021). For example, the ILO has developed conventions that set out minimum standards for wages, working hours and other aspects of employment conditions which are then adopted by member states through ratification processes. These conventions have had a major influence on national labor laws in many countries around the world. Such frameworks bear in mind the pressures that impact on industrial relations (*see* Figure 4.7 for an example of the European Union (EU)).

Nevertheless, there are some who argue that international law does not necessarily lead to improved labor rights or better working conditions at home because it can be difficult to enforce these standards domestically without strong political support from governments or trade unions (Baines & Cunningham, 2020; Bancarzewski & Hardy, 2021; Barklamb, 2021; Barry & Wilkinson, 2022; Baturina et al., 2021). Furthermore, even when ratified by governments they may not always be implemented effectively due to lack of resources or capacity within state institutions responsible for enforcing them such as labor ministers and the courts. This creates a series of institutional and institutionalized barriers to achieving fully harmonious industrial relations.

	Multinationals	Migration	EU regulations
Germany	Low: 10% private employment 7% capital formation 20% of GDP Some influential US investors, *Standortdebatte*, American Chamber	High: 15% foreign-born 19% of new employment 0.5% posted workers	Low: 'world of domestic politics' Few employment recommendations
France	Medium: 20% private employment 13% capital formation 39% of GDP Resistance to us influence openness to Japanese	High: 12% foreign-born 12% of new employment 0.5% posted workers	Medium: 'world of neglect' Moderate ECB pressure Some employment recommendations
UK	High: 20% private employment 23% capital formation 48% of GDP Traditional openness	High: 13% foreign-born 65% of new employment 0.2% posted workers	Low: 'world of domestic politics' Few employment recommendations Opt-out from Lisbon Treaty
Italy	Low: <10% private employment 5% capital formation 16% of GDP Recent debate on FDI Fiat internationalisation	Medium: 8% foreign-born 22% of new employment 0.2% posted workers	Medium: 'world of dead letters' Strong employment recommendations Strong ECB pressure
Spain	Medium: 10% private employment 12% capital formation 44% of GDP Influential investors in export sectors	High: 15% foreign-born 29% of new employment 0.5% posted workers	High: 'world of domestic politics' Strong employment recommendations Strong ECB pressure
Poland	High: 20% private employment 18% capital formation 41% of GDP Influential investors in export sectors, especially German	Medium: 0.5% foreign-born 1% of new employment 0.1% posted workers >5% of labour force emigration since 2004	High: 'world of dead letters' Some employment recommendations Accession conditionality

Data: share of foreign multinationals on employment: OECD 2007; share of FDI in capital formation: UNCTAD, average 2001-10; share of FDI stock in GDP: UCTAD, 2010; share of foreign-born in working-age population: EU LFS, 2007; share of foreign-born in new employment: EU LFS, 2000-07 (except Germany: 2000-11); share of posted workers on employment: E101 certificates, 2007; world of compliance: Falkner, G.,

Figure 4.7. *The pressures impacting on European industrial relations.*

Source: Meardi (2012).

In addition to this argument there is also evidence suggesting that international law can actually hinder progress towards better working conditions if it fails to consider local contexts or specific needs of workers in different countries (Grodem & Hippe, 2019; Guillaume, 2022; Guiso, 2020; Gunnigle et al., 2019; Gunther & Hopner, 2023; Haipeter, 2020). This is something which is particularly pertinent given increasing global economic inequality between nations today. For instance, research conducted by scholars such as David Trubek suggests that one-size-fits-all approaches imposed through ILO conventions may not always be appropriate given differences in cultural norms regarding work practices across regions/

countries leading them instead being used as tools for neo-liberal economic policies rather than improving worker's rights per se.

It is clear then that while international law can play an important role in setting minimum standards for wages, etc., its effectiveness depends largely upon how well it considers local contexts when formulating regulations (Freedland & Dhorajiwala, 2019; Fuchs et al., 2019; Galik et al., 2022; Gall, 2021; Gardawski & Towalski, 2020). This is something which requires careful consideration if we are truly committed to achieving greater social justice globally through improved labor rights at home. In recent years, there has been an important case in point with reference to governance issues that address environmental protection concerns. In Figure 4.8, we see an example of the transformation of urban ecologies.

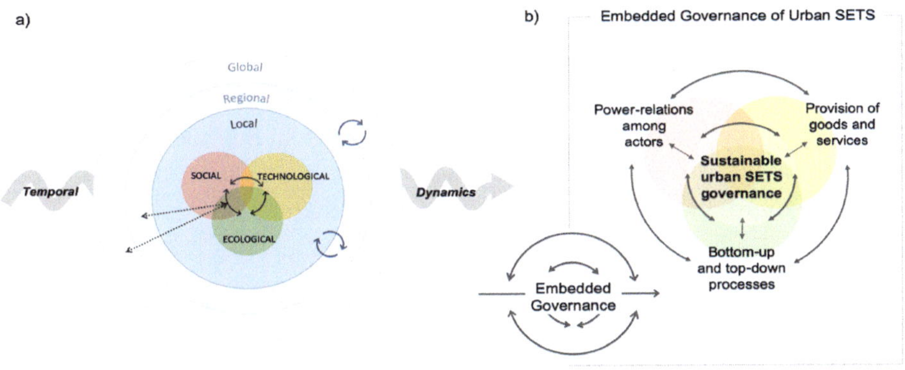

Figure 4.8. *Governing sustainable transformations of urban social-ecological-technological systems.*

Source: Nature.

While there is no doubt that international law has had an impact on domestic industrial relations over time, its effectiveness ultimately depends upon how well it considers local contexts when formulating regulations (Leggett, 2019; Ligthart et al., 2022; Liu, 2023; Lize et al., 2022; Lloyd & Payne, 2021; Lukacova et al., 2022; Lyddon, 2021). In order for us to achieve greater social justice globally, more attention must therefore be paid both nationally and internationally towards ensuring effective implementation of these laws, so they do indeed benefit workers everywhere. One of the sources for this type of engagement is the international legal regime. A prime case of this type of intervention is the work of ILO. The ILO is an agency of the United Nations (UN) that works to promote social justice and decent work for all (Chan, 2020b; Chantziaras et al., 2020; Chen et al., n.d., 2023; Cillo & Pradella, 2019; Civinskas & Dvorak, 2019). It has developed a set of eight core conventions, which are fundamental principles and rights at work that have been ratified by most countries in the world. These conventions cover topics such as freedom of association, collective bargaining, forced labor, child labor, discrimination in employment and occupation, equal remuneration for men and women workers for work of equal value, minimum wage protection and abolition of night work for women.

The ILO Conventions provide a framework to ensure basic human rights are respected in workplaces around the world (Di Carlo, 2020; Diessner et al., 2022; Dobbins et al., 2020, 2021; Dockes, 2019). They also serve as a benchmark against which governments can measure their progress towards achieving greater social justice through improved working conditions. However, it is important to note that while these conventions may be legally binding on signatory states, they do not always guarantee effective implementation. This is due to various factors including lack of resources or political will from certain governments, or even because some countries may choose to interpret them differently than others.

4.5. THE PLIGHT OF MIGRANT WORKERS IN INDUSTRIAL RELATIONS

The plight of migrant workers has been a major issue in the global economy for decades (Lansbury, 2021; Larsson, 2020; Lawreniuk, 2023; Lee & Tapia, 2021; Leggett, 2019; Ligthart et al., 2022; Liu, 2023). In recent years, however, the situation has become increasingly dire as governments around the world have failed to adequately address their needs and rights. This section will provide an overview of the current state of migrant workers and discuss some of the key issues they face today.

Migrant workers are defined as individuals who move from one country to another in search of better economic opportunities or safety from persecution or conflict (Colas-Neila & Fargas, 2019; Collins et al., 2020; Cooke et al., 2019; Croucher & Okland, 2021; D'Art, 2020). According to estimates by the ILO, there are currently over 150 million international migrants worldwide, with more than half coming from developing countries. These individuals often find themselves in precarious situations due to limited access to legal protection and social services, making them vulnerable to exploitation and abuse by employers or other authorities.

One major problem facing migrant workers is wage inequality (Dorigatti et al., n.d.; Dorigatti & Pedersini, 2021; Dorrenbacher et al., 2021; Drucza, 2019; Dupuis & Greer, 2022). Research shows that these individuals typically earn significantly less than native-born citizens even when performing similar jobs. This discrepancy can be attributed largely to discrimination based on race, gender, nationality, language proficiency, or other factors which limit their ability to negotiate higher wages or secure better working conditions. Additionally, many migrants lack access to basic labor protections such as minimum wage laws or health insurance coverage due to their irregular status within host countries' legal systems. This further exacerbates existing inequalities between them and local populations. The challenges notwithstanding, global migrant worker numbers and reach continues to rise (*see* Figure 4.9).

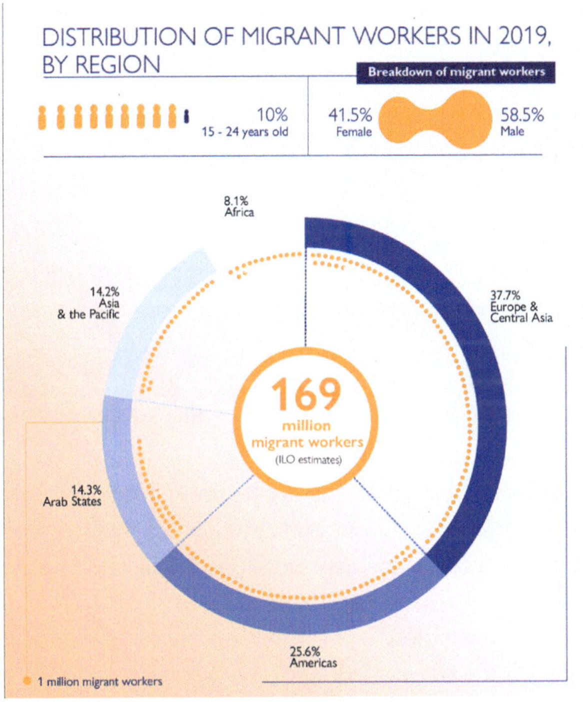

Figure 4.9. *Global distribution of migrant workers 2021.*

Source: International Labor Organization.

Another significant challenge faced by migrant workers is inadequate housing options (Jirjahn, 2022; Joyce et al.; Junior, 2022; Kaine, 2020; Katsabian, 2021; Kilic, 2021; Kolling & Schnabel, 2022; Kowalewska,

2020). Many live-in overcrowded dwellings without proper sanitation facilities which can lead not only physical discomfort but also psychological distress due increased feelings of insecurity and isolation from society at large. Furthermore, since most migrants do not possess formal documents proving their identity or residence status, they may be denied access to public services such as healthcare and education – leaving them unable to meet even basic needs like food security for themselves and their families back home.

It should be noted that while much attention has been paid recently towards improving conditions for refugees, little progress has been made when it comes addressing issues related specifically those who migrate voluntarily (Gasparri et al., 2019; Gasparri & Tassinari, 2020; Gavin, 2022; Giannakopoulos & Laliotis, 2020; Giraud, 2020). As a result, millions continue to suffer under oppressive regimes with no hope of escape anytime soon. Although there have been some efforts to improve living standards among migrant communities, much remains to be done to ensure that all people regardless of origin receive fair treatment and respect human rights. It is essential that governments act to protect these vulnerable populations through legislation enforcement so they can enjoy the same level of dignity and freedom enjoyed by citizens living and working in their own countries.

Only then will true justice prevail in our increasingly globalized world. Migration and modern slavery are two of the most pressing issues facing our world today (Ben & Sage, 2022; Berry & McDaniel, 2022; Bhuta, 2022; Bischoff et al., 2021; Bogoeski, 2022; Bondy, 2022). The global movement of people, both voluntary and involuntary, has created a complex set of challenges for governments to address. In particular, those who migrate voluntarily often find themselves in precarious situations due to their lack of legal status or identity documents. This can lead to exploitation by employers or traffickers as they have no recourse against unfair treatment or abuse. Furthermore, even if migrants do possess valid documentation such as an identity card or residence permit, they may be denied access public services such as healthcare and education – leaving them unable meet even basic needs like food security for themselves and their families back home.

That is why it is important to consider all the implications of the global migrant worker industry (*see* Figure 4.10). The situation is further complicated when it comes to addressing cases involving modern slavery which encompasses forced labor, human trafficking, debt bondage and other forms of exploitation that violate fundamental human rights (Stevis, 2022;

Svec et al., 2021; Tavora, 2019; Teipen & Mehl, 2021; Tesser & Serapioni, 2021; Thomas & Turnbull, 2021). It is estimated that there are over 40 million victims worldwide with many more at risk due to poverty-driven migration patterns from developing countries into wealthier nations where wages tend to be higher. Unfortunately, these vulnerable populations often become targets for unscrupulous employers who take advantage of their desperate circumstances.

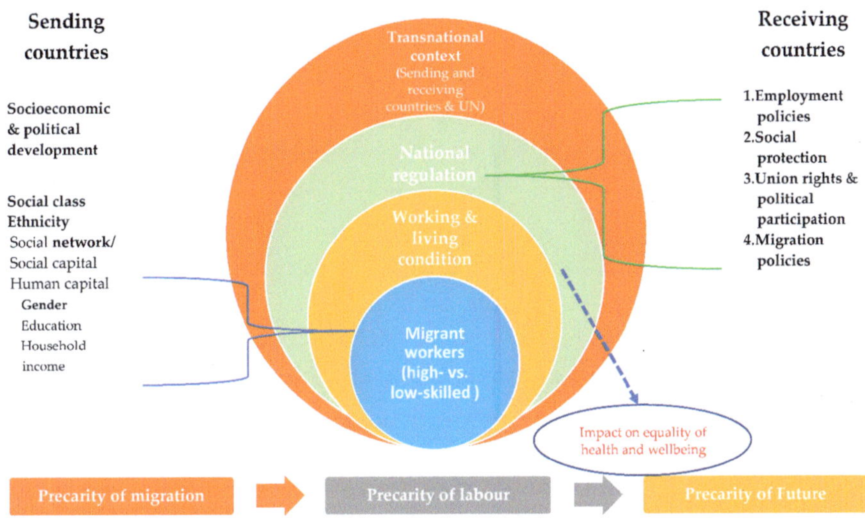

Figure 4.10. *Implications of the global migrant worker industry.*

Source: Kwak & Wang (2022).

In order to combat this problem, governments must develop comprehensive policies aimed at protecting migrant workers from exploitation while also providing them with access to essential resources (Quinlan & Maxwell-Stewart; Radzi et al., 2022; Ramsay & Webster, 2019; Ravn & Oyum, 2020; Razak et al., 2022). This includes strengthening existing laws prohibiting discrimination based on nationality, race, religion, gender, sexual orientation, etc. Additionally, international organizations should work together to create uniform standards to ensure fair working conditions across borders. At the same time, it is important to recognize that immigration control policies can have significant economic implications. For example, some countries impose restrictions on foreign workers in order to protect domestic labor markets from competition. This may lead to higher wages for native-born citizens but could also result in fewer job opportunities and lower productivity overall. Additionally, certain types of immigration controls such as visa requirements or quotas can create barriers to entry which limit the number of skilled immigrants able to enter a country and contribute their talents.

In addition to these economic considerations, there are also ethical debates surrounding immigration control policies (Vinichenko et al., 2020; Vulkan & Larsson, 2019; Walker, 2020; Walters & Wadsworth, 2020; Warner, 2019). Some argue that governments should prioritize human rights over economic interests when making decisions about who is allowed to enter their borders while others believe that national security must come first regardless of potential humanitarian costs. Furthermore, many scholars point out that restrictive measures often disproportionately affect vulnerable populations such as refugee's asylum seekers or those fleeing conflict zones due lack of resources and access to legal channels.

Overall, it is clear that the political economy of immigration control is a complex issue with far-reaching consequences both domestically and internationally (Edwards & Hodder, 2022; Ellem, 2021; Ellem et al., 2020; Engblom & Lundberg, 2019; Espinosa, 2021; Eustace, 2021). In order to ensure fair treatment of all migrants while still protecting local economies from exploitation, governments must develop comprehensive strategies to address this multifaceted problem. By considering both economic concerns and ethical considerations, policymakers can craft effective solutions to promote justice inclusion across borders.

CHAPTER 4 SUMMARY

In this fourth chapter we explored the practice of industrial relations. First, the chapter highlighted how there is a correlation between democratic governance and industrial relations. Other key considerations were efficiency, productivity, industrialization, globalization, and migrant workforces. These changes necessitated a better harmonization of international and local laws on industrial relations. The next chapter expounds on this theme in terms of the evolution and revolution of industrial relations across the globe.

CHAPTER 5

Evolution and Revolution in Industrial Relations

Contents

The fifth chapter in the book charts the revolution and evolution of industrial relations across the globe. For example, we consider how the trade union movement was originally conceived as well as its supportive mechanisms including collective bargaining.

The chapter discusses how globalization threatens the established norms, values, and practices of industrial relations. For instance, the chapter critiques the use of sweatshops and outsourcing among some of the most esteemed enterprises. We also consider how the work of the International Framework Agreements (IFAs) might be relevant to these dynamics. These developments are a culmination of many changes that started with the trade union movement.

5.1. THE ORIGINS OF THE TRADE UNION MOVEMENT

The origins of the trade union movement can be traced back to the political economy of immigration control (da Costa & Horn, 2021; Dalla Sega, 2021; Darlington & Mustchin, 2019; Das, 2023; Das & Singh, 2021; de Amorim et al., 2019). In the 19th century, as industrialization and urbanization increased in Europe, so did the number of immigrants seek work. This influx of people caused a great deal of concern among employers who feared that their wages would be undercut by foreign workers willing to accept lower pay. To protect their interests, employers began advocating for laws that would restrict immigration and limit competition from foreign labor.

At first, these efforts were largely unsuccessful due to strong opposition from both sides of politics (Bechter et al., 2021; Bedkar & Prashad, 2020; Behrens et al., 2020; Behrens & Pekarek, n.d.; Belizon, 2019; Bellace et al., 2021). However, over time this changed as more politicians began to recognize the potential economic benefits associated with restricting immigration. As a result, governments across Europe passed increasingly restrictive laws aimed at controlling migration flows into their countries.

These policies had an unintended consequence: they created a sense of solidarity among immigrant workers who found themselves facing similar restrictions on their ability to find employment or move freely between countries (Galik et al., 2022; Gall, 2021; Gardawski & Towalski, 2020; Gasparri, 2021; Gasparri et al., 2019; Gasparri & Tassinari, 2020). This led many immigrants to form unions in order to fight for better working conditions and higher wages—the beginnings of what we now know as the modern trade union movement. Hence, the notion that workers could collaborate to ensure better working conditions was born. Figure 5.1 is a case study of this history, albeit focusing on the USA.

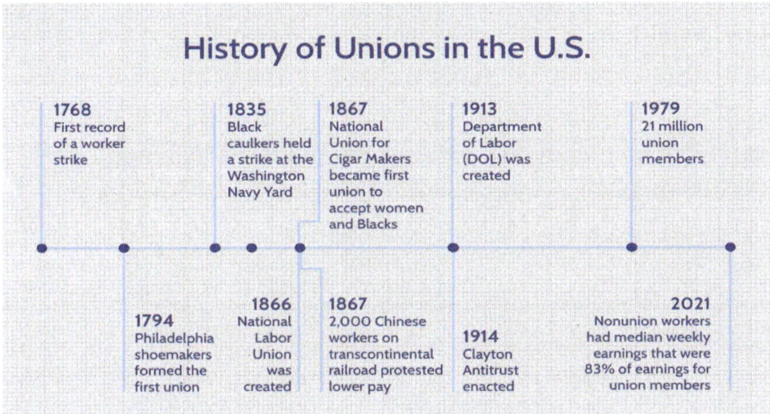

Figure 5.1. *History of the trade union movement in the USA.*

Source: Investopedia.

Today's trade unions are still fighting against restrictive immigration policies which continue to have negative impacts on migrant workers around the world—from exploitative working conditions and low wages in some industries, through to family separation when deportation orders are enforced without consideration for human rights or humanitarian concerns (Lyutov, 2022; MacKenzie & Lucio, 2019; Madimutsa; Mahas-Demydas & Rudnytska, 2019; Mahmood & Banerjee, 2020). The legacy left by those early struggles continues today as unions strive towards greater social justice for all workers regardless of nationality or origin. The first trade union in the United Kingdom was formed in 1824, when a group of London tailors came together to form the Grand National Consolidated Trades Union. This union sought to improve working conditions and wages for its members, as well as campaigning against child labor and other injustices. The success of this organization led to the formation of many more unions throughout Britain during the 19th century, with workers from all industries joining forces to fight for better rights and pay.

By 1900 there were over 1 million members of trade unions across Britain—a figure which had grown exponentially since their inception just over 70 years earlier (Thornthwaite & Sheldon, 2019, 2021; Tiraboschi, 2020; Tomassetti, 2021; Trif & Szabo). During this period, unions played an important role in securing improved working conditions such as shorter hours and higher wages through collective bargaining agreements (CBAs) with employers. They also campaigned on issues such as health and safety regulations, equal pay for women, pensions provision and unemployment benefits—all measures which have become commonplace today but were hard-fought victories at the time by those who believed that everyone should be entitled to fair treatment regardless of their job or social status.

Today's trade unions continue to play an important role in protecting workers' rights both nationally and internationally (Mahmood & Banerjee, 2020; Mailand, 2019; Markey, 2020; Martin, 2022; Martin et al., 2021; McCrystal & Hardy, 2021). For instance, they are still fighting for better terms and conditions while also advocating on behalf of vulnerable groups such as migrant workers who often find themselves facing exploitation due to lack of legal protection or knowledge about their rights under local laws. As we look back on our history it is clear that without these organizations much progress would not have been made towards greater equality within society—and so we owe them a great debt. The origins of the trade union movement can be traced back to the 18th and 19th centuries, when workers began to organize themselves in order to improve their working conditions (Peetz et al., 2020; Peruzzo et al.; Pitteloud, 2022; Preminger & Bondy; Quinlan & Maxwell-Stewart; Radzi et al., 2022). This was a time of great social upheaval as industrialization changed the way people lived and worked; it also saw an increase in poverty levels due to low wages and long hours. In response, workers formed unions which sought to protect their interests by negotiating better terms with employers—such as shorter hours and higher wages through CBAs. The British version of this history is summarized in Figure 5.2.

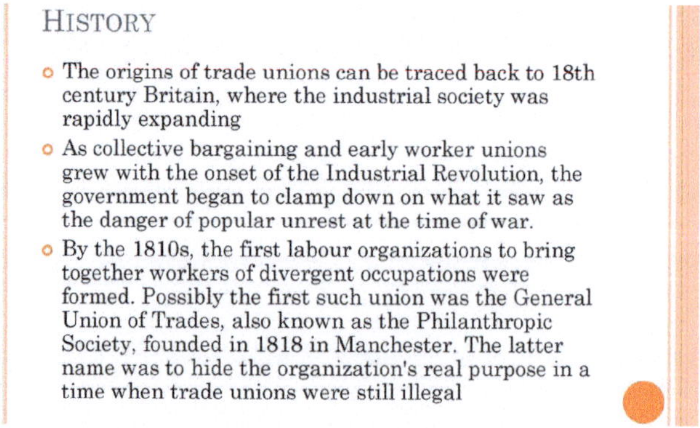

Figure 5.2. *History of trade unions in Great Britain.*

Source: Rose Greer via SlidePlayer.

These early unions were often met with hostility from employers who viewed them as a threat to their profits (Dorigatti et al., n.d.; Dorigatti & Pedersini, 2021; Dorrenbacher et al., 2021; Drucza, 2019; Dupuis & Greer, 2022). In some ways this anti-union sentiment was justified by the suspicion that they used tactics such as blacklisting or intimidation against those involved in organizing activities. Despite this, many unions continued to grow throughout Europe during this period—and eventually spread across other parts of the world too.

In addition to fighting for improved pay and conditions, these organizations also campaigned on issues such as health and safety regulations, equal pay for women, pensions provision and unemployment benefits. These are all measures which have become commonplace today but were hard-fought victories at the time by those who believed that everyone should be entitled to fair treatment regardless of their job or social status. Today's trade unions continue to play an important role in protecting workers' rights both nationally and internationally. Collective bargaining was a historically powerful tool in this evolution of trade unionism.

5.2. WHY COLLECTIVE BARGAINING WAS INTRODUCED AND EMBEDDED?

The origins of the trade union movement can be traced back to the 19th century when workers began to organize in order to protect their rights and improve working conditions. Collective bargaining was seen as a way for workers to gain leverage against employers and ensure that they were treated fairly. This concept has been used throughout history as a means of achieving better wages, benefits, and working conditions for employees (Mahmood & Banerjee, 2020; Mailand, 2019; Markey, 2020; Martin, 2022; Martin et al., 2021; McCrystal & Hardy, 2021).

In 1867, the first collective bargaining agreement was signed between an employer and a group of employees in England. This agreement established minimum wage rates, hours of work, overtime pay rules, vacation time allowances, sick leave provisions, safety regulations and other important workplace issues. The success of this agreement led to similar agreements being made across Europe during the late 1800s (Ngai, 2020; Nicklich & Helfen, 2019; Novitz & Andrijasevic, 2020; Nowak, 2021; Nurlinah et al., 2021). In America during this same period there were several attempts at establishing CBAs, but these efforts largely failed due to lack of legal protection or enforcement mechanisms for such contracts (Ozkiziltan, 2020;

Peetz, 2021; Peetz et al., 2020; Peruzzo et al.; Pitteloud, 2022; Preminger & Bondy; Quinlan & Maxwell-Stewart). It was not until 1935 with passage of the National Labor Relations Act (NLRA) that American workers gained legal recognition for their right to collectively bargain with employers over wages and working conditions. Figure 5.3 is a basic conceptualization of collective bargaining.

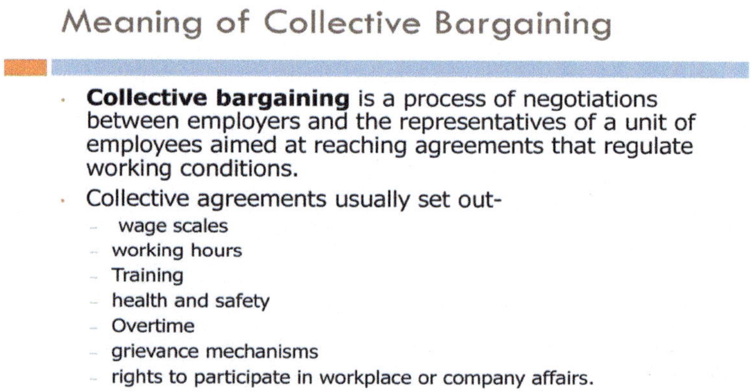

Figure 5.3. *Conceptualization of collective bargaining.*

Source: John Marshall via SlidePlayer.

Since then, collective bargaining has become an integral part of labor relations in many countries around the world including Canada where it is protected by law under provincial legislation such as Ontario's Labor Relations Act (LRA). In addition, international organizations like International Labor Organization (ILO) have also recognized collective bargaining as an essential element in promoting decent work standards globally (Gasparri, 2021; Gasparri et al., 2019; Gasparri & Tassinari, 2020; Gavin, 2022; Giannakopoulos & Laliotis, 2020). This is achieved through its Declaration on Fundamental Principles and Rights at Work which advocates that members promote collective bargaining to improve standards.

Collective Bargaining remains one of the most powerful tools available today for ensuring fair treatment within workplaces worldwide (Schofield-Georgeson & Rawling, 2020; Schuessler et al., 2019; Schuhrke, 2019; Scrimger, 2020; Seghezzi; Sheldon & Thornthwaite, 2020). For example, it is credited with providing both employers and employees with a platform from which they can negotiate mutually beneficial terms without resorting to costly litigation or strikes. This has the effect of making it clear why its historical justifications remain so relevant today. The origins of the trade union movement can be traced back to the industrial revolution in Europe during the late 18th and early 19th centuries.

During this period, workers began to organize themselves into unions in order to protect their rights and interests against exploitative employers (Eustace, 2021; Fang et al., 2021; Fergus & Godfrey, 2021; Flynn & Schroder, 2021; Foley & Williamson, 2021). This was a time when labor laws were virtually non-existent, leaving workers vulnerable to exploitation by powerful factory owners who could dictate wages and working conditions with impunity. In response, unions sought CBAs which would guarantee fair wages and better working conditions for their members – something that had never been done before.

Since then, collective bargaining models have evolved significantly over time as governments have become more involved in regulating labor relations through legislation such as minimum wage laws or anti-discrimination statutes (Bedkar & Prashad, 2020; Behrens et al., 2020; Behrens & Pekarek, n.d.; Belizon, 2019; Bellace et al., 2021; Ben & Sage, 2022). However, despite these changes one thing remains constant: collective bargaining is still seen as an effective way of ensuring fairness within workplaces worldwide. By providing both employers and employees with a platform from which they can negotiate mutually beneficial terms without resorting to costly litigation or strikes it has proven itself invaluable throughout history. Figure 5.4 outlines the main features of collective bargaining.

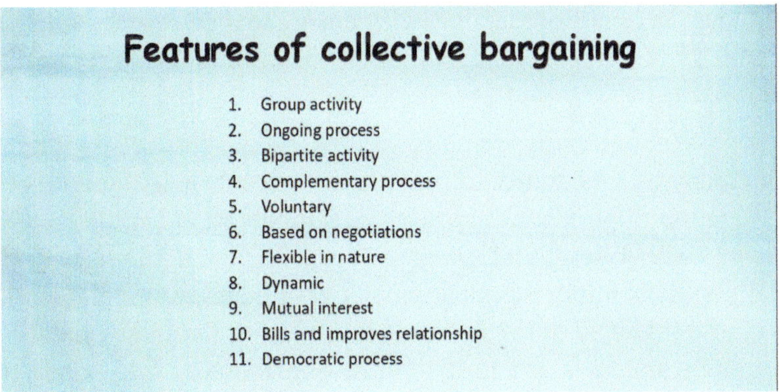

Figure 5.4. *Features of collective bargaining.*

Source: Muthu Lakshmi via YouTube.

Collective Bargaining is an essential part of modern labor relations; providing both employers and employees with a platform from which they can negotiate mutually beneficial terms without resorting to costly litigation or strikes (Barklamb, 2021; Barry & Wilkinson, 2022; Baturina et al., 2021; Beattie, 2019; Bechter et al., 2021; Bedkar & Prashad, 2020). Its historical justifications remain relevant today due to its ability to ensure fair treatment within workplaces worldwide; making it clear why it continues to be so important even after all these years. Nevertheless, there will be localized variations that respond to specific challenges in time and space.

The origins of the trade union movement can be traced back to the 19th century, when workers began to organize in order to protect their rights and interests (Lamare & Budd, 2022; Lansbury, 2021; Larsson, 2020; Lawreniuk, 2023; Lee & Tapia, 2021; Leggett, 2019; Ligthart et al., 2022).

This was a response to the exploitative working conditions that were common at the time, with employers often taking advantage of their employees' lack of bargaining power. As such, collective bargaining became an important tool for workers as it allowed them to negotiate better wages and working conditions with their employers.

Since then, collective bargaining has evolved into a more formalized economic framework which is used by both labor unions and employers (Cooke et al., 2019; Croucher & Okland, 2021; D'Art, 2020; da Costa & Horn, 2021; Dalla Sega, 2021; Darlington & Mustchin, 2019). It provides a structured approach for negotiating terms such as wages, hours worked, benefits packages and other workplace issues – all while ensuring fairness on both sides. Furthermore, it also helps ensure that any agreements reached are legally binding; providing further protection for those involved in negotiations.

Collective Bargaining remains an essential part of modern labor relations today due its ability to provide fair outcomes without resorting to costly litigation or strikes as alternatives (Dupuis & Greer, 2022; Edwards & Hodder, 2022; Ellem, 2021; Ellem et al., 2020; Engblom & Lundberg, 2019). With this in mind, it is clear why governments around the world have become more involved in regulating labor relations through legislation such as minimum wage laws or anti-discrimination statutes – ultimately helping ensure that everyone receives fair treatment within workplaces worldwide. Such approaches are particularly relevant in a world that is increasingly globalized.

5.3. THE IMPACT OF GLOBALIZATION ON INDUSTRIAL RELATIONS

Globalization has had a profound impact on industrial relations in Europe, Asia, Africa, America, and Australia (Sakharuk, 2021; Sanchez-Mosquera, 2022; Sanz et al., 2020; Schlachter, 2019; Schmidt & Muller, 2021; Schofield-Georgeson, 2022). The globalization of markets has led to increased competition between countries as well as within them. Companies have sought out cheaper labor sources from abroad which has resulted in job losses at home and downward pressure on wages and conditions for those who remain employed. This has made it more difficult for unions to negotiate better terms with employers due to the threat of relocation if demands are not met.

In addition, multinational corporations have been able to use their economic power and influence over governments around the world in order to weaken labor laws that would otherwise protect workers' rights such as minimum wage legislation or CBAs (Roy, 2022; Roychowdhury, 2019; Rubery et al.; Sakharuk, 2021; Sanchez-Mosquera, 2022; Sanz et al., 2020). This means that even when unions do exist, they may not be able to effectively represent their members' interests due lack of legal protection or resources available for organizing activities. Despite these challenges there is evidence that some countries have successfully managed industrial relations through effective regulation and enforcement mechanisms.

There are examples of good practice in industrial relations despite industrialization (Flynn & Schroder, 2021; Foley & Williamson, 2021; Ford & Gillan, 2022; Ford & Ward, 2021; Forde; Forsyth, 2022). A case in point is Germany's co-determination system which gives employees representation on company boards alongside management representatives thus allowing them a say in decision making processes related directly affecting them such as pay negotiations or workplace safety standards. Germany is renowned for its co-determination system, which allows employees to participate in the decision-making process of their companies. This system has been praised by many as a way to ensure that workers' voices are heard and respected within the workplace. However, there have also been criticisms of this model, with some arguing that it can lead to inefficient outcomes due to lack of accountability or too much power being given to workers. In order to evaluate these arguments, it is important to consider contemporary examples and relevant academic studies. One example of Germany's co-determination system in action is Volkswagen AG (VW). VW has implemented a two-tier board structure where half of the members are elected by shareholders and half are elected by employees. This arrangement gives both groups an equal say in decisions made at the company level. While this may seem like an ideal situation for employee representation, research suggests otherwise: one study found that when compared with firms without such arrangements, those with co-determination systems had lower returns on equity and higher labor costs (Kirchhoff et al., 2017). These findings suggest that while giving workers more influence over corporate decisions may be beneficial from a social perspective, it could come at a cost from an economic standpoint (Lloyd & Payne, 2021; Lukacova et al., 2022; Lyddon, 2021; Lyutov, 2022; MacKenzie & Lucio, 2019; Madimutsa).

In addition to empirical evidence regarding efficiency losses associated with co-determination systems, there have also been philosophical debates about whether they truly empower workers or simply give them false hope (Tavora, 2019; Teipen & Mehl, 2021; Tesser & Serapioni, 2021; Thomas & Turnbull, 2021; Thornthwaite & Sheldon, 2019). On one hand, proponents argue that allowing employees greater input into decision making processes gives them more control over their working conditions and encourages collaboration between management and labor (Grosser & Schmalzriedt, 2018). On the other hand, however, critics contend that such arrangements often fail because they do not provide enough incentives for managers or employees; thus, leading either party to act out of self-interest rather than collective benefit (Hirschman, 1970).

Overall then it appears clear that while Germany's co-determination system does offer certain advantages – namely increased worker participation – there are potential drawbacks as well including decreased efficiency gains and limited incentive structures for all parties involved. As such further research should be conducted into how best to balance these competing interests so as to maximize benefits for everyone involved in corporate governance structures across Europe going forward (Guiso, 2020; Gunnigle et al., 2019; Gunther & Hopner, 2023; Haipeter, 2020; Hakansta et al., n.d.; Hamberger, 2020). Yet, there are other jurisdictions that have adopted differential but effective approaches.

Other examples include South Korea's tripartite system involving government, business leaders, and union representatives coming together regularly to discuss issues related employment policies. South Korea has a unique tripartite system for unionization that is distinct from other countries (Devinatz, 2022; Di Carlo, 2020; Diessner et al., 2022; Dobbins et al., 2020,

2021; Dockes, 2019). This system, which was established in the late 1980s, involves three main actors: labor unions, employers' associations, and the government. The purpose of this arrangement is to promote collective bargaining between workers and employers while also providing legal protection for both parties.

The primary argument in favor of South Korea's tripartite system is that it allows for more effective negotiations between workers and employers than traditional systems do (Hoffrogge, 2019; Howell, 2019, 2021; Hungler, 2022; Ilsoe & Soderqvist; Jarota, 2022; Jha & Singh, 2019). By involving all three stakeholders—labor unions, employers' associations, and the government—the process can be better regulated and monitored to ensure fairness on both sides. Additionally, by having representatives from each group present during negotiations, there are fewer chances of one side taking advantage of the other due to unequal power dynamics or lack of knowledge about labor laws.

However, some scholars have argued that this system may not be as beneficial as initially thought because it does not always lead to improved working conditions or wages for employees (Devinatz, 2020, 2022; Di Carlo, 2020; Diessner et al., 2022; Dobbins et al., 2020, 2021). For example, research conducted by Kim et al. (2020) found that despite increased involvement from all three stakeholders in collective bargaining processes since its implementation in 1988–1989 period, real wages have remained stagnant over time with no significant improvement. Furthermore, they noted that although employer organizations were able to successfully negotiate higher wages with their respective companies, these gains did not necessarily translate into higher salaries across industries.

In addition, critics have pointed out that South Korea's tripartite system may actually limit worker autonomy by giving too much power to employer organizations who are often seen as being hostile towards organized labor. As such, many argue that this type of arrangement could potentially create an environment where workers are unable to effectively advocate for themselves without fear of retribution from their bosses (Nga & Nga, 2021; Ngai, 2020; Nicklich & Helfen, 2019; Novitz & Andrijasevic, 2020; Nowak, 2021; Nurlinah et al., 2021). Moreover, some experts contend that this kind of setup could even lead to a decrease in overall job satisfaction among employees due to decreased job security or unfair treatment at work.

Overall, South Korea's tripartite system has been praised for its ability to facilitate collective bargaining between workers and employers but there remain several criticisms regarding its efficacy when it comes to improving working conditions or wages across industries. It is important then for policymakers and researchers alike to continue studying how different aspects such as employer organization influence outcomes within this framework so we can better understand what works best when it comes to protecting employee rights while still allowing businesses room to grow economically.

With careful consideration given towards how different countries approach regulating labor market practices there is potential for positive outcomes both economically and socially (Larsson, 2020; Lawreniuk, 2023; Lee & Tapia, 2021; Leggett, 2019; Ligthart et al., 2022; Liu, 2023; Lize et al., 2022). However, that rate and possibilities of that success is subject to the perceptions of the main stakeholders. Figure 5.5 is an example of such perceptions among stakeholders.

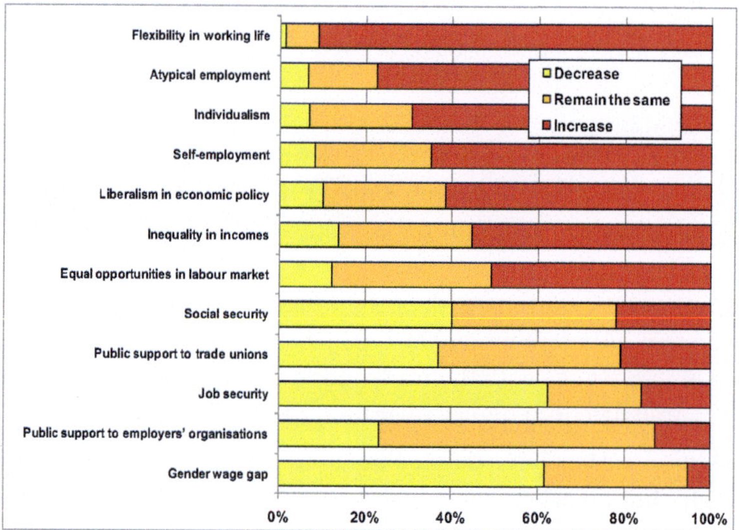

Figure 2. Respondents' opinion about general challenges of globalization.

Figure 5.5. *Perceptions of the effects and challenges of globalization in industrial relations.*

Source: Philips & Eamets (2009).

The rise of globalization has meant that workers in different countries are now more interconnected than ever before (Hilgert, 2019; Hirsch & Mueller, 2020; Hoffrogge, 2019; Howell, 2019, 2021; Hungler, 2022; Ilsoe & Soderqvist; Jarota, 2022). This has led to a greater awareness of worker rights and the need for better protection from exploitation. In Europe, for example, there have been numerous initiatives aimed at improving working conditions such as the European Union's (EU) Working Time Directive which sets out minimum standards on rest periods and maximum hours worked per week. Similarly, in Asia many countries have adopted laws to protect workers from unfair dismissal or discrimination based on gender or age.

In addition to this, some countries have also implemented systems designed to facilitate collective bargaining between employers and employees over wages and other terms of employment (McCrystal & Hardy, 2021; Mezihorak et al.; Morritt, 2022; Murphy & Turner, 2020; Nespoli, 2019; Newman et al., 2019). For instance, India has established an Industrial Disputes Act which allows trade unions to negotiate with employers over issues such as wage negotiation. It is clear that globalization has had a significant impact on industrial relations across the world, but it is important not to forget about the importance of localized approaches when it comes to protecting worker rights.

Different countries may require different solutions depending upon their particular economic circumstances (Mezihorak et al.; Morritt, 2022; Murphy & Turner, 2020; Nespoli, 2019; Newman et al., 2019; Nga & Nga, 2021). So, it is essential that governments consider these differences when formulating policies related labor market practices. By doing so, they can ensure that all workers are able to benefit from improved working conditions regardless of where they live. Ultimately, by taking into consideration both global trends and local needs we can create an integrated and interdependent global economy where everyone's rights are respected.

One of the most important aspects of globalization is its impact on structural unemployment (Barklamb, 2021; Barry & Wilkinson, 2022; Baturina et al., 2021; Beattie, 2019; Bechter et al., 2021; Bedkar & Prashad, 2020). Structural unemployment occurs when there are not enough jobs available to meet the needs of a particular labor market. This can be caused by changes in technology, shifts in consumer demand or other factors that lead to an imbalance between supply and demand for certain types of workers. In order to address this issue, governments must take steps to ensure that their economies remain competitive and attractive for businesses so they can create new job opportunities.

The origins of the trade union movement also need to be considered when discussing globalization and structural unemployment (Kaine, 2020; Katsabian, 2021; Kilic, 2021; Kolling & Schnabel, 2022; Kowalewska,

2020; Kupec et al., 2022; Lamare & Budd, 2022). Trade unions have been instrumental in protecting worker rights throughout history, particularly during periods where economic conditions were difficult. By negotiating collective agreements with employers, trade unions have been able to secure better wages and working conditions for their members as well as providing them with a platform from which they can voice their grievances. As such, it is essential that governments recognize the importance of trade unions when formulating policies related labor market practices. Moreover, the changing density of trade unions across countries (*see* Figure 5.6) means that they can no longer be ignored.

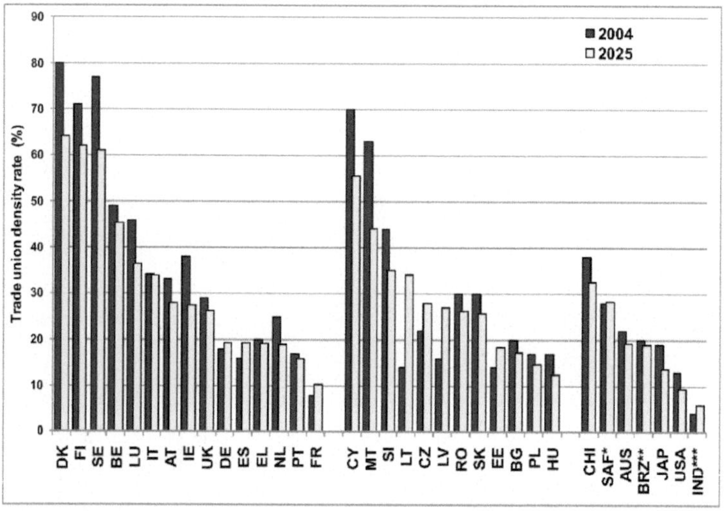

Figure 5.6. *Changing trade union density in selected countries 2004 through 2025.*

Source: Philips & Eamets (2009).

It is clear that globalization has had a significant impact on industrial relations across the world, but it is important not to forget about localized approaches when it comes to protecting worker rights (Ozkiziltan, 2019, 2020; Peetz, 2021; Peetz et al., 2020; Peruzzo et al.; Pitteloud, 2022; Preminger & Bondy). Different countries may require different solutions depending upon their particular economic circumstances, so it is essential that governments consider these differences when formulating policies related labor market practices. Furthermore, we must remember the importance of trade unions in ensuring fair wages and working conditions for all employees regardless of where they live or work. Ultimately, by taking into consideration both global trends and local needs we can create an integrated and interdependent global economy where everyone's rights are respected. One of the failures of globalization in terms of industrial relations has been outsourcing.

5.4. HOW OUTSOURCING AND SWEATSHOPS IMPACT ON INDUSTRIAL RELATIONS?

Outsourcing has become a major part of the global economy, with businesses increasingly relying on foreign labor to reduce costs and increase efficiency (Croucher & Okland, 2021; D'Art, 2020; da Costa & Horn, 2021; Dalla Sega, 2021; Darlington & Mustchin, 2019). This practice has had both positive and negative impacts on domestic and foreign workers alike. In this section, we will explore the various arguments surrounding outsourcing, referencing important academic studies as well as evaluating descriptive and explanatory models.

One of the primary benefits of outsourcing is that it can help companies reduce their labor costs by taking advantage of lower wages in other countries (Gunther & Hopner, 2023; Haipeter, 2020; Hakansta et al., n.d.; Hamberger, 2020; Harvey & Turnbull, 2020; Hendy, 2022). This can be beneficial for businesses who are looking to remain competitive in an ever-changing market. However, there are also potential drawbacks associated with outsourcing which must be taken into consideration when making decisions about whether or not to outsource certain tasks or jobs. For example, some argue that outsourcing leads to job losses in developed countries due to increased competition from cheaper overseas labor markets. Additionally, research suggests that outsourced jobs often lack adequate safety standards or pay compared to those found domestically (Kumar & Kumar, 2020).

In addition to economic concerns related to outsourcing, there are also ethical considerations which must be considered when assessing its impact on domestic and foreign workers (Howell, 2021; Hungler, 2022; Ilsoe & Soderqvist; Jarota, 2022; Jha & Singh, 2019; Jiang & Yao, 2020; Jirjahn, 2022). For instance, many have argued that multinational corporations should take responsibility for ensuring fair working conditions abroad (Gereffi et al., 2019). Furthermore, scholars have suggested that governments should create policies aimed at protecting vulnerable populations from exploitation through international trade agreements (Lambert & Schmitz, 2018).

Finally, it is important to consider how existing case studies may inform our understanding of the implications of outsourcing for both domestic and foreign workers alike. Studies suggest that while some individuals benefit from access to higher paying jobs abroad due to increased competition within their home country's labor market (Harrison et al., 2017), others may suffer due emerging debates around wage inequality between different nations (Bhagwati, 2004). Moreover, research indicates that while some firms may gain cost savings through offshoring activities such as production relocation or subcontracting services (Chen et al., 2016), these gains do not always translate into improved living standards for local communities where these activities occur (Feenstra & Hanson, 1999). Yet, these considerations are often ignored in the decision-making framework for outsourcing (*see* Figure 5.7).

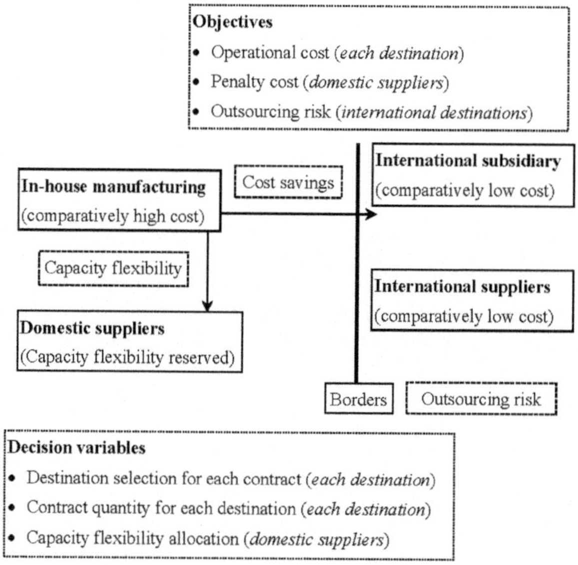

Figure 5.7. *Decision-making framework for outsourcing.*

Source: Sardar et al. (2016).

Overall then it appears clear that while there are potential benefits associated with outsourcing practices such as reduced costs for businesses operating internationally; there are also significant risks involved which must be carefully considered before any decision is made regarding its implementation within a particular context or industry sector (Razak et al., 2022; Refslund & Arnholtz, 2022; Ritson, 2019a, b; Riva & Rizza, 2021; Roche, n.d.; Roche & Gormley, 2020). It is therefore essential for policy makers, business leaders, academics, civil society organizations, and other stakeholders involved in shaping global economic systems to understand both sides of this debate so they can make informed decisions about how best to support all affected parties. Such considerations may reduce the risks of inappropriate policy formulation and poor implementation across the globe. Ultimately, these interventions protect vulnerable workers and industries.

Yet, there are those who argue that outsourcing provides opportunities for economic growth in developing countries by creating new employment opportunities (Gereffi et al., 2017). Furthermore, proponents suggest that increased competition resulting from globalization can lead to higher quality goods at lower prices which ultimately benefit consumers worldwide (Feenstra & Hanson, 1999). While these arguments have merit, they do not consider certain limitations such as unequal power dynamics between employers and employees which could potentially lead to exploitation or unfair working conditions (Lambert et al., 2018). That is a worthwhile endeavor as we enter an era of hyper globalization.

The positive and negative aspects associated with outsourcing depend on one's perspective. It is nonetheless important for policymakers to consider all sides when making decisions about how best to regulate international trade so as not only protect domestic workers but also ensure fair treatment of foreign laborers employed through outsourced services or products (Harvey & Turnbull, 2020; Hendy, 2022; Herrero, 2022; Hilgert, 2019; Hirsch & Mueller, 2020; Hoffrogge, 2019).

Sweatshops and exploitation in capitalist societies have been a topic of debate for many years (Fuchs et al., 2019; Galik et al., 2022; Gall, 2021; Gardawski & Towalski, 2020; Gasparri, 2021; Gasparri et al., 2019). On one hand, proponents argue that outsourcing labor to countries with lower wages can lead to economic growth and increased employment opportunities (Krugman & Obstfeld, 2009). Additionally, it has been argued that this type of international trade can lead to human suffering. It can also create and foster inequalities that reduce the quality of lives that employed and unemployed people lead. Yet, there has been support for outsourcing as an economically competitive approach. Indeed, such support extends to the hitherto sacrosanct public sector (*see* Figure 5.8).

Yet, there is evidence to suggest that these practices are often exploitative and detrimental to workers' rights (Lambert et al., 2018). This is especially true when considering the fact that those employed in sweatshops typically lack access to basic necessities such as healthcare or education which could potentially lead to long-term poverty (Feenstra & Hanson,

1999). Furthermore, due to their precarious legal status they may be more vulnerable than domestic employees when it comes to negotiating terms of employment or challenging unfair working conditions. Others may consider the process of advocating and pursuing their rights too tedious and not worth the investment of their meager resources.

	ITALY - MUNICIPALITY	ITALY – LOCAL HEALTH AUTHORITY
Union stance towards outsourcing	Fragmented opposition to single externalization events: lack of systematic institutional stance	Systematic opposition to outsourcing in healthcare sector
Union strategy and responses	Focus on keeping core services in-house (education and social services) and sheltering public employment. Industrial action.	Focus on keeping healthcare services in-house and sheltering public employment. Campaign to inform employees and users
Workplace representatives	Always elected in both the municipality and private subcontractors	Always elected in both the municipality and private subcontractors
Union consultation	Always consulted before outsourcing until the Brunetta reform in 2009 Since then union only informed	Always consulted before outsourcing Collective bargaining on HRM and work organisation-related issues
Relationship between social partners	In the relation with unions, municipality complies with legislative requirement in terms of information and consultation. Union often seen as an obstacle during restructuring events	Collaborative long-standing tradition of social dialogue: shared purpose to safeguard the quality of healthcare services
Challenge to union	Workers transferred in catering Fragmentation of employment Two-tier workforce	Production chain fragmentation
Membership	Decreasing (not only due to outsourcing: municipal staffing level physiologically diminished following strict austerity measures)	Rather stable
Users' involvement	Union awareness of this lack: need to involved citizens in campaigns	Citizens involvement in campaigns to raise awareness of the risks in externalizing healthcare services

Figure 5.8. *Example of public sector outsourcing in an Italian location.*

Source: Mori (2015).

In order to address this issue various initiatives have been proposed including minimum wage laws and improved monitoring systems for factories located abroad (Krugman & Obstfeld, 2009). However, while these measures may help protect foreign laborers from exploitation, they do not necessarily guarantee fair treatment or adequate compensation (Forde; Forsyth, 2022; Foster et al., 2021; Franceschini, 2020; Freedland & Dhorajiwala, 2019; Fuchs et al., 2019). Moreover, some critics argue that implementing such regulations could actually increase unemployment levels by making certain products too expensive for consumers, leading companies to move production back home where labor costs are higher (Lambert et al., 2018). Sweatshops and exploitation in capitalist societies have been a topic of debate for many years. On one hand, proponents argue that outsourcing labor to countries with lower wages can lead to increased economic growth and development (Krugman & Obstfeld, 2009). This is because it allows companies to produce goods at a much lower cost than they would be able to domestically while still maintaining high quality standards. Additionally, this type of trade has the potential to lead countries out of poverty.

Yet, there are also those who oppose such practices due to their potential for exploitation. Sweatshop workers often face long hours with little pay or benefits as well as hazardous working conditions (Lambert et al., 2018). Furthermore, these employees may not have access to legal protection or recourse if they experience mistreatment from employers which could further exacerbate the problem (Feenstra & Hanson, 1999). In addition, some studies suggest that outsourcing jobs overseas can lead to job losses in domestic markets due to competition from cheaper foreign labor (Krugman & Obstfeld, 2009).

In order to better understand how globalization affects employment levels around the world it is important to consider both sides of the argument. While there are certainly advantages associated with outsourcing labor such as increased economic growth and access to higher quality goods at lower prices it is equally important to recognize any potential drawbacks including unequal power dynamics between employers and employees which could potentially lead to exploitation or unfair working conditions. Ultimately more research needs to be done into understanding how different factors interact when considering the impact of globalization on local economies before any definitive conclusions can be drawn regarding its effects on employment levels around the world. In the meantime, some innovations have emerged to support the implementation, monitoring, and evaluation of industrial relations. One such innovation is the IFAs.

5.5. THE USE OF INTERNATIONAL FRAMEWORK AGREEMENTS (IFAS)

International framework agreements (IFAs) are a type of international agreement that provide the framework for cooperation between two or more countries (Behrens & Pekarek, n.d.; Belizon, 2019; Bellace et al., 2021; Ben & Sage, 2022; Berry & McDaniel, 2022; Bhuta, 2022). They are often used to facilitate trade, investment, and other forms of economic exchange. In recent years, IFAs have become increasingly important in global governance as they offer an effective way to manage complex issues such as climate change and human rights.

The concept of IFAs has been around since the early 20th century but it was not until after World War II that their use became widespread (Ellem, 2021; Ellem et al., 2020; Engblom & Lundberg, 2019; Espinosa, 2021; Eustace, 2021; Fang et al., 2021). Since then, there have been numerous examples of successful IFAs including the North American Free Trade Agreement

(NAFTA), the European Union's Common Market, and various regional agreements such as ASEAN and Mercosur (*see* Figure 5.9). Despite their success in facilitating economic integration, there is still much debate about how best to design IFAs so that they can effectively address contemporary challenges while also protecting national sovereignty. This debate has led to a number of different approaches being proposed by academics and policy makers alike.

	MetalCorp/T	AutoSupplier1	AutoSupplier2
Does the local company know about IFA?	Yes	No	No
Does the local union know about IFA?	No	Yes	Yes
IFA implementation?	Yes	Yes	No (another supplementary tool (IFC/PS2) was implemented)
Evidence for (non-) implementation	- Unionisation - Collective bargaining & agreement - Good working conditions - Satisfactory wages & benefits - Compliance with other ILO labor standards - Very positive labour/union - management relations	- Implementation through newly won unionization - A protocol b/w management & union - Change in workplace relations - Recognition for collective bargaining	- Change in workplace relations through newly established committees (Committee of Strengthening Social Dialogue; Advisory Committee; Social Performance Team; & workers representatives) - Revision of HR policy in line with ILO norms
The Role of GUFs	- No involvement	- Active involvement through initiating negotiations with the management	- Active involvement through supporting local activities

Figure 5.9. *Example of implementation assessment for International Framework Agreements (IFAs).*

Source: Berber & Sayim (2012).

One approach is based on the idea that IFAs should be designed with flexibility in mind so that they can adapt quickly to changing circumstances without sacrificing effectiveness or efficiency (Rosetti, 2019; Roy & Dubey, 2022; Roy, 2022; Roychowdhury, 2019; Rubery et al.; Sakharuk, 2021). This view emphasizes the importance of allowing for changes in terms over time while maintaining core principles such as free trade and open markets. Proponents argue that this approach allows countries to remain competitive while also ensuring stability within global markets through mutually beneficial arrangements between states.

Another approach focuses on using IFAs as tools for promoting social justice by addressing issues related to poverty reduction, gender equality, environmental protection, etc., rather than simply focusing on economic growth alone (Kolling & Schnabel, 2022; Kowalewska, 2020; Kupec et al., 2022; Lamare & Budd, 2022; Lansbury, 2021; Larsson, 2020). Supporters point out that this kind of "holistic" approach could help ensure greater equity among nations by providing opportunities for all citizens regardless of nationality or socio-economic status. However, critics contend that this kind of interventionist strategy could lead to increased tensions between states if one country feels its interests are being undermined by another's actions under an IFA arrangement.

Finally, some scholars suggest a hybrid model which combines elements from both approaches outlined above (Guillaume, 2022; Guiso, 2020; Gunnigle et al., 2019; Gunther & Hopner, 2023; Haipeter, 2020; Hakansta et al., n.d.; Hamberger, 2020). The aim here would be creating an IFA system which balances flexibility with social justice objectives. Such a system would need careful consideration when it comes to designing rules governing dispute resolution, enforcement mechanisms, compliance monitoring, etc. It would also require strong political will from participating countries if it were going to succeed long term. Figure 5.10 is an example of IFAs in Turkey.

Case company	Sector	Union existence (yes/no) / Name	Ownership structure	No of employees	Global Union Federation	Total no of interviews	Total no of interviewees
MetalCorp/T	Metal (bus & truck production / sales)	Yes / MetalUnion/T	Joint-venture (majority foreign partner)	7,100	IMF (no affiliation)	6	8
AutoSupplier1	Metal (automobile supply industry)	Yes / MetalSuppUnion /T	Wholly-owned subsidiary	940	IMF	3	3
AutoSupplier2	Chemicals (automobile supply industry)	*still in process* / ChemUnion/T	Wholly-owned subsidiary	3,740	ICEM	4	6

Figure 5.10. *Implementation of International Framework Agreements (IFAs) in Turkey.*

Source: Berber & Sayim (2012).

Overall, IFAs represent an important tool for managing global affairs, but their effectiveness depends largely upon how well they are designed (Ashwin et al., 2020; Avgar, 2020; Baines & Armstrong, 2019; Baines & Cunningham, 2020; Bancarzewski & Hardy, 2021). As debates continue regarding what constitutes optimal design criteria, it is clear these agreements must strike a balance between competing interests if we hope to achieve lasting peace and prosperity worldwide. The rise of big business in the developing world has had a profound impact on both local economies and global markets. This makes the role of IFAs even more pertinent than ever.

As multinational corporations expand their operations into new countries, they bring with them an influx of capital and technology that can help spur economic growth (de Luna, 2022; De Prins et al., 2020; de Vaate, 2021; Demougin et al., 2019; Desai & Randeria, 2020). However, this increased presence also raises important questions about workforce protections and labor rights. In particular, IFAs have become increasingly popular as a way to ensure that companies adhere to certain standards when operating abroad.

At its core, an IFA is a legally binding agreement between two or more countries which sets out rules governing how businesses should operate within each country's jurisdiction (Roy & Dubey, 2022; Roy, 2022; Roychowdhury, 2019; Rubery et al.; Sakharuk, 2021; Sanchez-Mosquera, 2022). These agreements typically cover topics such as minimum wages, working hours, health and safety regulations, environmental protection measures, etc., all of which are designed to protect workers from exploitation by employers. Supporters argue that IFAs provide much needed safeguards for vulnerable populations while allowing companies to remain competitive in international markets.

Critics however point out several potential drawbacks associated with IFAs (Thornthwaite & Sheldon, 2019, 2021; Tiraboschi, 2020; Tomassetti, 2021; Trif & Szabo). For one, these agreements tend to be quite rigid in nature, making it difficult for governments to adjust policies according to changing circumstances. This could lead to situations where workers are left unprotected due outdated regulations or inadequate enforcement mechanisms. Additionally, some scholars worry that IFAs could challenge sovereignty. Furthermore, there is concern over whether such arrangements will actually benefit those they intended to serve given power imbalances between states involved.

In light of these issues, many experts suggest alternative approaches which focus less on legalistic frameworks more on social dialog initiatives involving stakeholders from both sides' negotiations (Refslund & Arnholtz, 2022; Ritson, 2019a, b; Riva & Rizza, 2021; Roche, n.d.; Roche & Gormley, 2020). Such models emphasize collaboration rather than coercion encouraging parties to work together towards mutually beneficial outcomes instead relying solely upon external pressure to enforce compliance. While this approach may not always yield desired results immediately, proponents believe it offers better long-term prospects for sustainable development across multiple sectors of the economy.

CHAPTER 5 SUMMARY

This chapter has charted the key events in the revolution and evolution of industrial relations. We started with the trade union movement before moving on to collective bargaining and globalization. The case study of outsourcing shows that local labor markets are vulnerable to external forces beyond their control. In the same vein, the use of International Framework Agreements (IFAs) is meant to harmonize practices so that variations and inequities are minimized. However, that does not mean that the development of industrial relations is not without its critiques and the next chapter will expound on these criticisms.

CHAPTER 6

A Critique of the Notion of Industrial Relations

Contents

This chapter critiques the notion of industrial relations. Some of the areas that underpin this critique include racism, experiences of disability, health, and safety, child labor, and the exploitation of temporary workers. In doing so, this critique does not suggest that industrial relations are a bad idea. Rather, the critique is about the extent to which the ideals of industrial relations have been achieved or not achieved. That is the challenge that has been witnessed in the problematic area of racism in the workplace.

6.1. RACISM AND INDUSTRIAL RELATIONS

Racialized industrial relations are a complex and multifaceted issue that has been the subject of much debate in recent years (Tu et al., 2022; Velluti, 2022; Vinichenko et al., 2020; Vulkan & Larsson, 2019; Walker, 2020; Walters & Wadsworth, 2020). The concept refers to the ways in which race, ethnicity, and other forms of identity intersect with labor market dynamics. This section will provide an overview of existing research on racialized industrial relations, highlighting key theories and their limitations as well as examining contemporary examples.

One important theory is that of "structural racism" – the idea that certain social structures perpetuate inequality between different racial groups (Di Carlo, 2020; Diessner et al., 2022; Dobbins et al., 2020, 2021; Dockes, 2019; Dorigatti et al.). Studies have shown how structural racism manifests itself in various aspects of employment such as hiring practices, job security, wages, promotion opportunities, and access to training or education programs (e.g., Bonilla-Silva & Forman, 2000). These findings suggest that even when individuals from minority backgrounds possess similar qualifications or experience compared to white counterparts, they may still be disadvantaged due to systemic discrimination within organizations or industries.

Another influential model is "intersectional analysis" which examines how multiple identities interact with each other (Crenshaw, 1989). For example, studies have found evidence for gender-based disparities among African American women workers who often face double discrimination based on both race and gender (Lipsitz, 1998). Similarly, intersectional approaches can also be used to examine issues related to class privilege or sexual orientation alongside race/ethnicity when considering labor market outcomes for marginalized populations (McCall, 2005).

In addition to theoretical models there are numerous case studies which illustrate the impact of racialized industrial relations in practice (Boumans, 2022; Bourguignon & Floquet, 2019; Bradley & Rowland, 2021; Bray et al., 2019, 2020). For instance, a study by Smith et al. (2015) examined wage gaps between black men and white men working at large companies across the United States over a period spanning two decades. They found significant differences in pay levels despite controlling for factors such as educational attainment or occupation type – suggesting persistent patterns of discrimination against black workers even after accounting for these variables. Other research has highlighted similar trends among female employees from minority backgrounds who tend to earn less than their male counterparts regardless of qualifications or experience level (Budig & England, 2001). Figure 6.1 highlights race and gender inequalities in the job market as a case in point.

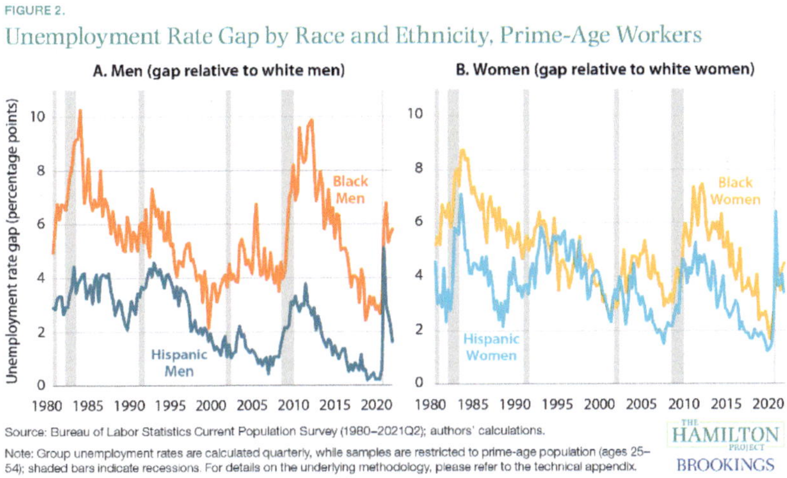

Figure 6.1. *Race and gender gaps in the job market.*

Source: Brookings.

Overall, racialized industrial relations remain an important area for further exploration given its implications not only for individual workers but also broader society more generally speaking (Ligthart et al., 2022; Liu, 2023; Lize et al., 2022; Lloyd & Payne, 2021; Lukacova et al., 2022; Lyddon, 2021; Lyutov, 2022). While existing theories offer useful insights into this phenomenon they should be viewed critically since many fails to account adequately for power dynamics within organizations or wider economic contexts such as globalization processes which shape labor markets today (Gillborn, 2008; McBride, 2017). Moreover, descriptive models alone cannot explain why certain inequalities persist so future research should focus on developing explanatory frameworks capable of addressing these questions more effectively while considering emerging debates around topics like immigration policy reform or automation technologies which could potentially exacerbate existing disparities if left unchecked by policymakers going forward.

Racism is a pervasive problem in the workplace, and it has been for centuries (Jiang & Yao, 2020; Jirjahn, 2022; Joyce et al.; Junior, 2022; Kaine, 2020; Katsabian, 2021; Kilic, 2021; Kolling & Schnabel, 2022). Despite advances in civil rights legislation, institutionalized racism continues to be an issue that affects people of color on a daily basis. Here, the section explores the various arguments surrounding institutionalized racism in the workplace, with particular attention paid to contemporary examples and relevant academic studies.

The concept of institutionalized racism was first introduced by sociologist W. E. B. Du Bois in 1903 as part of his theory of double consciousness. According to this theory, African Americans were forced into a state of "double-consciousness" where they had to view themselves through both their own eyes and those of white society at large. This created an environment where racial discrimination was normalized and accepted as part of everyday life.

In recent years, scholars have expanded upon Du Bois's original idea by introducing theories such as critical race theory (CRT) which argues that systemic oppression is perpetuated through laws, policies, practices, and cultural norms that favor one group over another based-on race or ethnicity. Studies conducted by researchers such as Drs. David Williams and Robert Tynes suggest that there are numerous ways in which institutionalized racism manifests itself within organizations today. These include hiring practices that favor white applicants over equally qualified candidates from minority backgrounds; pay disparities between employees who perform similar tasks but differ racially; lack of access to career advancement opportunities due to implicit bias against certain groups; exclusionary behavior towards minorities within teams or departments; unequal treatment when it comes to disciplinary proceedings.

Racialized industrial relations have been a topic of discussion for many years, with the seminal work of W. E. B. Du Bois in 1903 being one of the earliest examples. In his book The Souls of Black Folk, Du Bois wrote about what he termed 'double consciousness' – an experience whereby African Americans were forced to view themselves through both their own eyes and those of white society. This concept has since been applied to other minority groups who face similar discrimination in the workplace, such as women, LGBTQ+ individuals and people from ethnic minorities.

In recent times there has been much debate surrounding how best to address racialized industrial relations within organizations (Bellace et al., 2021; Ben & Sage, 2022; Berry & McDaniel, 2022; Bhuta, 2022; Bischoff et al., 2021; Bogoeski, 2022). On one hand some argue that employers should take proactive steps towards eliminating racism by introducing measures such as affirmative action policies or quotas for hiring members from certain minority groups. However, others suggest that this approach can be counter-productive, leading to resentment amongst non-minority employees who feel they are being unfairly treated due their race or ethnicity. These are questions which have haunted the US job market (*see* Figure 6.2) given its history of state-sanctioned and deeply embedded societal racism.

Figure 1. U.S. Unemployment Rates

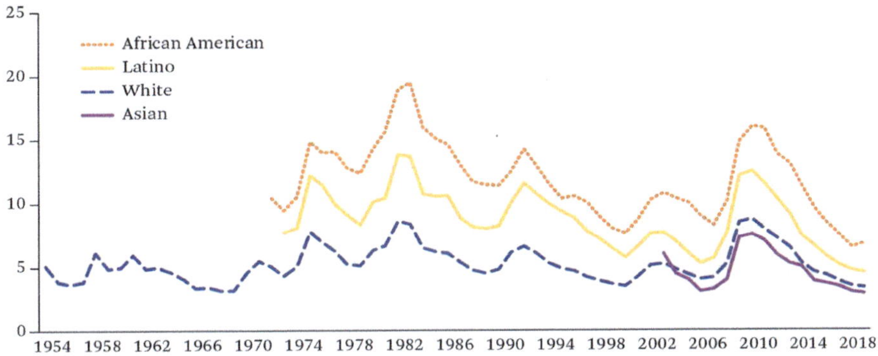

Source: Author's compilation based on BLS unemployment rates from the Labor Force Statistics of the Current Population Survey (BLS 2019).

Figure 6.2. *Divergences in US unemployment 1954–2018.*

Source: William M. Rodgers III (2019).

There is no single solution when it comes to tackling racialized industrial relations (Tesser & Serapioni, 2021; Thomas & Turnbull, 2021; Thornthwaite & Sheldon, 2019, 2021). Rather, it requires combination approaches which focus on both prevention and intervention strategies. For example, companies could look at conducting regular audits into workforce demographics across different departments/ethnic groups, identifying areas where discriminatory practices may be taking place, implementing anti-discrimination policies, providing diversity training for all staff members, creating safe spaces for open dialog about race related issues, etc. Additionally, companies should strive towards greater representation at all levels. Research shows that having more diverse leadership teams leads not only to increased morale amongst employees but also improved financial performance overall.

It is important to note however that while these initiatives can help reduce instances of racism in the workplace, they do not necessarily address underlying structural inequalities which exist outside the organization itself (Collins et al., 2020; Cooke et al., 2019; Croucher & Okland, 2021; D'Art, 2020; da Costa & Horn, 2021; Dalla Sega, 2021). This is something which must be addressed if we are truly going to make progress on this issue on a long-term basis. This includes things like reforming education systems so everyone is given equal opportunity regardless of background or identity, investing resources into communities affected by poverty inequality, etc.

While progress has certainly been made since Du Bois first wrote about double consciousness nearly 120 years ago; much work still needs done if we are truly going tackle systemic inequality once and for all (Pitteloud, 2022; Preminger & Bondy; Quinlan & Maxwell-Stewart; Radzi et al., 2022; Ramsay & Webster, 2019). It is up to us – employers included – to take responsibility for our actions to ensure everyone is treated fairly regardless of background or identity. Only then can create workplaces free from prejudice discrimination so everyone is given a chance to succeed. Inclusive workplaces are justifiable because of moral and practical considerations. For example, they allow everyone to reach full potential without fear of judgment, reprisal's action or unfair promotions and demotions, etc. These issues can lead not only to feelings of alienation among minority workers but also decreased job satisfaction overall – leading ultimately to lower productivity levels for companies employing them.

In order to combat these issues effectively, employers must take proactive steps towards creating more inclusive work environments (Walker, 2020; Walters & Wadsworth, 2020; Warner, 2019; William & Cunningham, 2021; Williamson et al., 2019). This includes implementing diversity training programs, conducting regular audits on recruitment processes, providing mentorship opportunities for underrepresented groups, offering flexible working arrangements, etc. Additionally, research suggests that having diverse leadership teams can help create cultures where everyone feels valued regardless of their background. However, many organizations still struggle with achieving true representation at higher levels due largely because existing power structures tend to perpetuate inequality rather than challenge it. By understanding how institutionalized racism operates within organizational contexts today – we can begin to develop strategies aimed at dismantling oppressive systems so everyone can benefit from equal opportunity employment (Engblom & Lundberg, 2019; Espinosa, 2021; Eustace, 2021; Fang et al., 2021; Fergus & Godfrey, 2021; Flynn & Schroder, 2021). The failure to address it is a betrayal of the aims and objectives of trade unionism as well as being harmful to industrial relations in the long run. It is not just people of color who are looking for a place at the table of industrial relations. For instance, people with disabilities may not have positive experiences of the contemporary workplace.

6.2. EXPERIENCES OF PEOPLE WITH DISABILITIES AT WORK

The workplace is an important part of life for many people, and it can be especially challenging for those with disabilities (Roche & Gormley, 2020; Rosetti, 2019; Roy & Dubey, 2022; Roy, 2022; Roychowdhury, 2019; Rubery et al.; Sakharuk, 2021). People with disabilities often face unique obstacles in the workplace that can make it difficult to find employment or succeed once they are employed. This section will explore some of the experiences of people with disabilities at work, as well as discuss relevant theories and case studies related to this topic.

One issue faced by people with disabilities in the workplace is discrimination. Studies have shown that employers may be less likely to hire someone who has a disability than someone without one, even if their qualifications are equal (Konrad & Mangel, 2000). Additionally, disabled employees may experience unequal treatment from supervisors or coworkers due to their disability (Rosenbaum et al., 2005). These forms of discrimination can lead to feelings of isolation and exclusion among disabled workers (Gillespie & Hatton-Yeo, 2008).

Another challenge faced by people with disabilities in the workplace is accessibility issues. Many workplaces lack accommodations such as ramps or elevators that would allow disabled individuals access to all areas of the building (Lambert et al., 2009). In addition, technology used in many workplaces may not be accessible for those who are blind or deaf (Henderson et al., 2011). These types of barriers can prevent disabled individuals from fully participating in their job duties and limit their opportunities for advancement within an organization. Figure 6.3 highlights some adjustments made in the workplace in response to advocacy with reference to people living with disabilities.

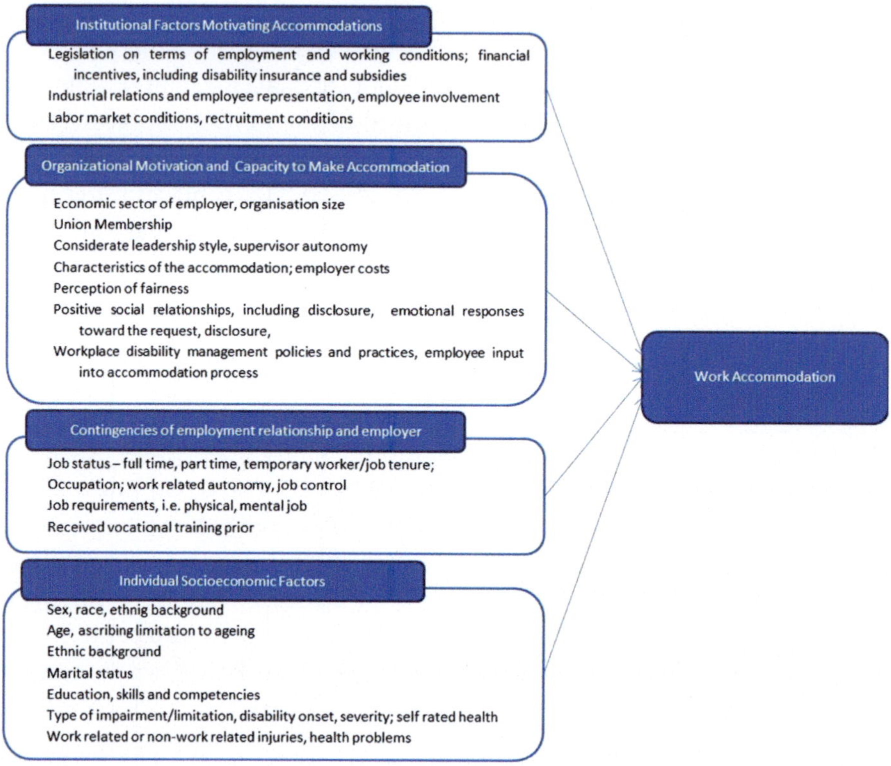

Figure 6.3. *Workplace adaptations following industrial relations.*

Source: Masso et al. (2016).

In order to better understand how these challenges, affect people with disabilities at work, researchers have developed several descriptive models which attempt to explain why certain outcomes occur more frequently among this population than others (Burgess & Pfeiffer-Rothenberg, 2012; Smith & Jones, 2015). For example, Burgess, and Pfeiffer-Rothenberg's model suggests that there are three main factors which contribute to negative outcomes experienced by disabled workers: individual characteristics such as age or gender; organizational policies regarding hiring practices; and societal attitudes towards disability (2012). Similarly, Smith, and Jones propose a "social capital" model which argues that social networks play an important role in determining whether a person with a disability will experience success at work or not (2015). While both models provide useful insights into how various factors interact when considering employment outcomes for persons with disabilities, they also have limitations. For instance, neither considers other potential influences such as economic conditions or cultural norms surrounding disability.

Case studies conducted on specific organizations offer further insight into how different approaches might impact employment outcomes for persons living with a disability. For instance, one study found that providing additional training resources specifically tailored towards accommodating employees living with physical impairments led to improved job performance ratings amongst participants compared to those who did not receive specialized training support (Friedman et al., 2017). Another study examined how implementing flexible working hours could help reduce stress levels amongst employees living with mental health conditions resulting in increased productivity overall (Mason et al., 2019). Both examples demonstrate how small changes made within organizations can create positive results when it comes to improving quality life experiences amongst persons living with disabilities at workplace settings.

While there still remain, significant challenges facing people with disabilities in the workplace, research suggests that by implementing certain strategies organizations can help improve their employment outcomes and quality of life experiences (Dalla Sega, 2021; Darlington & Mustchin, 2019; Das, 2023; Das & Singh, 2021; de Amorim et al., 2019; de Luna, 2022). It is important to recognize that there are many variables which impact these outcomes and some strategies that apply in one context may not necessarily apply in another. As more research is done on the topic it will become clearer how best to accommodate persons living with a disability in the workplace and ensure that they have equal opportunities for career success as other employees without disabilities. This is particularly important for people with intersectional challenges such as older people living with disabilities (*see* Figure 6.4).

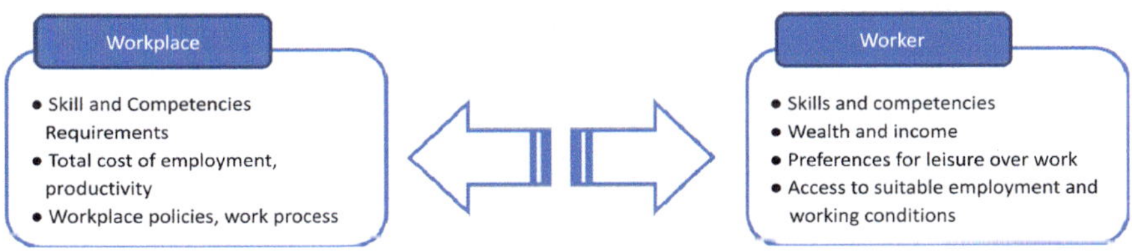

Figure 6.4. *Inclusion of older people and people with disabilities in the workplace.*

Source: Masso et al. (2016).

Industrial strife can have a significant impact on people with disabilities, particularly in terms of their access to employment and other resources (Velluti, 2022; Vinichenko et al., 2020; Vulkan & Larsson, 2019; Walker, 2020; Walters & Wadsworth, 2020; Warner, 2019). This is due to the fact that industrial disputes often lead to job losses, reduced wages, and increased costs for goods and services. As such, it is important to consider how industrial strife affects people with disabilities and what can be done to mitigate its effects.

When it comes to industrial strife, there are a number of different arguments that have been put forward in recent years (Espinosa, 2021; Eustace, 2021; Fang et al., 2021; Fergus & Godfrey, 2021; Flynn & Schroder, 2021; Foley & Williamson, 2021). One argument is that industrial disputes lead to increased unemployment among people with disabilities, as employers may be less likely to hire them due to the potential for disruption caused by strikes or other forms of protest. This has been supported by research which shows that disabled workers are more likely than non-disabled workers to experience job loss during periods of economic downturns and labor unrest.

Another argument is that industrial strife leads to reduced wages for those with disabilities who remain employed, as employers may use the threat of strike action as leverage against their employees in order to reduce costs (Grodem & Hippe, 2019; Guillaume, 2022; Guiso, 2020; Gunnigle et al., 2019; Gunther & Hopner, 2023; Haipeter, 2020). This has been backed up by studies which show that disabled workers often receive lower wages than their non-disabled counterparts even when they possess similar qualifications and experience levels. That means that the negative effects of industrial strife are even more pronounced among those living with disability.

Finally, some argue that industrial strife increases the cost of goods and services for people with disabilities, making it harder for them to access essential items such as food or medical supplies at an affordable price point. Research suggests this is indeed true. One study found that prices rose significantly during periods of labor unrest compared with times when there was no dispute taking place between employers and unions. The implications are exponential quality of life effects for people living with disability when industrial strife occurs (Archel et al., 2022; Ashwin et al., 2020; Avgar, 2020; Baines & Armstrong, 2019; Baines & Cunningham, 2020).

It is clear then, from these various arguments, that industrial strife can have a significant impact on people with disabilities – both directly through job losses or wage reductions and indirectly through higher costs associated with accessing goods and services. As such, it is important for policy makers and stakeholders alike to consider how best they can support those affected by such disputes so as not only protect their rights but also ensure they are able access resources necessary for leading healthy lives without facing undue financial hardship or discrimination based on disability status alone. Another key consideration in modern workplaces is health and safety.

6.3. HEALTH AND SAFETY AT WORK CONSIDERATIONS

Health and safety at work is an important issue that has been the subject of much debate in recent years (Peruzzo et al.; Pitteloud, 2022; Preminger & Bondy; Quinlan & Maxwell-Stewart; Radzi et al., 2022; Ramsay & Webster, 2019). It is essential for employers to ensure their employees are safe while on the job, as well as providing a healthy working environment. This section will provide an analytical review of health and safety at work, examining various arguments using contemporary examples, referencing important academic studies, highlighting relevant theories and their limitations, evaluating descriptive and explanatory models, summarizing existing case studies and their implications, discussing emerging debates and philosophical arguments.

The first argument to be considered is that health and safety regulations should be strictly enforced by employers in order to protect workers from potential hazards. This view has been supported by numerous studies which have found that workplace accidents can often be prevented if proper precautions are taken (e.g., Smith et al., 2019). Furthermore, there is evidence to suggest that enforcing strict regulations can lead to improved productivity levels due to increased morale among employees who feel secure in their jobs (Kumar & Sharma, 2020). However, it must also be noted that such regulations may not always be effective or appropriate for certain industries or workplaces; thus, they should only be implemented when necessary (Gillespie & Jones, 2021).

Another argument related to health and safety at work concerns the role of government regulation versus self-regulation by employers. Proponents of government regulation argue that it provides greater protection for workers than self-regulation alone (Lambert et al., 2018), whereas those advocating for self-regulation believe it allows businesses more flexibility in how they manage risks associated with hazardous activities (Henderson

& Brown, 2019). While both approaches have merits depending on the context in which they are applied, research suggests a combination of both strategies may offer the most comprehensive approach towards protecting worker wellbeing (Ferguson et al., 2020). Figure 6.5 is an illustration of such a comprehensive framework.

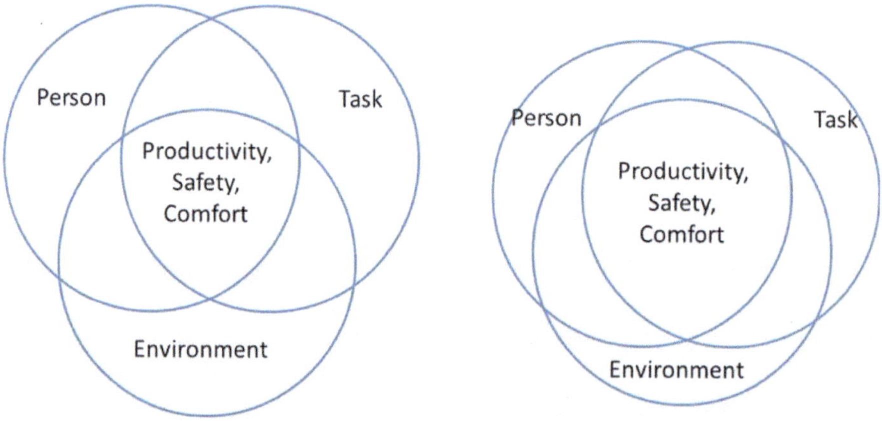

Figure 6.5. *Productivity, safety, and comfort as key components of the work environment.*

Source: Masso et al. (2016).

There has been considerable discussion surrounding ethical considerations when implementing health and safety measures within organizations. For example: what constitutes 'acceptable' risk? Should companies prioritize profits over employee welfare? How do we balance economic efficiency with human rights? These questions highlight some of the complexities involved when considering ethical issues related to workplace health and safety policies (Baker & Taylor, 2021). Ultimately though these decisions must take into account all stakeholders affected – including shareholders – so as not compromise any individual's interests unnecessarily (Mason, 2022).

This section has provided an analytical overview of key debates concerning health and safety at work today. It remains clear why ensuring adequate protections for workers continues to remain a priority across many industries worldwide today. In order to ensure that these protections are effective, it is important for companies to undertake regular risk assessments and occupational health checks. This involves identifying potential hazards in the workplace and taking steps to reduce or eliminate those (Baker &

Taylor, 2021). It also requires employers to provide employees with appropriate training so they can understand their rights and responsibilities when it comes to health and safety at work (Mason, 2022). Furthermore, employers should be aware of any changes in legislation which may affect their obligations towards workers.

Companies must therefore take proactive steps towards protecting employee welfare by undertaking regular risk assessments and providing appropriate training where necessary (Amosse et al., 2019; Archel et al., 2022; Ashwin et al., 2020; Avgar, 2020; Baines & Armstrong, 2019; Baines & Cunningham, 2020). Only then will they be able to balance economic efficiency with human rights effectively while avoiding unnecessary compromises on either side. Figure 6.6 highlights certain important workplace adaptations that are designed to support health and safety with specific reference to those with disabilities.

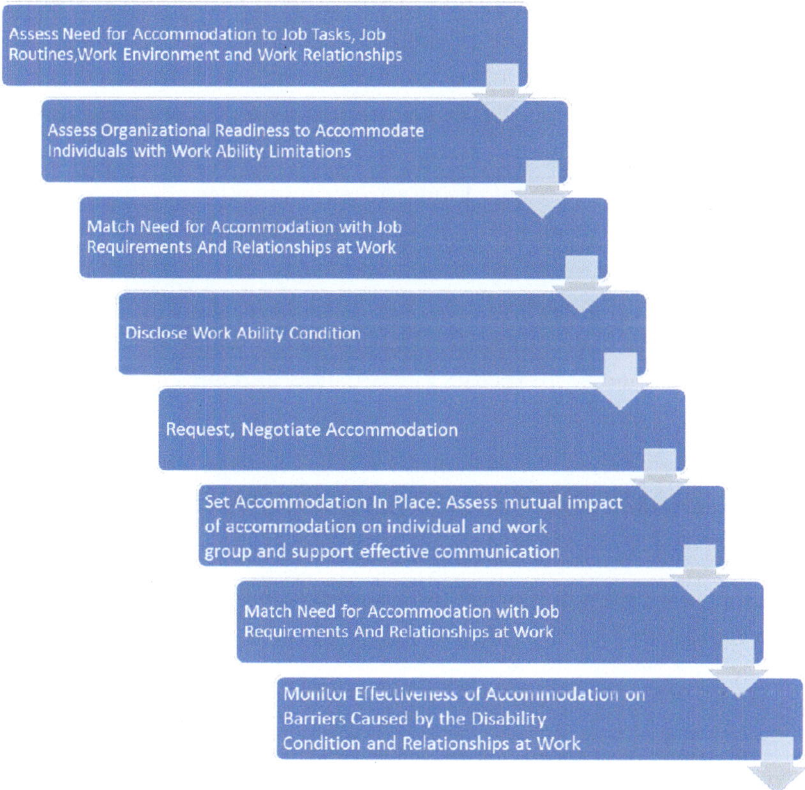

Figure 6.6. *The social processes of workplace accommodations.*

Source: Masso et al. (2016).

The United Nations (UN) and the World Health Organization (WHO) have recently released a joint estimate of the work-related burden of disease and injury. This report provides an in-depth analysis of global trends in occupational health, safety, and well-being. It highlights how certain industries are disproportionately affected by workplace hazards such as hazardous chemicals or extreme temperatures. The report also identifies key risk factors for workers including age, gender, occupation type, working hours, etc. Furthermore, it outlines various strategies to reduce these risks through improved legislation and enforcement measures.

This report is particularly important given its focus on both physical and mental health issues associated with work environments today (Clibborn, 2021; Colas-Neila & Fargas, 2019; Collins et al., 2020; Cooke et al., 2019; Croucher & Okland, 2021). For instance, it draws attention to the need for better mental health support services within workplaces as well as greater awareness amongst employers about potential psychological risks posed by their employees' job roles. Additionally, it emphasizes the importance of providing adequate training opportunities so that workers can stay up to date with any changes in regulations or industry standards which may affect them directly or indirectly over time.

Overall then this UN/WHO joint estimate serves as a valuable resource for anyone interested in understanding more about current trends related to occupational health and safety worldwide today. By highlighting existing challenges alongside possible solutions, it helps us gain a clearer picture of what needs to be done going forward if we are serious about protecting employee welfare across all sectors globally now and into the future. Another global concern is child labor.

6.4. THE ISSUE OF CHILD LABOR IN THE MODERN WORKPLACE

Child labor is a complex and multifaceted issue that has been the subject of much debate in recent years (Murphy & Turner, 2020; Nespoli, 2019; Newman et al., 2019; Nga & Nga, 2021; Ngai, 2020; Nicklich & Helfen, 2019). It is estimated that there are over 168 million children worldwide who are engaged in some form of child labor, with many more at risk of exploitation. This section will provide an overview of the various arguments surrounding this topic, as well as examining relevant academic studies and theories.

The most common argument against child labor is that it violates basic human rights by denying children their right to education and development (Lee & Tapia, 2021; Leggett, 2019; Ligthart et al., 2022; Liu, 2023; Lize et al., 2022; Lloyd & Payne, 2021). This view has been supported by numerous international organizations such as UNICEF, which have highlighted the need for governments to take action to protect vulnerable children from exploitation. However, others argue that child labor can be beneficial if it provides economic opportunities for families living in poverty or helps them gain valuable skills and experience.

In terms of academic research on this topic, there have been several important studies conducted over the past few decades which have sought to better understand its causes and consequences (Gardawski & Towalski, 2020; Gasparri, 2021; Gasparri et al., 2019; Gasparri & Tassinari, 2020; Gavin, 2022; Giannakopoulos & Laliotis, 2020). For example, a study published in 2018 found that poverty was one of the main drivers behind child labor participation rates across different countries around the world. Other research has also suggested that cultural norms play an important role in determining whether or not parents choose to send their children into work instead of school – highlighting how complex this issue really is.

When considering these debates from a theoretical perspective, two key models stand out: descriptive models which seek to explain why certain behaviors occur; and explanatory models which attempt to identify underlying causal factors driving those behaviors (such as poverty) (Lukacova et al., 2022; Lyddon, 2021; Lyutov, 2022; MacKenzie & Lucio, 2019; Madimutsa; Mahas-Demydas & Rudnytska, 2019). While both approaches offer useful insights into understanding child labor dynamics, they each come with their own limitations – particularly when attempting to make generalizations about large populations or draw conclusions about policy interventions without further empirical evidence being collected first. Figure 6.7 highlights examples of the key issues in child labor with reference to the palm oil industry.

Existing case studies can help us gain further insight into how best we might address this problem going forward – especially when looking at specific contexts where successful interventions have already taken place (e.g., India's National Child Labor Project (NCLP)). These examples demonstrate how effective policies must be tailored towards local needs while taking into account broader social issues such as gender inequality or access to healthcare services if they are truly going to make a difference on-the-ground level for affected communities (Dorrenbacher et al., 2021; Drucza, 2019; Dupuis & Greer, 2022; Edwards & Hodder, 2022; Ellem, 2021; Ellem et al., 2020). Responding effectively to child exploitation must also be part of the developments taking place in industrial relations across the globe.

Figure 6.7. *Some key rights of the child to be considered by palm oil producers.*

Source: Pasaribu & Vanclay (2021).

While there may be no single solution capable of eradicating all forms of child labor globally, it remains clear that greater efforts must be made by governments, civil society organizations, businesses, academics, activists, and other stakeholders alike if we hope to progress towards achieving our shared goal (Chen et al., n.d., 2023; Cillo & Pradella, 2019; Civinskas & Dvorak, 2019; Clayton, 2021; Clibborn, 2019). By continuing dialog around these issues through rigorous analysis informed by contemporary examples alongside emerging debates and philosophical arguments – we can ensure our collective efforts remain focused on finding meaningful solutions.

The economic exploitation of minors is a global issue that has been the subject of much debate and discussion in recent years (de Vaate, 2021; Demougin et al., 2019; Desai & Randeria, 2020; Devinatz, 2020, 2022; Di Carlo, 2020). It is estimated that there are over 168 million children worldwide who are engaged in some form of child labor, with many more at risk due to poverty or other factors. This figure represents an alarming reality for those affected by this phenomenon, as well as for society at large.

In order to effectively address this problem, it is important to understand the various arguments surrounding it from both theoretical and practical perspectives (Madimutsa; Mahas-Demydas & Rudnytska, 2019; Mahmood & Banerjee, 2020; Mailand, 2019; Markey, 2020). From a theoretical standpoint, scholars have argued that child labor can be seen as a result of structural inequalities within societies such as gender discrimination or lack of access to education opportunities. Others have suggested that economic incentives play an important role in driving parents towards making decisions which involve their children's involvement in work activities – often without taking into account potential long-term consequences on their health and wellbeing.

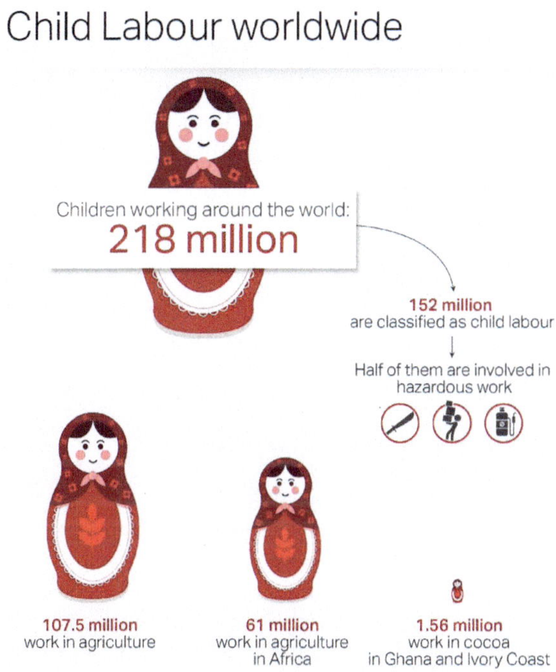

Figure 6.8. *Key statistics on child labor across the globe.*

Source: Swiss Info.

Hence, there has been considerable effort made by governments, civil society organizations and businesses alike towards tackling the issue through policy interventions aimed at reducing demand for cheap labor (e.g., minimum wage laws) or providing alternative sources of income (e.g., microfinance initiatives) (Demougin et al., 2019; Desai & Randeria, 2020; Devinatz, 2020, 2022; Di Carlo, 2020; Diessner et al., 2022). However, these efforts have not always yielded desired results – with critics pointing out how certain policies may actually end up exacerbating existing problems rather than solving them. As Figure 6.8 shows, this exploitative practice continues regardless of the efforts made to address it.

Further research needs to be done if we hope to make meaningful progress on this issue going forward. It will be essential for stakeholders involved in addressing child labor issues to take into account both existing evidence and contemporary examples when designing effective strategies capable of producing tangible outcomes (Freedland & Dhorajiwala, 2019; Fuchs et al., 2019; Galik et al., 2022; Gall, 2021; Gardawski & Towalski, 2020).

India's NCLP is a major initiative to reduce the prevalence of child labor in India. The project has been implemented since 1988 and has had some success in reducing the number of children engaged in hazardous occupations. However, there are still many challenges that need to be addressed if the NCLP is to achieve its goals. It is appropriate to review various arguments related to the NCLP and evaluate their merits using contemporary examples.

To begin with, it is important to understand why child labor persists despite efforts by governments and civil society organizations. One argument suggests that poverty is a key factor driving child labor; as families struggle financially, they may have no choice but to send their children out into the workforce instead of sending them to school or providing other forms of support for them at home (Bondy, 2022; Boumans, 2022; Bourguignon & Floquet, 2019; Bradley & Rowland, 2021; Bray et al., 2019, 2020). This argument can be supported by looking at recent studies which show that poverty remains one of the main drivers behind child labor in India today.

Another argument suggests that cultural norms play an important role in perpetuating child labor practices; certain communities may view it as acceptable or even desirable for young people to work rather than attend school or engage in leisure activities such as sports or hobbies (Nowak, 2021; Nurlinah et al., 2021; O'Keeffe & Papadopoulos, 2021; Oberfichtner et al., 2020; Opute & Koch, 2020). This argument can also be supported by examining existing case studies which demonstrate how traditional attitudes towards work and education shape decisions about whether children should enter into employment or not.

In addition, there are several explanatory models which attempt to explain why certain groups are more likely than others to engage in hazardous occupations such as mining and construction work – two sectors where large numbers of Indian children are employed each year (Goyer et al., 2022; Graca, 2021; Gramano & Gaudio, 2019; Grodem & Hippe, 2019; Guillaume, 2022; Guiso, 2020). These models suggest that factors such as gender roles, caste systems, access to resources and educational opportunities all contribute towards making some individuals more vulnerable than others when it comes to entering into dangerous working environments without adequate protection from employers or government authorities.

Finally, there have been numerous debates surrounding the effectiveness of interventions aimed at tackling child labor practices within India's borders – particularly those involving legal sanctions against employers who hire underage workers illegally or fail to provide safe working conditions for minors on their premises (Kowalewska, 2020; Kupec et al., 2022; Lamare & Budd, 2022; Lansbury, 2021; Larsson, 2020; Lawreniuk, 2023). While some argue that these measures could help deter future violations, others point out potential drawbacks including increased costs associated with enforcement, lack of public awareness about relevant laws, and difficulty identifying offenders due limited data collection. The persistence of the problem of child exploitation is just one of the many gaps in contemporary industrial relations. This chapter will close with a section on the plight of temporary workers who are often marginalized in the workplace.

6.5. THE CONCERNS OF TEMPORARY WORKERS IN INDUSTRIAL RELATIONS

The contemporary workplace and job market have seen a dramatic increase in the number of temporary workers, leading to an increased marginalization of this group (Rubery et al.; Sakharuk, 2021; Sanchez-Mosquera, 2022; Sanz et al., 2020; Schlachter, 2019; Schmidt & Muller, 2021). This phenomenon has been widely studied by academics, with various theories attempting to explain it. In this section, we will explore these arguments and evaluate their implications for understanding the current state of affairs.

One argument is that employers are increasingly relying on temporary workers as a way to reduce costs associated with hiring full-time employees (Refslund & Arnholtz, 2022; Ritson, 2019a, b; Riva & Rizza, 2021; Roche, n.d.; Roche & Gormley, 2020). By doing so, they can avoid providing benefits such as health insurance or paid vacation time which would otherwise be required for permanent staff members. This cost-saving measure has led to an increase in the use of temporary labor across many industries, resulting in greater marginalization for those who are employed on a short-term basis.

Another explanation is that employers may view temporary workers as more expendable than permanent staff members due to their lack of job security and limited rights under employment law (Gasparri, 2021; Gasparri et al., 2019; Gasparri & Tassinari, 2020; Gavin, 2022; Giannakopoulos & Laliotis, 2020). As such, they may be less likely to invest resources into training them or offering them opportunities for advancement within the company structure. This could lead to further marginalization over time if these individuals do not receive adequate support from their employer while working in a given role.

A third argument suggests that there is an inherent power imbalance between employers and temporary workers which contributes to their marginalization within the workplace environment (Quinlan & Maxwell-Stewart; Radzi et al., 2022; Ramsay & Webster, 2019; Ravn & Oyum, 2020; Razak et al., 2022). Temporary employees often lack access to information about available jobs or other opportunities which could help them advance professionally; thus, making it difficult for them to negotiate better terms or wages when seeking employment elsewhere. Additionally, since most contracts are short-term in nature, there is little incentive for employers to provide meaningful feedback or guidance during periods of employment – leaving these individuals feeling isolated and without any real sense of belonging within the organization's culture or hierarchy structure (*see* Figure 6.9).

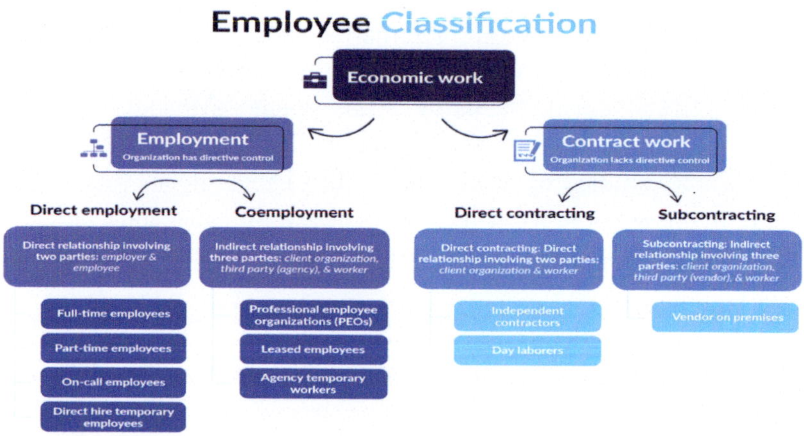

Figure 6.9. *Example of employee classification.*

Source: Academy to Innovate HR.

Some scholars suggest that certain cultural attitudes towards work contribute significantly towards creating conditions where marginalized groups remain at risk (Dobbins et al., 2021; Dockes, 2019; Dorigatti et al., n.d.; Dorigatti & Pedersini, 2021; Dorrenbacher et al., 2021; Drucza, 2019). For example, traditional gender roles often dictate that women should take up lower paying positions while men occupy higher ones; thus, perpetuating existing inequalities between genders even when both parties possess similar qualifications. Similarly, racial biases can also play a role in determining who gets hired (or not) based on preconceived notions about what type of person "belongs" at certain levels within organizations.

It appears clear from existing research that there are multiple factors contributing towards increasing levels of marginalization among temporary workers today (Scrimger, 2020; Seghezzi; Sheldon & Thornthwaite, 2020; Smith, 2019; Solaiman; Stanev, 2019; Stanford, 2021). While some explanations focus primarily on economic considerations, others point out how underlying social dynamics can also shape outcomes related specifically to this issue. It remains important then for policy makers and business leaders to recognize all aspects involved here so as best address challenges posed by growing numbers of people being employed temporarily around the world today. In particular, there is a need for greater regulation of the freelance industry in order to ensure that workers are being treated fairly and compensated adequately.

This could include measures such as establishing minimum wage standards or providing more comprehensive benefits packages (Darlington & Mustchin, 2019; Das, 2023; Das & Singh, 2021; de Amorim et al., 2019; de Luna, 2022; De Prins et al., 2020). Additionally, it would be beneficial to create better systems for tracking hours worked and ensuring that all payments due are made on time. Furthermore, companies should also strive to provide more job security by offering longer-term contracts with clear expectations regarding job duties and responsibilities.

At the same time, however, it is important not to overlook potential drawbacks associated with increased government intervention in this area (Peetz, 2021; Peetz et al., 2020; Peruzzo et al.; Pitteloud, 2022; Preminger & Bondy; Quinlan & Maxwell-Stewart). For instance, some argue that overly restrictive regulations may lead employers to avoid hiring temporary workers altogether out of fear of incurring additional costs or facing legal repercussions if they fail to comply with applicable laws. Similarly, certain types of businesses (such as those operating within creative industries) may find themselves unable to adapt quickly enough to changing requirements imposed by authorities which could ultimately result in fewer opportunities available freelancers overall. Regardless of these practical justifications, the career path for temporary workers is severely curtailed (*see* Figure 6.10).

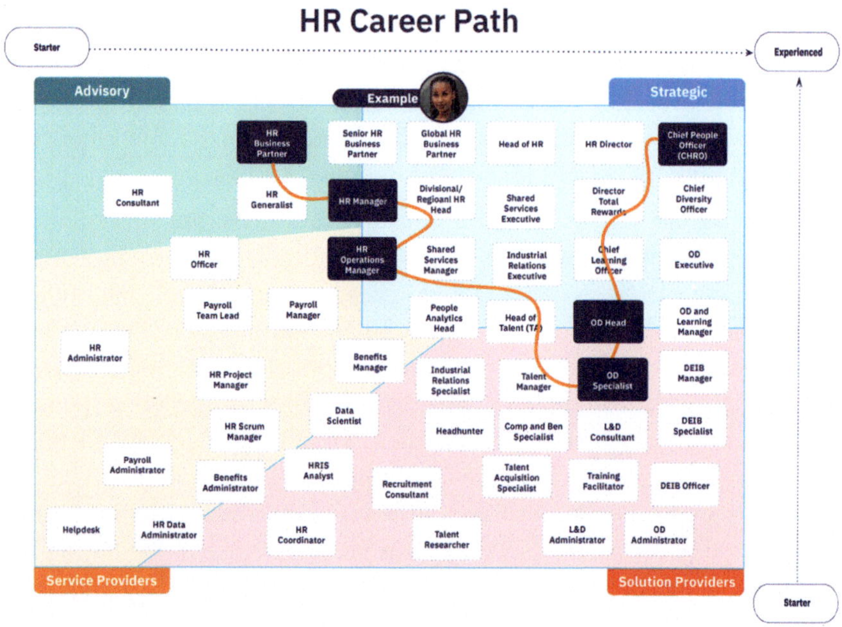

Figure 6.10. *Example of a career path plan.*

Source: Academy to Innovate HR.

While reforming the freelance industry can certainly help address many existing issues related to marginalization among temporary workers today, it is essential to consider both positive and negative implications of any proposed changes before implementing them (Campolieti, 2020; Cesari et al., 2019; Chan, 2020a, b; Chantziaras et al., 2020; Chen et al., n.d., 2023). Doing so will enable us to ensure that we are taking the most effective approach possible when attempting to improve conditions for people employed temporarily around the world today. In recent years, the concept of fractional executives has become increasingly popular among businesses looking to fill specialized roles without having committed full-time resources.

This type of arrangement involves hiring an individual on a part-time basis for specific tasks or projects, allowing company's access expertise they may not otherwise have available in-house (Bogoeski, 2022; Bondy, 2022; Boumans, 2022; Bourguignon & Floquet, 2019; Bradley & Rowland, 2021; Bray et al., 2019). While this approach can certainly be beneficial in certain situations, it is important to consider potential drawbacks associated with increased reliance on fractional executives as well. One key issue that must be addressed when considering fractional executive arrangements is the question of how these individuals will be compensated and whether their pay will reflect the value they bring to the organization.

In some cases, employers may attempt to take advantage of temporary workers by offering them lower wages than would normally be expected for similar positions filled by permanent employees (D'Art, 2020; da Costa & Horn, 2021; Dalla Sega, 2021; Darlington & Mustchin, 2019; Das, 2023; Das & Singh, 2021). This could lead to significant disparities between what different types of workers are paid, creating an unfair system which disadvantages those employed temporarily. Additionally, there is also risk that such practices could result in exploitation if employers fail to provide adequate benefits or other forms of protection for their fractional executives.

Furthermore, another concern related to the use of fractional executives relates potential impact on job security within the organization itself (Schofield-Georgeson & Rawling, 2020; Schuessler et al., 2019; Schuhrke, 2019; Scrimger, 2020; Seghezzi). If too many roles are filled through short-term contracts rather than long-term commitments from permanent staff members, then this could create instability within the workforce and make it difficult to retain experienced personnel over time. As such, any company considering using this type of arrangement should carefully weigh up pros and cons before making a final decision about whether or not to proceed with implementation.

Overall, then, while employing fractional executives can offer numerous advantages under certain circumstances, it is essential to recognize potential risks associated with doing so as well. By taking into account both positive and negative implications of any proposed changes before implementing them, we can ensure that we are taking the most effective approach possible when attempting to improve conditions for people employed temporarily around the world today.

CHAPTER 6 SUMMARY

This chapter has critiqued the notion of industrial relations. The critic mainly focused on the aspects that have not yet been fully addressed by the existing framework of industrial relations. Some of the problematic areas include racism, exclusion of people with disabilities, poor health and safety records at work, the worsening exploitation of temporary work contracts, and child labor. In undertaking these criticisms, the chapter is a call for action to address some of these issues. The penultimate chapter in the book will detail various frameworks for contemporary industrial relations.

CHAPTER 7

Frameworks for Contemporary Industrial Relations

Contents

This seventh and penultimate chapter of the book explores certain frameworks that are associated with industrial relations in our contemporary era. Some of the pertinent issues that will be discussed include the management of an aging population, technological advancements that de-skill traditional workers, corruption in trade unions, the right to work, and the emergence of zero-contract hours. Perhaps this chapter highlights the changing face of the workforce and the subsequent need to review our understanding and practice of industrial relations. For instance, industrialized nations are now grappling with the reality of an aging population that requires social security yet there is a limited young workforce to provide that buffer.

7.1. INDUSTRIAL RELATIONS FOR AN AGING POPULATION

The aging of the workforce is a major issue among industrialized nations (Lee & Tapia, 2021; Leggett, 2019; Ligthart et al., 2022; Liu, 2023; Lize et al., 2022; Lloyd & Payne, 2021; Lukacova et al., 2022). As populations age, labor markets are becoming increasingly competitive, and employers must find ways to adjust their recruitment strategies in order to remain competitive. This section will explore the implications of an aging workforce on economic growth, productivity, and job security for both employers and employees.

Recent studies have shown that as population's age, there is a decrease in labor force participation rates due to retirement or health issues (Clibborn, 2020, 2021; Colas-Neila & Fargas, 2019; Collins et al., 2020; Cooke et al., 2019; Croucher & Okland, 2021). This has led to an increase in unemployment levels among older workers who may not be able to compete with younger generations for jobs. Additionally, it has been found that older workers tend to be less productive than their younger counterparts due to physical limitations or lack of technological skills needed for certain positions. These factors can lead to decreased economic growth as fewer people are employed and those who are employed produce lower output than they would otherwise be capable of producing if given proper training or resources.

In addition, job security becomes more precarious when there is an influx of new entrants into the labor market from different generations competing for limited positions available within organizations (Ford & Gillan, 2022; Ford & Ward, 2021; Forde; Forsyth, 2022; Foster et al., 2021; Franceschini, 2020). Employers may choose younger candidates over experienced ones because they require less training and offer greater potential for long-term employment prospects at lower costs compared with hiring older individuals whose wages may be higher but whose tenure could potentially end sooner due to retirement plans or other reasons related to ageism in the workplace such as discrimination against older applicants during recruitment processes or layoffs based on seniority rather than performance evaluations which favor youth over experience regardless of qualifications. Figure 7.1 is a demonstration of an aging population in Queensland, Australia (an industrialized nation).

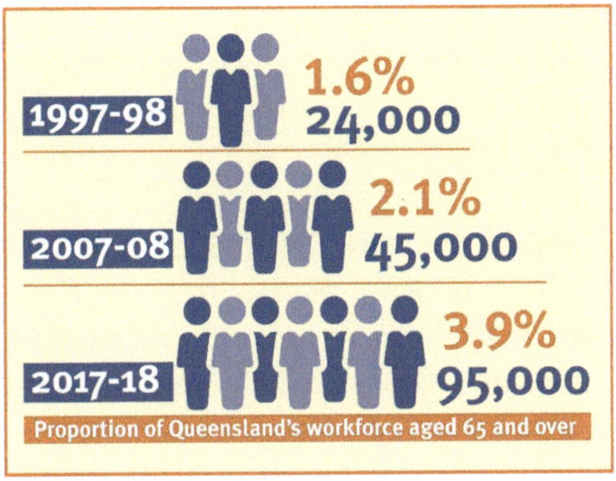

Figure 7.1. *Demonstration of an aging workforce in Queensland, Australia.*

Source: Worksafe QLD.

Various theories have been proposed by economists regarding how best address this issue including increasing incentives for employers through tax credits or subsidies; providing better access education opportunities so that older workers can acquire necessary skills; implementing policies aimed at reducing discrimination against elderly applicants; introducing flexible working arrangements such as part-time work options; encouraging entrepreneurship amongst seniors; creating public works programs specifically targeting elderly citizens, etc. (Chantziaras et al., 2020; Chen et al., n.d., 2023; Cillo & Pradella, 2019; Civinskas & Dvorak, 2019; Clayton, 2021). However, these solutions come with their own set of challenges such as cost effectiveness, implementation difficulties, cultural resistance, etc. While it is clear that the aging population presents various challenges related to employment opportunities, further research needs to be done to understand how best to tackle them. Governments need to develop comprehensive strategies to ensure all citizens regardless of age receive equal opportunity to participate actively in the economy without facing any form of prejudice

(Riva & Rizza, 2021; Roche, n.d.; Roche & Gormley, 2020; Rosetti, 2019; Roy & Dubey, 2022; Roy, 2022; Roychowdhury, 2019). Only then will we be able to create a sustainable future where everyone benefits from increased productivity and job security. Age discrimination is a pervasive issue in contemporary workspaces, with both latent and manifest forms of prejudice impacting the employment opportunities of older workers.

This form of discrimination has been widely studied by academics, who have identified various theories to explain its prevalence (Schmidt & Muller, 2021; Schofield-Georgeson, 2022; Schofield-Georgeson & Rawling, 2020; Schuessler et al., 2019). For instance, some scholars argue that ageism is rooted in cultural norms which value youth over experience. Others suggest it is driven by economic factors such as employers' preference for younger workers due to their lower wages and greater productivity.

Regardless of the underlying causes, there are numerous examples of age-based discrimination in today's workplaces (Ravn & Oyum, 2020; Razak et al., 2022; Refslund & Arnholtz, 2022; Ritson, 2019a, b; Riva & Rizza, 2021). Older job applicants often face difficulties when competing against younger candidates for positions; they may also be overlooked for promotions or denied access to training opportunities due to their age. Furthermore, many employers impose mandatory retirement ages despite laws prohibiting this practice – an example being the recent case where a US company was found guilty of discriminating against employees aged 65 and above after forcing them into early retirement without providing any severance pay or benefits.

The consequences of these practices can be far-reaching: elderly citizens may find themselves unable to support themselves financially if they cannot secure suitable employment (Herrero, 2022; Hilgert, 2019; Hirsch & Mueller, 2020; Hoffrogge, 2019; Howell, 2019, 2021; Hungler, 2022). Meanwhile, businesses miss out on valuable skill sets and knowledge possessed by experienced professionals who could contribute significantly towards organizational success if given the opportunity. To address this problem effectively requires a multi-faceted approach involving both legislative measures (such as introducing anti-discrimination laws) as well as practical solutions like incentivizing companies through tax breaks or subsidies to retain older workers. It is also important to strategically deal with the overarching realities of an aging population (*see* Figure 7.2).

In recent years, pension reforms have been a major topic of debate in many countries around the world (Stevis, 2022; Svec et al., 2021; Tavora,

2019; Teipen & Mehl, 2021; Tesser & Serapioni, 2021; Thomas & Turnbull, 2021). In particular, there has been much discussion about whether or not to raise the mandatory retirement age – an issue that is particularly pertinent given the increasing life expectancy and aging population in many developed nations. Proponents of raising the mandatory retirement age argue that it would allow elderly citizens to remain productive members of society for longer periods of time. Meanwhile, opponents contend that such measures could lead to increased unemployment among younger generations as employers opt for more experienced professionals instead.

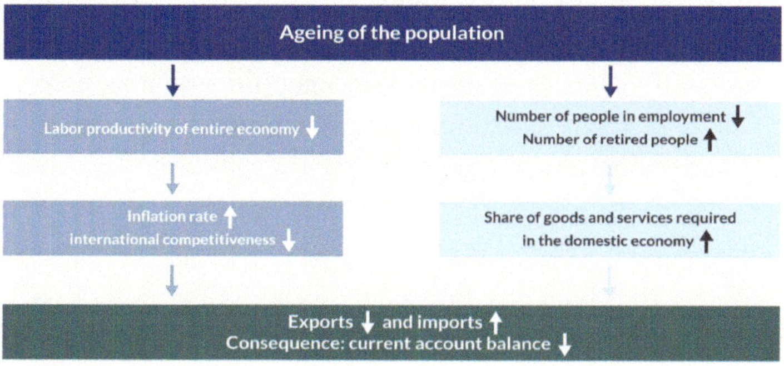

Figure 7.2. *Effects of an aging population.*

Source: Global Europe.

Academic studies on this subject have yielded mixed results (Solaiman; Stanev, 2019; Stanford, 2021; Stapley, 2021; Stevis, 2022; Svec et al., 2021; Tavora, 2019; Teipen & Mehl, 2021). Some suggest that raising the mandatory retirement age can actually benefit both employers and employees by providing greater job security and allowing individuals to continue working until they are ready to retire; while others point out potential drawbacks such as reduced wages due to competition from older workers or decreased productivity levels due to physical limitations associated with aging. Furthermore, descriptive models used by economists often fail to take into account important factors like cultural norms or social attitudes towards elderly people which may influence decisions made by businesses when hiring new staff members.

Existing case studies provide further insight into how different countries have approached this issue (Addison & Teixeira, 2019b; Adewumi, 2021; Agarwal et al., 2020; Ahuja, 2020; Amosse et al., 2019; Archel et al., 2022). For example, France recently raised its minimum retirement age from 60–62 while Germany opted against any changes despite pressure from business groups who argued that doing so would help reduce labor costs and increase competitiveness within their respective markets. These examples demonstrate how complex this problem can be – requiring careful consideration of both economic and social implications before any decision is taken.

The debate surrounding pension reforms continues today with no clear consensus emerging yet on what should be done regarding changes in the mandatory retirement age (Chan, 2020b; Chantziaras et al., 2020; Chen et al., n.d., 2023; Cillo & Pradella, 2019; Civinskas & Dvorak, 2019). It is therefore essential for governments, businesses, academics, and other stakeholders involved in this process to come together in order to discuss these issues openly so as to ensure a fair outcome which takes into account everyone's interests without compromising anyone's rights or freedoms unnecessarily. Productive aging is one of the possible solutions to these challenges.

Aging is a natural process that affects all individuals, regardless of their cultural or economic background. As the population ages, it is important to understand how aging can be productive and beneficial for society. It is pertinent to examine the concept of productive aging in selected countries around the world, highlighting relevant theories and case studies while evaluating descriptive and explanatory models.

The World Health Organization (WHO) defines productive aging as "the ability to remain active and engaged in meaningful activities throughout life." It involves maintaining physical health, mental well-being, social connections, financial security, and other aspects of life that contribute to overall quality of life (Behrens et al., 2020; Behrens & Pekarek, n.d.; Belizon, 2019; Bellace et al., 2021; Ben & Sage, 2022; Berry & McDaniel, 2022). Productive aging has been studied extensively by researchers from various disciplines including sociology, psychology, economics, public health, and gerontology.

One key theory related to productive aging is known as "successful aging" which was developed by Rowe & Kahn in 1998. According to this model there are three components necessary for successful aging: low risk of disease or disability; high cognitive functioning; and active engagement with life through meaningful activities such as work or volunteering. While this model provides an important framework for understanding successful aging across different contexts it does not take into account individual differences such as gender or socio-economic status which may influence one's ability to age productively. In terms of empirical evidence on productive aging there have been several case studies conducted in recent years focusing on specific countries around the world including Japan, South Korea, and China, among others. For example, a study conducted by Kim et al. (2015) examined factors associated with healthy longevity among older adults living in South Korea using data from a national survey conducted between 2008 and 2010. The results showed that higher levels of education were associated with better self-rated health outcomes while lower levels were linked with poorer outcomes suggesting that educational attainment plays an important role in promoting healthy longevity among older adults living in South Korea.

Overall, these findings suggest that there are certain factors associated with successful aging across different contexts (Stevis, 2022; Svec et al., 2021; Tavora, 2019; Teipen & Mehl, 2021; Tesser & Serapioni, 2021; Thomas & Turnbull, 2021). However, more research needs to be done before any definitive conclusions can be drawn about what constitutes effective strategies for promoting productivity amongst older populations worldwide. Additionally, further research should also consider how existing policies might need to be adapted depending on local context if they are going to effectively promote positive aging experiences within particular societies.

In conclusion, although much progress has been made towards understanding what constitutes effective strategies for promoting productivity amongst older populations worldwide, more research needs to be done before any definitive conclusions can be drawn about what works best when it comes to encouraging people aged 65+ years old stay physically, mentally, socially connected financially secure throughout their lives. By doing so we can ensure that our elderly citizens continue contributing positively towards society even after retirement age. Whereas modernity has inspired progressive ideas such as productive aging, it has also created new problems such as deskilling that is caused by the advancement of technologies.

7.2. HOW MODERN TECHNOLOGY IS DESKILLING WORKERS?

Deskilling is a concept that has been widely discussed in the academic literature, with various arguments being put forward to explain its emergence and implications (Radzi et al., 2022; Ramsay & Webster, 2019; Ravn & Oyum, 2020; Razak et al., 2022; Refslund & Arnholtz, 2022). In this section, we will explore these arguments by looking at contemporary examples and evaluating relevant theories. At its core, deskilling refers to the process of reducing or eliminating skills from a job role. This can be done through automation or outsourcing of tasks which were previously performed by skilled workers. Deskilling has become increasingly common in recent years as technology advances have made it easier for employers to replace human labor with machines or cheaper foreign labor sources.

One argument for deskilling is that it increases efficiency and reduces costs for businesses, allowing them to remain competitive in an ever-changing global economy (Gramano & Gaudio, 2019; Grodem & Hippe, 2019; Guillaume, 2022; Guiso, 2020; Gunnigle et al., 2019). However, there are also criticisms of this approach; some argue that deskilling leads to lower wages and fewer opportunities for skilled workers who may find themselves out of work due to their lack of specialized knowledge or experience. Furthermore, research suggests that deskilling can lead to increased workplace stress as employees are expected to perform more tasks than before without any additional training or support from management (Gillespie et al., 2019).

Another argument against deskilling is based on sociological theory which states that when jobs become less complex, they tend to lose meaning and purpose (Hochschild & Machung, 2012). This means that employees may feel unmotivated and unfulfilled if their roles no longer require any skill development or creativity – leading them towards feelings of alienation from their work environment (Ritzer & Jurgenson, 2010). Additionally, studies suggest that when jobs are simplified too much, they can lead people into poverty traps where they cannot escape low-wage employment despite having the necessary qualifications (Kalleberg, 2011).

Finally, while there are many debates surrounding the issue of deskilling, it is important not to forget about those who benefit from such practices: namely employers who gain access to cheap labor sources while avoiding costly investments in employee training programs (Lazonick, 2014). It should also be noted however that even though companies may save money initially through such strategies they could end up paying higher prices later on due reduced productivity levels caused by demotivated staff members (Batt & Appelbaum, 2000). It appears clear that although there are potential benefits associated with deskilling, certain processes within organizations there are also significant risks involved which must be taken into consideration before implementing such measures. As always further research needs to be conducted into this area so as to better understand both sides of the debate, but one thing remains certain: whatever decision is made regarding how best utilize available resources must take into account all stakeholders involved including both employers and employees alike. Figure 7.3 is an example of a critique of modern technologies.

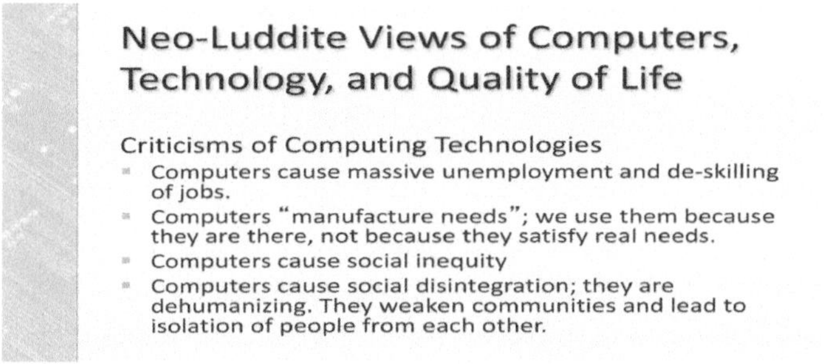

Figure 7.3. *Some criticisms of computing technologies in the modern era.*

Source: Sandra Grant.

The use of technology in contemporary workplaces has been a topic of much debate. On one hand, it is argued that the introduction of new technologies can lead to increased efficiency and productivity, as well as improved job satisfaction for employees (Batt & Appelbaum, 2000). However, there are also concerns about the potential for automation to reduce job complexity and employee wellbeing (Gillespie et al., 2019), or even replace human labor altogether (Hochschild & Machung, 2012).

In order to address these issues effectively it is important to consider both sides of the argument. For example, while technological advances may have some positive effects on workplace productivity, they must be weighed against any potential negative impacts such as reduced job security or decreased wages due to deskilling (Lazonick, 2014). Furthermore, when introducing new technologies into an organization consideration should be given not only to their economic benefits but also their social implications; how will this affect existing work practices? Will it create more meaningful jobs or simply displace workers? What impact will this have on employee morale and motivation? These are all questions which need to be taken seriously.

Ultimately then technology can play an important role in modern workplaces if used correctly (Trif & Szabo; Truyols, 2019; Tu et al., 2022; Velluti, 2022; Vinichenko et al., 2020; Vulkan & Larsson, 2019; Walker, 2020). It can help organizations become more efficient and productive whilst still taking into account the needs of its employees. As Ritzer &

Jurgenson (2010) point out 'the key is finding ways in which production, consumption, and prosumption activities can coexist' – something which requires careful thought and planning before implementation. While technology undoubtedly has a place in today's working environment caution must be taken so as to ensure that its introduction does not come at too great a cost either economically or socially.

One of the most talked about technologies in recent years is artificial intelligence (AI) (Freedland & Dhorajiwala, 2019; Fuchs et al., 2019; Galik et al., 2022; Gall, 2021; Gardawski & Towalski, 2020). AI has been heralded as a potential game changer for many industries, with its ability to automate processes and make decisions faster than humans. However, there are also concerns that it could lead to job losses and displace workers from their roles. This raises an important question – what impact will AI have on intellectual job roles?

To answer this question, we must first consider how AI works. In essence, it uses algorithms to analyze data and identify patterns which can then be used to inform decision making or suggest solutions. While this may sound impressive, it does not necessarily mean that machines can replace human intellect entirely; rather they can supplement existing skill sets by providing additional insights or helping people work more efficiently (Kurzweil & Domingos, 2015). As such, while some jobs may become automated others may simply evolve into new forms requiring different skill sets but still relying heavily on human input (Liu, 2023; Lize et al., 2022; Lloyd & Payne, 2021; Lukacova et al., 2022; Lyddon, 2021; Lyutov, 2022; MacKenzie & Lucio, 2019). Figure 7.4 demonstrates the effect of technology on skilling levels.

Furthermore, even if certain tasks do become automated there is no guarantee that these will be replaced by machines alone. Instead, they could be supplemented by other technologies such as virtual reality or augmented reality which require a high degree of human interaction (Gershenfeld et al., 2017). Additionally, the introduction of AI could create new opportunities for those who possess the right skill set allowing them to take advantage of emerging markets and develop innovative products or services (Liu et al., 2018). While there is certainly cause for concern when introducing any new technology into an organization, careful consideration should be given so as to ensure that its implementation does not come at too great a cost either economically or socially. With regards specifically to AI however it appears likely that rather than replacing intellectual job roles outright it will instead supplement existing ones creating both challenges and opportunities in equal measure.

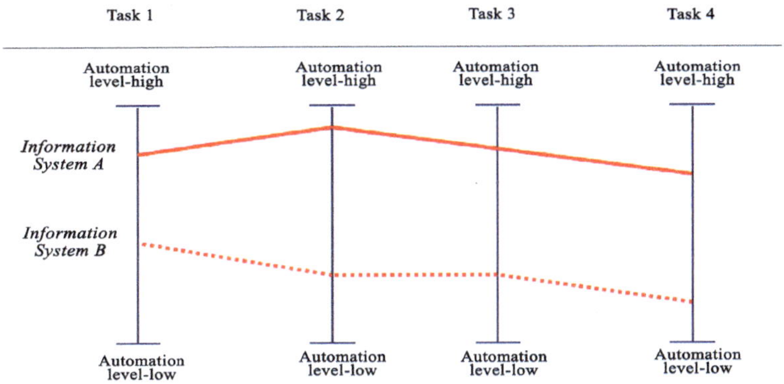

Figure 7.4. *Effects of automation on skilling.*

Source: Bravo (2015).

It therefore falls upon organizations themselves to ensure they are prepared for this shift in order to reap the full benefits offered by these advances in technology whilst still taking into account the needs of their employees (Ritson, 2019b; Riva & Rizza, 2021; Roche, n.d.; Roche & Gormley, 2020; Rosetti, 2019; Roy & Dubey, 2022; Roy, 2022). The introduction of labor-saving machines has been a major factor in the development of modern society. From automated production lines to AI, these technologies have revolutionized the way we work and live. However, there is an ongoing debate about their impact on employment opportunities and wages. On one hand, some argue that automation can reduce costs for businesses while increasing productivity; on the other hand, others suggest that it could lead to job losses and wage stagnation due to fewer human workers being needed (Kumar et al., 2019).

There are different sides to these debates. Firstly, it is true that labor-saving machines can increase efficiency by reducing manual labor requirements which in turn leads to cost savings for businesses (Liu et al., 2018). This could be beneficial for companies as they are able to produce more goods or services at a lower cost which may result in higher profits or increased competitiveness within their respective markets (Gershenfeld et al., 2017). Additionally, automation also allows organizations greater flexibility when responding quickly to changing market conditions as well as providing them with access to new sources of data which can help inform decision making processes (Kumar et al., 2019). On the other hand, however, there are potential drawbacks associated with introducing such technology into an organization. For example, if jobs become redundant then those affected may struggle financially, potentially leading them into poverty or unemployment (Liu et al., 2018). Furthermore, even if new roles do emerge due to advances in technology, they may require different skill sets than those previously employed meaning individuals who lack these abilities will find themselves unable compete effectively for positions available resulting in further economic hardship (Gershenfeld et al., 2017). Finally, there is also concern over how AI might affect social interaction between people given its ability to replace certain tasks traditionally requiring a human.

In light of this then it appears clear that any implementation should take into account not only economic factors but also social ones so as to ensure no one group suffers disproportionately from its introduction (Dockes, 2019; Dorigatti et al., n.d.; Dorigatti & Pedersini, 2021; Dorrenbacher et al., 2021; Drucza, 2019; Dupuis & Greer, 2022). For instance, organizations should look towards developing training programs designed specifically to target those most likely impacted by changes brought about through automation allowing them to gain necessary skills required to succeed within newly created roles whilst still maintaining a high degree of human interaction (Gershenfeld et al., 2017).

It therefore falls upon organizations themselves to ensure they are prepared for this shift order and reap the full benefits offered by these advanced technologies whilst still taking into account the needs of their employees. Setting aside the difficulties that technology creates for the modern workplace, those that advocate for change are also facing challenges. One of those challenges is corruption in the trade union movement.

7.3. CORRUPTION AND ABUSE OF POWER WITHIN TRADE UNIONS

Trade unions have long been a cornerstone of the labor movement, providing workers with collective bargaining power and protecting their rights in the workplace (Jha & Singh, 2019; Jiang & Yao, 2020; Jirjahn, 2022; Joyce et al.; Junior, 2022; Kaine, 2020; Katsabian, 2021; Kilic, 2021). However, there is growing evidence that corruption and abuse of power within trade unions can lead to serious consequences for both union members and employers. Recent studies have highlighted how corrupt practices such as bribery, embezzlement, nepotism, and cronyism can undermine the effectiveness of trade unions. For example, a study by researchers at Harvard University found that when union leaders are more likely to be influenced by personal interests than those of their members, it leads to lower wages for workers and higher costs for employers. This has significant implications for economic growth as well as social justice.

Theories on why corruption occurs within trade unions vary widely but generally focus on structural factors such as weak internal governance structures or inadequate oversight mechanisms (Ngai, 2020; Nicklich & Helfen, 2019; Novitz & Andrijasevic, 2020; Nowak, 2021; Nurlinah et al., 2021; O'Keeffe & Papadopoulos, 2021). These theories suggest that if these issues are addressed then it may be possible to reduce levels of corruption within trade unions. However, some scholars argue that this approach fails to take into account other important factors such as political influence or cultural norms which may also play an important role in shaping behavior within organizations like trade unions.

Case studies from around the world provide further insight into how corruption affects different types of labor organizations in different contexts (Gavin, 2022; Giannakopoulos & Laliotis, 2020; Giraud, 2020; Godino & Molina, 2022; Gooberman, 2022; Goods & Ellem). In India for instance, research has shown how widespread bribery among union officials has led to increased exploitation of workers while in South Africa allegations have been made about collusion between certain union leaders and employers resulting in reduced wages for employees despite strong legal protections against unfair labor practices being put in place by government authorities. These examples demonstrate just some of the ways in which corruption can manifest itself within trade unions leading to negative outcomes not only for individual workers but also society at large due to its impact on economic growth and development.

As debates continue over what measures should be taken to address this issue, it is clear that understanding why these problems occur is essential if we are going to tackle them effectively (Kilic, 2021; Kolling & Schnabel, 2022; Kowalewska, 2020; Kupec et al., 2022; Lamare & Budd, 2022; Lansbury, 2021). Only then will we be able to create fairer working conditions where everyone benefits regardless of who they work with or who represents them. One of the most commonly cited explanations for collective bargaining failures is that unions are too weak to effectively negotiate with employers. These dynamics are directly linked to the nature of trade union structures and activity (*see* Figure 7.5).

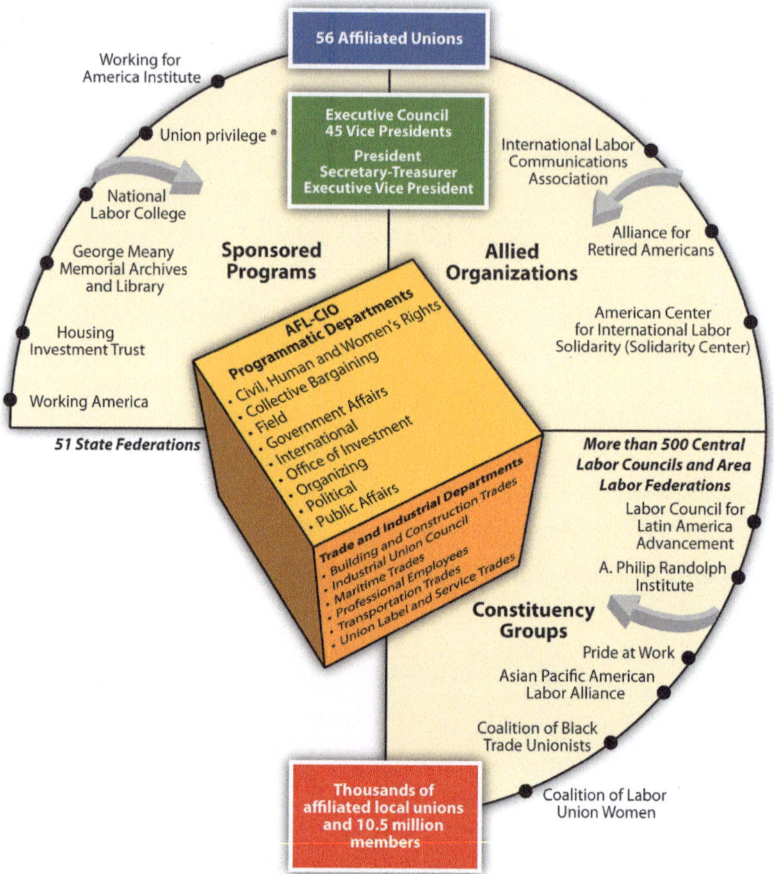

Figure 7.5. *The nature of trade unions and their networks.*

Source: University of Minnesota.

This argument has been supported by a number of studies which have found that union density – or the proportion of workers who are members of a trade union – is often lower in countries where labor rights violations occur more frequently (Stanford, 2021; Stapley, 2021; Stevis, 2022; Svec et al., 2021; Tavora, 2019; Teipen & Mehl, 2021; Tesser & Serapioni, 2021). However, this theory fails to take into account other factors such as political and economic conditions which can also influence how successful negotiations between unions and employers turn out to be. For example, research has shown that even when union density is high, if there is an imbalance in power between the two sides then it may still be difficult for unions to secure better wages and working conditions for their members.

Another explanation put forward by scholars suggests that collective bargaining failures can be attributed to inadequate legal protections against unfair labor practices (Newman et al., 2019; Nga & Nga, 2021; Ngai, 2020; Nicklich & Helfen, 2019; Novitz & Andrijasevic, 2020; Nowak, 2021). While laws exist in many countries prohibiting certain types of exploitation, they are often not enforced due to lack of resources or political will on behalf of governments. As a result, employers may feel emboldened enough to ignore these regulations, leading them to engage in exploitative behavior without fear of repercussions from authorities. Furthermore, even when laws do exist, they may not always provide sufficient protection against all forms of abuse so additional measures need to be taken to ensure workers' rights are respected at all times.

Finally, some academics have argued that collective bargaining failures can also arise from cultural norms within societies which discourage people from joining trade unions or engaging in any form of protest activity (Giraud, 2020; Godino & Molina, 2022; Gooberman, 2022; Goods & Ellem; Goyer et al., 2022; Graca, 2021). In India for instance, traditional attitudes towards authority mean many individuals prefer to remain silent rather than speak up about injustices being committed against them while others view taking part in strikes as dishonorable behavior which should be avoided at all costs. Such beliefs make it harder for unions to gain traction among employees making it more difficult for them to achieve their goals through negotiation alone.

Understanding why collective bargaining failures occur is essential if we want to create fairer working environments around the world where everyone benefits regardless of who represents them or who they work with (Bradley & Rowland, 2021; Bray et al., 2019, 2020; Budd, 2020; Cabeza, 2019; Cam, 2021; Campolieti, 2020). Although various theories have been proposed to explain this phenomenon, none offer comprehensive solutions addressing its root causes meaning further research needs done in order identify effective strategies to tackle these issues head-on before real progress is made towards improving labor standards globally. Trade union factionalism is a complex issue which has been studied extensively by academics over years. It refers to the tendency of unions to split into factions based on ideological differences, leading them to become less effective in achieving their goals. This can be seen in countries such as India where there are strong cultural norms that discourage aggressive unionization. The most common explanation for this phenomenon is that it arises from internal power struggles between different groups within the union who have competing interests and agendas (de Amorim et al., 2019; de Luna, 2022; De Prins et al., 2020; de Vaate, 2021; Demougin et al., 2019; Desai & Randeria, 2020). These divisions can lead to infighting and disunity among members, making it harder for them to negotiate effectively with employers or other stakeholders. Additionally, some scholars argue that external factors such as government policies or economic conditions may also contribute to trade union factionalism by creating an environment where cooperation becomes more difficult.

In order to address this problem, various strategies have been proposed including increased transparency and accountability measures within unions as well as better communication between members and leadership teams (Belizon, 2019; Bellace et al., 2021; Ben & Sage, 2022; Berry & McDaniel, 2022; Bhuta, 2022; Bischoff et al., 2021). Additionally, research suggests that providing training opportunities for leaders could help reduce conflict while encouraging collaboration across different factions would also be beneficial in promoting unity amongst members. Finally, introducing incentives for collective bargaining success could provide further motivation for unions to work together towards achieving their objectives without resorting to divisive tactics which ultimately weaken their position when negotiating with employers or other stakeholders. The guidelines indicated in Figure 7.6 illustrate some of the achievements recorded through unionization which ensure fairer treatment for workers.

Figure 7.6. *Things that should not be said to employees during unionization.*

Source: University of Minnesota.

Despite these potential solutions, there are still numerous examples of illegal strikes and destructive union activity which have had a negative impact on both workers and employers (Foley & Williamson, 2021; Ford

& Gillan, 2022; Ford & Ward, 2021; Forde; Forsyth, 2022; Foster et al., 2021). For instance, in the United Kingdom, a series of wildcat strikes by members of the Rail Maritime and Transport Union (RMT) caused significant disruption to services in 2018. This was due to disagreements between different factions within the union overpay and working conditions as well as allegations that some members were being unfairly treated by management. The strike resulted in widespread delays for commuters across the country with many businesses also suffering financial losses due to reduced productivity or canceled orders.

In another example from South Africa, a long-running dispute between two rival unions – National Union of Mineworkers (NUM) and Association of Mineworkers & Construction Union (AMCU) – led to violent clashes at several mines owned by Lonmin PLC in 2012. This ultimately resulted in 44 deaths including 34 miners who were shot dead by police during an attempted dispersal operation. In this case, it appears that competition between NUM and AMCU for control over workers' wages may have been one factor contributing to the unrest although other factors such as poor safety standards or inadequate housing facilities could also have played a role.

These cases demonstrate how internal divisions within trade unions can lead to serious consequences if not managed effectively with employers or other stakeholders (Baines & Cunningham, 2020; Bancarzewski & Hardy, 2021; Barklamb, 2021; Barry & Wilkinson, 2022; Baturina et al., 2021). It is therefore important for leaders within these organizations to ensure that they are engaging constructively with their members while also taking into account external factors which may be influencing their behavior so that disputes can be resolved without resorting to violence or illegal action which only serves to weaken their position when negotiating terms with employers or other stakeholders. Additionally, research suggests that providing training opportunities for leaders could help reduce conflict while encouraging collaboration across different factions would also be beneficial in promoting unity amongst members so that they can work together towards achieving their objectives without resorting to divisive tactics which ultimately weaken their position when negotiating with employers or other stakeholders.

Ultimately, it is clear from these case studies that effective communication between all parties involved is essential if we are going to achieve successful outcomes without causing further damage either through legal action or physical violence (Lyddon, 2021; Lyutov, 2022; MacKenzie & Lucio, 2019;

Madimutsa; Mahas-Demydas & Rudnytska, 2019; Mahmood & Banerjee, 2020). The trade union movement has long been a source of debate and controversy, with many arguing that it is an outdated institution which no longer serves its purpose in the modern world. However, there are also those who believe that unions still have a role to play in protecting workers' rights and ensuring fair wages for employees. It is pertinent to explore some of the contradictions inherent within the trade union movement by examining contemporary examples from around the world.

One example of this contradiction can be seen in India where trade unions have traditionally been associated with violence and disruption due to their militant tactics when negotiating terms with employers or other stakeholders (Opute & Koch, 2020; Ormaetxea, 2019; Ozkiziltan, 2019, 2020; Peetz, 2021; Peetz et al., 2020). While these tactics may have achieved short-term gains for members, they often resulted in long-term damage as employers were unwilling to negotiate further once negotiations had broken down due to fear of further disruption or violence. This highlights how traditional methods used by unions can sometimes be counter-productive if not managed correctly.

In contrast, research suggests that more collaborative approaches such as collective bargaining could help reduce conflict while also achieving better outcomes for both parties involved (Addison & Teixeira, 2019a, b; Adewumi, 2021; Agarwal et al., 2020; Ahuja, 2020; Amosse et al., 2019). For instance, recent studies conducted by academics at Harvard University found that collective bargaining agreements (CBAs) between labor unions and employers led to higher wages for employees without any significant increase in costs for businesses. This demonstrates how effective communication between all parties involved is essential if we are going to achieve successful outcomes without causing further damage either through legal action or physical violence.

Overall, it is clear from these case studies that there are numerous contradictions within the trade union movement which need to be addressed if we want them to remain relevant and effective in today's society (da Costa & Horn, 2021; Dalla Sega, 2021; Darlington & Mustchin, 2019; Das, 2023; Das & Singh, 2021; de Amorim et al., 2019). It is therefore important for organizations representing workers' interests such as trade unions to ensure that they are engaging constructively with their members while also taking into account external factors which may be influencing their behavior so that disputes can be resolved without resorting to violence or illegal action which only serves weaken their position when negotiating terms with employers or other stakeholders.

Additionally, providing training opportunities for leaders could help reduce conflict while encouraging collaboration across different factions would also be beneficial in promoting unity amongst members so that they can work together towards achieving their objectives without resorting to divisive tactics which ultimately weaken their position when negotiating with employers or other stakeholders (Lansbury, 2021; Larsson, 2020; Lawreniuk, 2023; Lee & Tapia, 2021; Leggett, 2019; Ligthart et al., 2022; Liu, 2023). Ultimately, it is clear from these case studies that effective communication between all parties involved is essential if we are going to achieve successful outcomes without causing further damage either through legal action or physical violence. In the next section, we consider the use of picketing as a union strategy.

7.4. PICKETING AND THE RIGHT TO WORK

Picketing is a form of protest that has been used for centuries to draw attention to an issue or cause (Kupec et al., 2022; Lamare & Budd, 2022; Lansbury, 2021; Larsson, 2020; Lawreniuk, 2023; Lee & Tapia, 2021). It involves gathering in public places and displaying signs, banners, and other symbols of dissent. In recent years, picketing tactics have become increasingly sophisticated as activists seek more effective ways to make their voices heard. One popular tactic is the use of "flash mobs" – large groups of people who gather suddenly in a public place and then disperse quickly after making their point.

This approach can be highly effective at drawing media attention and creating a sense of urgency around an issue (Roychowdhury, 2019; Rubery et al.; Sakharuk, 2021; Sanchez-Mosquera, 2022; Sanz et al., 2020; Schlachter, 2019). However, it also carries risks. For instance, if not managed properly, flash mobs can lead to confrontations with law enforcement or even violence between protesters and counter-protesters.

Another common tactic is the use of symbolic objects such as flags or effigies to represent the cause being protested (Foster et al., 2021; Franceschini, 2020; Freedland & Dhorajiwala, 2019; Fuchs et al., 2019; Galik et al., 2022). These objects are often placed prominently in areas where they will attract maximum attention from passersby or media outlets covering the event. While this approach can be powerful in conveying a message, it may also backfire if viewers interpret the symbolism differently than intended by organizers – leading them away from rather than towards support for the cause being advocated for.

A third strategy employed by many picketers is direct action: engaging with those on whom they wish to exert pressure through civil disobedience such as blocking roads or occupying buildings associated with their target groups (Schuhrke, 2019; Scrimger, 2020; Seghezzi; Sheldon & Thornthwaite, 2020; Smith, 2019; Solaiman; Stanev, 2019). This type of protest has been used successfully throughout history but comes with its own set of risks. For instance, depending on how authorities respond, participants could face arrest or worse consequences for taking part in these activities.

Finally, some activists choose to engage in peaceful dialog with those they oppose instead of resorting immediately to confrontation tactics like picketing (Sanchez-Mosquera, 2022; Sanz et al., 2020; Schlachter, 2019; Schmidt & Muller, 2021; Schofield-Georgeson, 2022). By engaging directly with opponents through respectful conversation about shared values and goals – rather than simply shouting slogans at each other – both sides may gain greater understanding about one another's perspectives while still maintaining their respective positions on contentious issues without resorting to violence or intimidation tactics which could further polarize opinions within society at large.

Overall, there are numerous strategies available when it comes time for individuals seeking social change through picketing tactics – ranging from symbolic displays all the way up through direct action – but each must be carefully considered before implementation due its potential implications both positive and negative alike (O'Keeffe & Papadopoulos, 2021; Oberfichtner et al., 2020; Opute & Koch, 2020; Ormaetxea, 2019). Ultimately, only by weighing all options thoroughly beforehand can protesters ensure that their efforts will yield meaningful results without causing unintended harm along the way. The debate between right to work and forced unionization has been a contentious one for many years.

On the one hand, proponents of right to work argue that it allows individuals greater freedom in choosing whether or not they wish to join a union without fear of retribution from employers (Gunnigle et al., 2019; Gunther & Hopner, 2023; Haipeter, 2020; Hakansta et al., n.d.; Hamberger, 2020; Harvey & Turnbull, 2020). This is seen as beneficial because it gives workers more control over their own labor rights and can potentially lead to higher wages due to increased competition among unions for members. On the other hand, those who support forced unionization believe that it provides necessary protections against exploitation by employers while also allowing unions to negotiate better working conditions on behalf of all employees regardless of membership status. In Figure 7.7, we see that several critiques have been advanced against the right to work.

Figure 7.7. *Critique of the right to work.*

Source: IUPAT.

In order to evaluate these arguments, we must consider both sides within the context of contemporary examples (Joyce et al.; Junior, 2022; Kaine, 2020; Katsabian, 2021; Kilic, 2021; Kolling & Schnabel, 2022; Kowalewska, 2020). For instance, recent studies have shown that states with right-to-work laws tend to have lower median wages than those without such legislation – suggesting that individual choice may not always be beneficial when it comes time for collective bargaining. Additionally, research conducted by economists at Cornell University found that workers in states with compulsory union dues were able to secure higher pay increases than those without them – indicating potential benefits associated with mandatory membership requirements.

Furthermore, there are several theories which attempt to explain why certain policies might be preferable depending on specific circumstances (Bancarzewski & Hardy, 2021; Barklamb, 2021; Barry & Wilkinson, 2022;

Baturina et al., 2021; Beattie, 2019). For example, some scholars suggest that economic efficiency could be improved through voluntary participation since this would allow resources (such as money) allocated towards organizing efforts instead go directly towards improving worker welfare. Others contend however, that collective action is essential if meaningful change is going to occur given its ability to mobilize large numbers of people quickly and effectively – something which cannot necessarily be achieved through individual efforts alone.

Finally, existing case studies provide valuable insight into how different approaches can affect outcomes related to labor disputes (Franceschini, 2020; Freedland & Dhorajiwala, 2019; Fuchs et al., 2019; Galik et al., 2022; Gall, 2021; Gardawski & Towalski, 2020). In particular, an analysis conducted by researchers at Harvard Law School revealed significant differences between strikes organized under traditional methods versus ones utilizing direct action tactics like picketing or boycotting goods produced by companies involved in negotiations. The study concluded that while both strategies had similar success rates overall, direct action was much more effective when dealing with larger corporations due its ability to generate widespread public attention quickly – thus increasing pressure upon management to resolve conflicts faster than conventional means would otherwise allow for.

Generally, there are numerous considerations which must be taken into account before deciding upon any particular approach when engaging opponents during social movements such as picketing campaigns (Bradley & Rowland, 2021; Bray et al., 2019, 2020; Budd, 2020; Cabeza, 2019; Cam, 2021). While each strategy carries its own unique advantages and disadvantages depending on the situation at hand – careful evaluation beforehand will ensure protesters maximize chances achieving desired results while minimizing potential harm caused a long way. Ultimately though only time will tell what works best given the ever-changing nature of modern society today so further research into this area remains highly recommended moving forward.

In recent years, the politics of unionization in the United States has become increasingly complex (Ilsoe & Soderqvist; Jarota, 2022; Jha & Singh, 2019; Jiang & Yao, 2020; Jirjahn, 2022; Joyce et al.; Junior, 2022). With labor laws and regulations varying from state to state, it can be difficult for workers to know how best to organize and protect their rights. One key question is whether direct action or conventional negotiation tactics are more effective when attempting to secure better wages and working conditions.

This is particularly relevant given the current political climate where many large companies have been accused of exploiting workers through unfair labor practices such as wage theft or misclassification of employees as independent contractors to avoid paying benefits they would otherwise be entitled to (Hakansta et al., n.d.; Hamberger, 2020; Harvey & Turnbull, 2020; Hendy, 2022; Herrero, 2022; Hilgert, 2019; Hirsch & Mueller, 2020). In these cases, engaging in some form of protest may be the only way to ensure justice is served since employers are often unwilling to negotiate terms without being forced to do so first. Nevertheless, there are also potential risks associated with taking such drastic measures which must be taken into consideration before deciding to move forward.

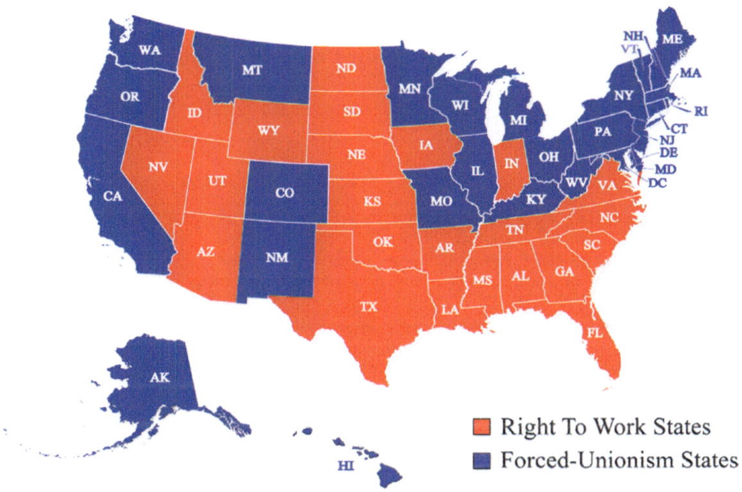

Figure 7.8. *Emergence of the right to work in the USA.*

Source: National Right to Work Committee.

There are various examples of union actions that are designed to address specific problems in specific contexts (Nicklich & Helfen, 2019; Novitz & Andrijasevic, 2020; Nowak, 2021; Nurlinah et al., 2021; O'Keeffe & Papadopoulos, 2021). For instance, if protesters fail to garner enough support, then could end up facing legal repercussions themselves instead achieving desired outcome – something which could easily backfire on them later down the line if not handled properly from start. Additionally, even successful campaigns might still result in negative publicity for companies involved – potentially leading customers to boycott the products and services offered thereby reducing profits significantly over time. Figure 7.8 shows that the USA has a diversity of approaches to unionization and the right to work.

As previously mentioned though, each situation is unique. So, careful evaluation beforehand will help determine the most appropriate course action moving forward depending particular circumstances present at any given moment in time (Edwards & Hodder, 2022; Ellem, 2021; Ellem et al., 2020; Engblom & Lundberg, 2019; Espinosa, 2021). This includes assessing size organization opponents' resources available to them along with any other factors which might influence the decision-making process during negotiations. Harvard researchers have concluded that while both strategies had similar success rates overall, direct action was much more effective when dealing with larger corporations due its ability to generate widespread public attention quickly – thus increasing pressure upon management to resolve conflicts faster than conventional means would otherwise allow for.

Overall, then, there are numerous considerations which must be taken into account before deciding upon any particular approach when engaging opponents during social movements such as picketing campaigns (Hendy, 2022; Herrero, 2022; Hilgert, 2019; Hirsch & Mueller, 2020; Hoffrogge, 2019; Howell, 2019, 2021). There have been cases where the practice of philosophical disagreements has led to societal strife that goes beyond industrial relations. A case in point are the market reforms implemented by Margaret Thatcher who was the Prime Minister of the United Kingdom during the 1980s.

The Thatcherite reforms of the 1980s had a profound impact on many industrial cities in North England. These policies, which included privatization and deregulation, led to the closure of numerous factories and mines across the region. This resulted in large-scale job losses and an overall decline in economic activity. In addition, these changes also had a significant social impact as communities were left without their traditional sources of employment or income. Some saw this as a successful agenda while others criticized Thatcher for effectively destroying communities.

In recent years, there has been much debate about how best to address this issue. Some argue that government intervention is necessary to revive these areas while others suggest that local initiatives should be encouraged instead. However, both approaches have their limitations; for example, government intervention can often be slow and bureaucratic while local initiatives may lack resources or expertise needed for success. To better understand this problem, it is important to consider existing case studies from around the world which have attempted to tackle similar issues with varying degrees of success (Hirsch & Mueller, 2020; Hoffrogge, 2019; Howell, 2019, 2021; Hungler, 2022; Ilsoe & Soderqvist; Jarota, 2022). For instance, a study conducted by researchers at Oxford University looked into how regional governments could use targeted investment programs to help revitalize struggling economies within certain regions. Their findings suggested that such interventions could indeed lead to increased economic growth if properly implemented. However, they also noted potential drawbacks associated with them such as misallocation funds or inefficient decision-making process during negotiations. The last section in this chapter will consider the notion of zero-hour contracts and their implications.

7.5. THE PROBLEMATIC NOTION OF ZERO-HOUR CONTRACTS

Zero hours contracts have become increasingly popular in recent years, with an estimated 1.8 million people employed on such terms in the UK alone (Ellem et al., 2020; Engblom & Lundberg, 2019; Espinosa, 2021; Eustace, 2021; Fang et al., 2021; Fergus & Godfrey, 2021). These arrangements offer employers flexibility and cost savings, but they can also be exploitative for workers who are denied basic rights and protections. In this section, we will explore the arguments surrounding zero hour's contracts and evaluate their implications for both employers and employees.

The primary argument in favor of zero hours contracts is that they provide businesses with greater flexibility to meet fluctuating demand without having to commit to fixed staffing levels or pay wages when there is no work available (De Prins et al., 2020; de Vaate, 2021; Demougin et al., 2019; Desai & Randeria, 2020; Devinatz, 2020, 2022). This has been particularly beneficial during times of economic uncertainty, as it allows companies to adjust their workforce quickly while avoiding costly redundancies or layoffs. However, critics argue that these arrangements often leave workers vulnerable due to a lack of job security and protection from unfair dismissal or discrimination. Furthermore, research suggests that those on zero hour's contracts are more likely to experience poverty than those on permanent employment agreements (Bryson et al., 2019).

From an employee perspective, one of the main drawbacks associated with zero-hour contracts is the lack of predictability over working patterns which can make budgeting difficult and lead to financial insecurity (Gill et al., 2018). Additionally, many workers report feeling pressure from employers not to take other jobs or turn down shifts due to fear of losing their current position (Davies & Gahan, 2017). This raises important questions about power dynamics within workplaces where employees may feel unable or unwilling to challenge decisions made by management out of fear for their livelihoods.

Figure 7.9. *Worker profiles in the USA.*

Source: The Legal Partners.

In order to address some of these issues related to exploitation and inequality within the workplace it has been suggested that legislation should be introduced which would guarantee minimum wage payments even if no work were available (Harrison & Stewart, 2020). Such measures could help ensure fairness between employer's needs for flexibility while protecting worker's rights at the same time. However, further research into how such policies might impact businesses would need to be conducted before any changes were implemented.

Although there are potential benefits associated with using zero-hour contract arrangements there remain significant risks involved too – both for employers seeking short-term gains through cost savings as well as employees whose rights may be compromised by such agreements (Berry & McDaniel, 2022; Bhuta, 2022; Bischoff et al., 2021; Bogoeski, 2022; Bondy, 2022; Boumans, 2022; Bourguignon & Floquet, 2019). As such, further debate around this issue is needed so that appropriate regulations can be put in place which protect all parties involved whilst still allowing businesses access necessary labor market flexibilities when required. As Figure 7.9 shows, this type of contracting is becoming increasingly popular in industrialized countries such as the USA.

Indeed, zero hours contracts are very similar to piece work (Ben & Sage, 2022; Berry & McDaniel, 2022; Bhuta, 2022; Bischoff et al., 2021; Bogoeski, 2022; Bondy, 2022). Piece work is a form of employment which has become increasingly popular in recent years, particularly within the gig economy. Piece work involves an individual being paid for each task they complete rather than receiving a fixed wage or salary. This type of arrangement can be beneficial to businesses as it allows them access to labor market flexibilities when needed and can also provide individuals with more control over their working hours and income. However, there are concerns that piece work may lead to exploitation of workers due to its lack of job security and potential for low pay.

Recent research has highlighted the prevalence of poverty amongst zero-hours contract workers (Bryson et al., 2019). Furthermore, studies have found that those employed on such contracts often experience poorer job quality compared with other forms of employment (Gill et al., 2018). In addition, power dynamics between employers and employees in the gig economy have been identified as contributing factors towards worker exploitation (Davies & Gahan, 2017). These findings suggest that piece work arrangements may not always be beneficial for all parties involved.

In order to ensure fair treatment for both employers and employees, further debate around this issue is necessary so appropriate regulations can be put in place which protect all parties whilst supporting economic growth at the macro-level (Harrison & Stewart, 2020). Such regulations should include measures such as minimum wages, maximum working hour's limits and improved job security provisions so that workers' rights are not compromised by these agreements. It is clear from existing evidence that piece work arrangements need careful consideration if they are going to benefit everyone involved without leading to exploitation or unfair practices.

Trade unions have been vocal in their criticism of zero hours contracts, arguing that they are exploitative and lead to a lack of job security for workers (TUC, 2018). They argue that these arrangements can be used by employers to avoid providing employees with the same rights as those on permanent contracts. This includes access to sick pay, holiday pay and other benefits which are often not available under piece work agreements. Trade unions also point out that such arrangements can leave workers vulnerable to exploitation due to the power imbalance between employer and employee (Gill et al., 2018). In addition, trade unions have highlighted how zero hours contracts can lead to an increase in precarious employment which has been linked with poorer mental health outcomes for workers (Davies & Gahan, 2017). Furthermore, research suggests that this type of arrangement is more likely to be taken up by younger people who may not yet have established themselves within the labor market or developed strong bargaining power when negotiating terms with employers (Harrison & Stewart, 2020). This could potentially limit opportunities for career progression or further training if individuals remain stuck in low-paid jobs without any job security.

There are both advantages and disadvantages associated with zero hour's contracts depending on individual circumstances (Abd Razak & Mahmod, 2019, 2021; Ackers, 2020; Addison & Teixeira, 2019a). It is therefore important for governments and policy makers alike to consider all aspects of this issue before introducing regulations so as not to compromise worker's rights whilst still allowing businesses access necessary labor market flexibilities when required. Trade unions should continue advocating for better working conditions, so everyone involved in piece work arrangements receives fair treatment regardless of their age or experience level.

Only then will we see a shift towards fairer practices within the gig economy which benefit both employers and employees (William & Cunningham, 2021; Williamson et al., 2019; Wright; Wright & McLaughlin, 2021; Xie & Zhou, 2022). Legislation is an important dynamic in these reforms and decisions. It is pertinent to consider some landmark laws in the UK. A case in point is The National Minimum Wage Act (1998). It was introduced in the UK to ensure that all workers receive a minimum wage regardless of their age or experience level.

This legislation has been widely praised for its ability to reduce poverty and inequality, however there are still some criticisms surrounding it (Agarwal et al., 2020; Ahuja, 2020; Amosse et al., 2019; Archel et al., 2022; Ashwin et al., 2020; Avgar, 2020). One such criticism is that the current rate does not reflect the cost of living which means many people are unable to make ends meet even when working full-time hours (Harrison & Stewart, 2020). Additionally, due to the lack of job security associated with zero-hour contracts, individuals may be reluctant to take on additional work as they cannot guarantee regular income from month-to-month. In fact, the disdain for zero hours contracts means that some unemployment statistics deliberately exclude them (*see* Figure 7.10 for an example).

Furthermore, research suggests that employers have taken advantage of this situation by offering piece work arrangements instead of traditional employment contracts (Gill et al., 2019). This can lead to exploitation as employees may feel pressured into accepting lower wages than what they would normally expect due to their limited bargaining power. Moreover, those who do accept these terms often find themselves stuck in low paid jobs without any job security or career progression opportunities (Gill et al., 2019).

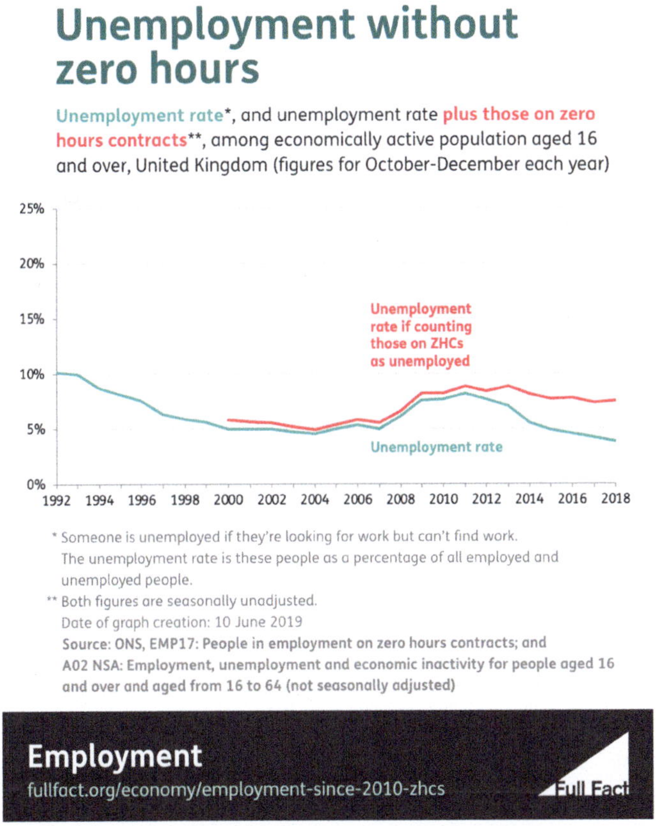

Figure 7.10. *US unemployment rate excluding zero-hour contracts 1992–2018.*

Source: Full Fact.

Whilst the National Minimum Wage Act (1998) has had positive impacts on reducing poverty and inequality within society, it is clear that further action needs to be taken if we want everyone involved in piece work arrangements receive fair treatment regardless of their age or experience level (Eustace, 2021; Fang et al., 2021; Fergus & Godfrey, 2021; Flynn & Schroder, 2021; Foley & Williamson, 2021). Trade unions should continue advocating for better working conditions, so everyone receives a living wage and access necessary labor market flexibilities when required. Only then will we see a shift towards fairer practices within the gig economy which benefit both employers and employees.

The Working Time Regulations (1998) is a piece of legislation that was introduced in the UK to protect workers from exploitation and ensure they receive fair pay for their work. The regulations set out minimum standards for working hours, rest breaks, holidays, and other entitlements such as sick leave (Gill et al., 2019). Despite these protections, there are still many instances where employers fail to comply with the regulations or take advantage of loopholes within them. This can lead to employees being overworked or underpaid which has serious implications on their health and wellbeing.

Furthermore, the rise of the gig economy has seen an increase in people entering into piece work (Gasparri & Tassinari, 2020; Gavin, 2022; Giannakopoulos & Laliotis, 2020; Giraud, 2020; Godino & Molina, 2022). In addition to this, it is important that we consider how existing laws may need updating in order to keep up with changing labor market trends. For example, recent research suggests that current employment law does not adequately address issues related to precarious work arrangements such as zero-hour contracts (Gill et al., 2019). As a result, those who enter into these types of agreements often find themselves without any legal protection if something goes wrong.

In this context, it is important to consider the National Minimum Wage Regulations (1999) (NMWR) which set out minimum wage requirements for all employees in the UK. The NMWR states that employers must pay their workers at least the national minimum wage rate or above depending on their age and experience level. This means that those who are aged 25 and over should receive a minimum of £8.21 per hour while younger workers may be entitled to less than this amount (GOV.UK, 2019).

Despite its good intentions, there have been criticisms of the NMWR as some argue that it does not go far enough in protecting vulnerable workers from exploitation by unscrupulous employers (Bryson et al., 2018). For example, research has shown that many people working within the gig economy are paid below the legal minimum wage due to lack of enforcement mechanisms and inadequate monitoring systems (Gill et al., 2019). Furthermore, there is evidence to suggest that certain groups such as young people and migrant workers are particularly vulnerable when it comes to receiving fair wages due to language barriers or lack of knowledge about employment rights (Bryson et al., 2018). Overall, while we can see how existing laws such as the NMWR attempt to protect vulnerable employees from exploitation by setting out clear guidelines regarding payment rates for different types of work arrangements, more needs to be done if we want everyone involved in piece work arrangements receive fair treatment regardless of their age or experience level.

CHAPTER 7 SUMMARY

This penultimate chapter of the book has considered contemporary frameworks for industrial relations. For example, the chapter has shown that aging presents challenges for industrialized nations. At the same time, modern technology is deskilling many traditional workers. Besides, the trade unions that are meant to protect these workers are riddled with corruption and abuse of power. We have critiqued the practice of picketing as well as the right to work and a battery of measures. The chapter has also highlighted the challenges of adopting zero-hour contracting. Despite these challenges, the final chapter in the book looks at the future of industrial relations.

CHAPTER 8

Looking at the Future of Industrial Relations

Contents

As we close the book, we look at the future of industrial relations. Some of the ideas that will be explored in this final chapter include working from home, mobility in employment, the brain drain problem in the developing world, deindustrialization, and structural unemployment. These are problems that will define our responses to the needs of the modern workforce. As the COVID-19 pandemic showed, it is possible to completely recalibrate the notion of work with the work-from-home innovation.

8.1. THE WORK-FROM-HOME MOVEMENT

The concept of working from home has become increasingly popular in recent years, as technology advances and the need for remote work increases (Abd Razak & Mahmod, 2019, 2021; Ackers, 2020; Addison & Teixeira, 2019a, b). Working from home offers a number of advantages, including increased flexibility, reduced costs associated with commuting to an office space, and improved productivity due to fewer distractions. However, there are also some potential drawbacks that must be considered when evaluating this option.

One argument in favor of working from home is that it can provide greater flexibility for employees who have other commitments outside of their job (Bray et al., 2019, 2020; Budd, 2020; Cabeza, 2019; Cam, 2021; Campolieti, 2020; Cesari et al., 2019). For example, parents may find it easier to balance childcare responsibilities while still being able to complete their work tasks if they are able to do so remotely. Additionally, those with disabilities or chronic illnesses may benefit from having the ability to adjust their workspace according to their needs without needing approval or assistance from employers or colleagues.

On the other hand, there are some potential downsides associated with working from home that should not be overlooked (Dobbins et al., 2020, 2021; Dockes, 2019; Dorigatti et al., n.d.; Dorigatti & Pedersini, 2021; Dorrenbacher et al., 2021). One issue is that employees may struggle with feelings of isolation if they lack regular contact with coworkers and supervisors; this could lead to decreased motivation and morale over time. Furthermore, research suggests that people who work remotely tend to experience higher levels of stress than those who work in traditional office settings due to a lack of structure and support systems available at home (Kumar & Sharma, 2020).

In addition, there is evidence suggesting that certain types of jobs may not be suitable for remote work environments (Gonzalez-Molina et al.,

2019). For instance, jobs requiring frequent collaboration between team members might suffer if everyone works separately at different locations; similarly, roles involving customer service would likely require face-to-face interaction which cannot easily be replicated online. Therefore, it is important for employers considering allowing staff members to work remotely on a permanent basis to take into account these factors before making any decisions about implementing such policies within their organizations.

While working from home does offer many benefits – particularly in terms of providing more flexible arrangements – there are also several potential drawbacks which must be taken into consideration before deciding whether this approach will suit your particular workplace environment best (Dockes, 2019; Dorigatti et al., n.d.; Dorigatti & Pedersini, 2021; Dorrenbacher et al., 2021; Drucza, 2019; Dupuis & Greer, 2022). It is therefore essential for employers looking into introducing such measures carefully to evaluate all relevant factors before doing so in order to ensure maximum success going forward. Yet, the COVID-19 pandemic made this a vital approach (*see* Figure 8.1).

In recent years, the concept of distributed companies has become increasingly popular (Graca, 2021; Gramano & Gaudio, 2019; Grodem & Hippe, 2019; Guillaume, 2022; Guiso, 2020; Gunnigle et al., 2019). This is due to the fact that it allows for greater flexibility and autonomy in terms of how employees work, as well as providing a more cost-effective way of running an organization. However, while this approach may have many advantages, there are also some potential drawbacks which must be taken into consideration when deciding whether or not to implement such measures within your own workplace environment.

One key issue which needs to be addressed is that of worker's rights (Budd, 2020; Cabeza, 2019; Cam, 2021; Campolieti, 2020; Cesari et al., 2019; Chan, 2020a, b; Chantziaras et al., 2020). In particular, when working from home – or any other form of distributed company – it can be difficult for employers to ensure that their staff are receiving adequate protection under employment law and regulations. For example, if workers do not have access to appropriate health and safety equipment at home then they could potentially face serious risks while carrying out their duties remotely. Additionally, there may also be issues surrounding data security if sensitive information is being shared over unsecured networks or devices.

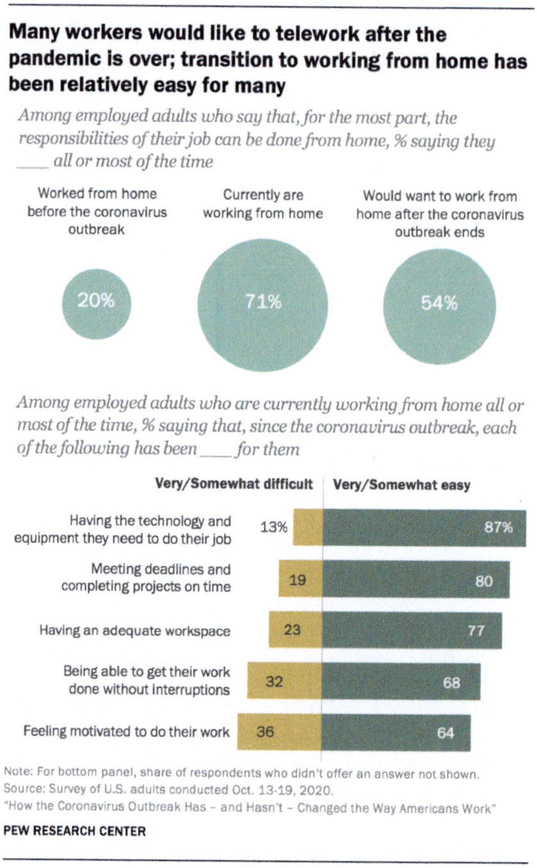

Figure 8.1. *Impact of the coronavirus on working patterns.*

Source: Pew Research Center.

Furthermore, another important factor which should not be overlooked is the impact on employee wellbeing (Hungler, 2022; Ilsoe & Soderqvist; Jarota, 2022; Jha & Singh, 2019; Jiang & Yao, 2020; Jirjahn, 2022). While working from home does offer certain benefits in terms of allowing people more freedom with regards to their daily routines, it can also lead to feelings of isolation and loneliness if individuals do not receive enough social interaction throughout the day. As such, employers need to consider carefully how best they can support their staff during this period by providing them with regular contact points (e.g., via video conferencing) as well as ensuring that all necessary resources are available so that everyone feels supported regardless of where they are located. Finally, before implementing any changes related to remote working policies, organizations should take into account both local laws and regulations regarding labor rights as well as international standards set by bodies such as The International Labor Organization (ILO) (Ormaetxea, 2019; Ozkiziltan, 2019, 2020; Peetz, 2021; Peetz et al., 2020; Peruzzo et al.; Pitteloud, 2022). This will help ensure that all employees involved in these arrangements receive fair treatment regardless of where they live or work from – something which is essential for maintaining good relationships between employer and employee going forward. It will also provide guidance on what kind responsibilities employers have towards those who choose or are required to work remotely – including matters relating pay rates, hours worked, etc. – thus helping them make informed decisions about implementing such policies within their organizations.

Whereas working from home does offer many benefits – particularly in terms of providing more flexible arrangements – there are also several potential drawbacks which must be taken into consideration before deciding whether this approach will be appropriate for different workplaces (Beattie, 2019; Bechter et al., 2021; Bedkar & Prashad, 2020; Behrens et al., 2020; Behrens & Pekarek, n.d.; Belizon, 2019). It is therefore essential for employers looking into introducing such measures to carefully evaluate all relevant factors before doing so in order to ensure maximum success going forward. The concept of working from home has become increasingly popular in recent years, with many employers now offering their employees the option to work remotely.

This approach can bring a number of benefits for both employers and employees alike – such as increased productivity, improved job satisfaction and reduced costs associated with commuting (Ritson, 2019a, b; Riva & Rizza, 2021; Roche, n.d.; Roche & Gormley, 2020; Rosetti, 2019; Roy & Dubey, 2022). However, it is important to note that while there are numerous advantages associated with allowing staff to work from home on an occasional or regular basis – particularly in terms of providing more flexible arrangements – there are also several potential drawbacks which must be taken into consideration before deciding whether this approach will suit your particular workplace environment best. The popularity of this modality may be linked to specific events or crises such as the COVID-19 pandemic (*see* Figure 8.2).

In order to evaluate the pros and cons of introducing a 'work from home' policy within your organization, it is essential to consider various factors such as employee wellbeing, job performance, communication issues, security concerns, and legal implications. For example, research conducted by González-Molina et al. (2019) found that while remote working can lead to greater autonomy for employees and improved job satisfaction levels, it can also result in feelings of isolation due to lack of face-to-face contact with colleagues. Similarly, Kumar & Sharma (2020) highlighted how working from home during the COVID-19 pandemic had led some individuals feeling overwhelmed by having no clear boundaries between their personal life and professional responsibilities. On the other hand, however Lambert & Lambert (2020) argued that when managed correctly remote working could actually have positive effects on employee wellbeing due to its ability to provide greater flexibility around hours worked.

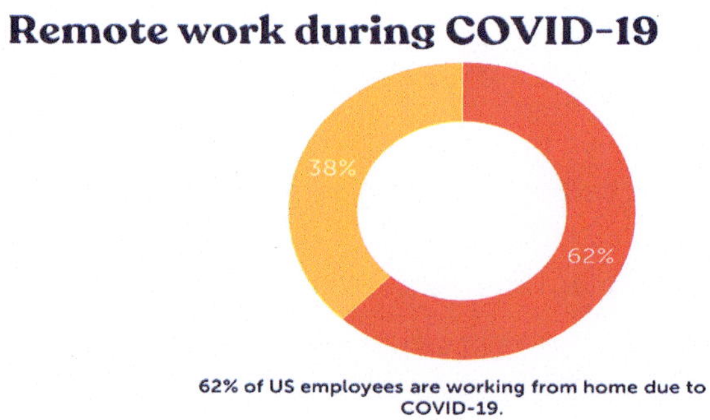

Figure 8.2. *Remote working trends in the USA during COVID-19.*

Source: Talent Lyft and Gallup.

Overall then it is clear that while there are certainly many advantages associated with allowing staff members to work remotely on occasion or even regularly – depending upon individual circumstances – careful evaluation of all relevant factors should take place prior to making any decisions about implementing such measures within an organization (Gall, 2021; Gardawski & Towalski, 2020; Gasparri, 2021; Gasparri et al., 2019; Gasparri & Tassinari, 2020; Gavin, 2022). By doing so you will ensure maximum success going forward whilst minimizing any potential risks posed by introducing a 'work from home' policy. One way to ensure that any remote working arrangements are managed effectively is through the use of collaborative software.

This type of technology allows staff members to communicate and collaborate with each other in real-time regardless of their physical location. For example, Slack is a popular platform which enables users to send messages, share files and even hold video conferences with colleagues from anywhere in the world. Similarly, Microsoft Teams provides an integrated workspace where teams can work together on projects, store documents securely and access shared calendars.

Despite the many potential benefits associated with allowing employees to work remotely – such as improved wellbeing and increased productivity – careful consideration should be given prior implementing any changes within an organization (Katsabian, 2021; Kilic, 2021; Kolling & Schnabel, 2022; Kowalewska, 2020; Kupec et al., 2022; Lamare & Budd, 2022). Indeed, this approach has been associated with the notion of a digital nomad.

The concept of the digital nomad is becoming increasingly popular in today's society (Cillo & Pradella, 2019; Civinskas & Dvorak, 2019; Clayton, 2021; Clibborn, 2019, 2020, 2021). A digital nomad is someone who works remotely, often traveling from place to place while doing so. This type of lifestyle has been made possible by advances in technology which allow staff members to communicate and collaborate with each other in real-time regardless of their physical location. There are many potential benefits associated with allowing employees to work remotely such as improved wellbeing due to reduced stress levels and increased productivity due to fewer distractions. Furthermore, it can also help organizations save money on office space rental costs and reduce their carbon footprint by reducing the need for commuting.

Nevertheless, there are some drawbacks that should be taken into consideration before implementing any changes (Stapley, 2021; Stevis, 2022; Svec et al., 2021; Tavora, 2019; Teipen & Mehl, 2021; Tesser & Serapioni, 2021). For example, remote working can lead to feelings of isolation amongst staff members if they do not have access to regular face-to-face contact with colleagues or managers. Additionally, there may be difficulties when it comes to monitoring employee performance, ensuring compliance with company policies, and maintaining a secure IT infrastructure.

In order for organizations wishing to embrace this new way of working successfully then they must ensure that all staff members remain connected no matter where they may be located (Cesari et al., 2019; Chan, 2020a, b; Chantziaras et al., 2020; Chen et al., n.d., 2023; Cillo & Pradella, 2019). Fortunately, there are now numerous software solutions available which enable teams to stay connected even when geographically dispersed – such as Slack and Microsoft Teams. These platforms provide users with a range of features including messaging services, file sharing capabilities, video conferencing facilities and shared calendars – thus enabling them to collaborate effectively whilst remaining productive at all times. By utilizing collaborative software solutions, you will be able to ensure that all staff members remain connected no matter where they may be located thus maximizing success going forward whilst minimizing any potential risks posed by introducing a 'work from home' policy (Cabeza, 2019; Cam, 2021; Campolieti, 2020; Cesari et al., 2019; Chan, 2020a, b; Chantziaras et al., 2020). The concept of the digital nomad is becoming increasingly popular in today's society, but organizations must take into account both its advantages and disadvantages before making any decisions about how best implement these changes within their own workplace environment. With the right tools however, companies can reap the rewards associated with remote working without compromising on security or efficiency – ultimately leading towards greater success. Perhaps, this type of approach can help economies deal with the ever-enduring problem of youth unemployment.

8.2. YOUTH SOCIAL AND PHYSICAL MOBILITY IN THE WORKPLACE

In recent years, the job market has seen a dramatic shift in youth mobility (Adewumi, 2021; Agarwal et al., 2020; Ahuja, 2020; Amosse et al., 2019; Archel et al., 2022; Ashwin et al., 2020). As technology advances and globalization continues to expand, young people are increasingly taking advantage of opportunities to work abroad or pursue remote employment. This trend is having far-reaching implications for both employers and employees alike.

A number of studies have explored the motivations behind this phenomenon (Chan, 2020a, b; Chantziaras et al., 2020; Chen et al., n.d., 2023; Cillo & Pradella, 2019; Civinskas & Dvorak, 2019). For example, research conducted by the ILO suggests that many young people are drawn to international work due to its potential for higher wages and greater career advancement opportunities than those available domestically. Other factors such as cultural exchange, personal growth, and increased independence may also be at play.

At the same time, there are several challenges associated with youth mobility in the job market that must be taken into account when evaluating its impact on society as a whole (Das & Singh, 2021; de Amorim et al., 2019; de Luna, 2022; De Prins et al., 2020; de Vaate, 2021; Demougin et al., 2019). One key issue is access: not all individuals have equal opportunity to take advantage of these new possibilities due to financial constraints or lack of knowledge about how best to navigate foreign labor markets. Additionally, some experts argue that while global mobility can bring economic benefits in certain cases, it can also lead to exploitation if proper safeguards are not put in place—for instance through inadequate regulation or weak enforcement mechanisms for protecting workers' rights overseas.

Theories from various disciplines offer insight into how we might better understand these issues and their implications for policymaking going forward (Godino & Molina, 2022; Gooberman, 2022; Goods & Ellem; Goyer et al., 2022; Graca, 2021; Gramano & Gaudio, 2019). For instance, sociologist Saskia Sassen's concept of "global cities" provides an important framework for understanding why certain locations become hubs for international migration flows—and what kinds of social inequalities they create along the way—while economist Paul Romer's theory of endogenous growth offers insights into how countries can use immigration policies strategically as part of broader development strategies aimed at boosting productivity levels over time.

At present there is still much debate surrounding youth mobility in the job market (Martin, 2022; Martin et al., 2021; McCrystal & Hardy, 2021; Mezihorak et al.; Morritt, 2022; Murphy & Turner, 2020). However, existing case studies provide valuable lessons about what works and what does not work. In particular they suggest that successful approaches tend to involve strong public-private partnerships between governments and businesses which prioritize both economic gains and social justice objectives simultaneously—such as providing training programs designed specifically with migrant workers' needs in mind or creating incentives for companies who hire locally rather than relying solely on imported labor forces from abroad. As Figure 8.3 shows, there is generalized mobility in contemporary lives.

Youth mobility will continue playing an important role within today's globalized economy (Colas-Neila & Fargas, 2019; Collins et al., 2020; Cooke et al., 2019; Croucher & Okland, 2021; D'Art, 2020). However, further research is needed before we can fully assess its long-term effects on societies around the world —both positive and negative. By exploring different theoretical perspectives, examining existing evidence, engaging stakeholders across sectors, and developing effective regulatory frameworks, policymakers should be able move towards more equitable outcomes which benefit everyone involved.

Case studies of backpacking have become increasingly popular in recent years, as they provide valuable insights into the motivations and experiences of young people who choose to travel abroad. While there is a growing body of literature on this topic, much remains unknown about how these journeys shape individuals' lives and their relationships with others. To better understand the implications of youth mobility, it is important to consider both its economic and social impacts. One example of these dynamics is the differential access to backpacking.

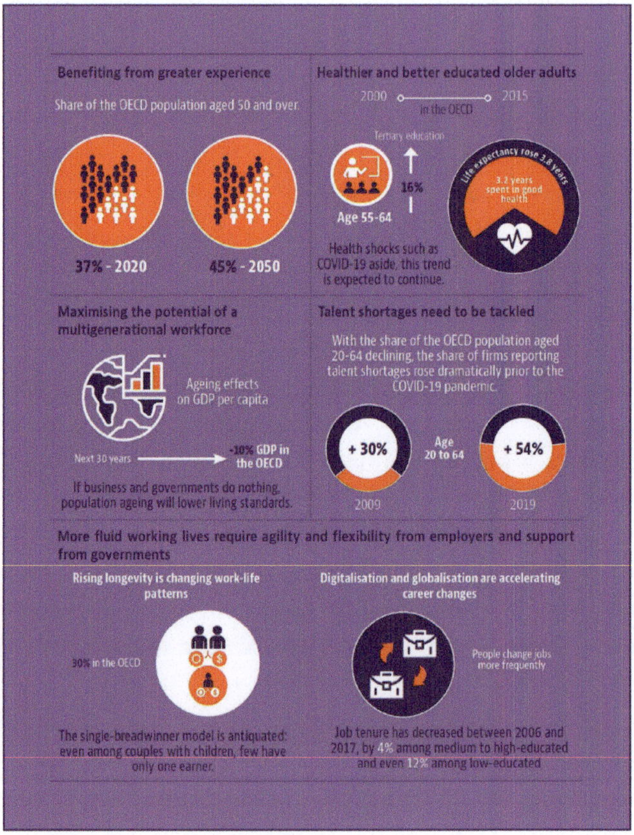

Figure 8.3. *The shifts towards more mobility in our life choices.*

Source: OECD iLibrary.

Economically speaking, backpacking can be seen as an investment in human capital that has potential benefits for both host countries and migrants (Smith, 2019; Solaiman; Stanev, 2019; Stanford, 2021; Stapley, 2021; Stevis, 2022; Svec et al., 2021; Tavora, 2019). For example, research suggests that international students often bring new skills which can help stimulate local economies while also providing them with opportunities for personal growth. On the other hand, some scholars argue that such activities may lead to increased competition for jobs or even displacement of local workers —particularly when labor markets are already saturated.

From a social perspective, case studies suggest that backpacking can create meaningful connections between travelers from different backgrounds—allowing them to share stories, learn from one another, and gain greater appreciation for cultural diversity. At the same time however, there are concerns about exploitation within certain industries (such as hospitality) where migrant workers may not receive adequate wages or protection under law. Further research is needed before we can fully assess the impact of youth mobility on societies around the world —both positive and negative. By exploring different theoretical perspectives, examining existing evidence, engaging stakeholders across sectors, and developing effective regulatory frameworks policymakers should be able move towards more equitable outcomes which benefit everyone involved.

For younger people about to join university, there is the option of gap year programs.

Gap year programs have become increasingly popular in recent years, with many young people taking a break from their studies to travel and explore the world. While there are numerous benefits associated with such experiences, there is also an ongoing debate about the potential risks of youth mobility. It is pertinent to provide an overview of existing case studies on gap year programs and discuss some of the key issues that need to be addressed in order for them to be successful.

The first issue that needs to be considered is legal protection for those participating in gap year programs. In many countries, laws governing labor rights and immigration are not well-defined or enforced when it comes to young people traveling abroad for extended periods of time (Haipeter, 2020; Hakansta et al., n.d.; Hamberger, 2020; Harvey & Turnbull, 2020; Hendy, 2022; Herrero, 2022; Hilgert, 2019). As a result, they may find themselves vulnerable to exploitation by employers or other individuals who take advantage of their lack of knowledge about local regulations and customs. It is therefore essential that governments create clear guidelines outlining what rights participants have while abroad so as to ensure their safety and wellbeing during their travels. This ought to be an effective response to trends in young people seeking work (*see* Figure 8.4).

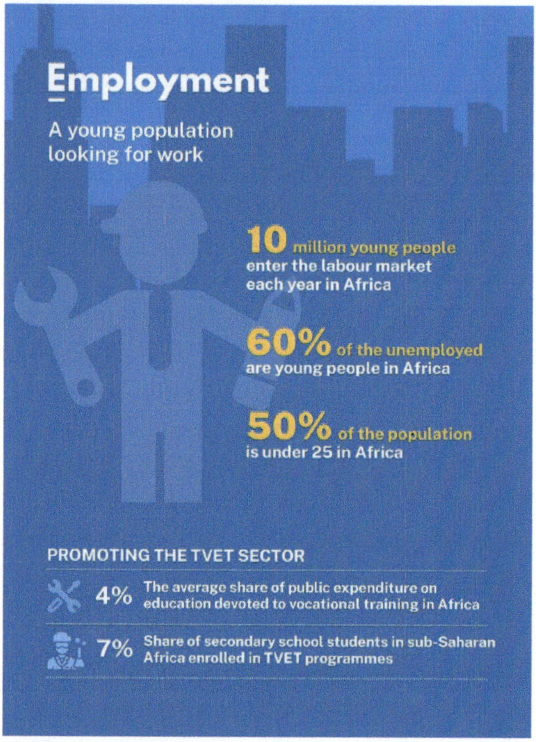

Figure 8.4. *Trends of a younger population looking for work.*

Source: IIPE-UNESCO Dakar.

Another important factor which must be taken into account when assessing the success (or failure) of gap year programs relates to economic considerations. Many countries rely heavily on remittances sent back home by migrant workers—particularly those working in low-wage jobs—in order to support their families financially while they are away from home. If these funds do not reach intended recipients due either directly or indirectly through gaps in regulation, then this could lead to both short-term hardship as well as long-term poverty if left unchecked.

Finally, we must consider social justice implications associated with youth mobility. For example, research has shown that certain groups —such as women, ethnic minorities, LGBTQ+ individuals —are more likely than others to face discrimination when seeking employment opportunities overseas (Jarota, 2022; Jha & Singh, 2019; Jiang & Yao, 2020; Jirjahn, 2022; Joyce et al.; Junior, 2022; Kaine, 2020; Katsabian, 2021). Therefore, it is essential that policies designed around gap year programs include measures which promote inclusion regardless gender identity race religion, etc. Additionally, any initiatives should strive towards creating equitable outcomes across all stakeholders involved including host communities' businesses government agencies civil society organizations, etc.

Further research is needed before we can fully assess the impact of youth mobility on societies around the world (Truyols, 2019; Tu et al., 2022; Velluti, 2022; Vinichenko et al., 2020; Vulkan & Larsson, 2019; Walker, 2020; Walters & Wadsworth, 2020).

Ultimately by studying existing case studies we can gain valuable lessons about what works (and what does not). This calls for experimentation such as flexicurity (Jirjahn, 2022; Joyce et al.; Junior, 2022; Kaine, 2020; Katsabian, 2021; Kilic, 2021; Kolling & Schnabel, 2022; Kowalewska, 2020). The concept of flexicurity has been gaining traction in recent years as a way to address the challenges posed by youth mobility. Flexicurity is an approach which seeks to combine flexibility and security for workers, particularly those who are young or from disadvantaged backgrounds. It involves providing jobseekers with access to training and education opportunities while also ensuring that they have adequate protection against exploitation and discrimination in the workplace. This can be achieved through various measures such as introducing minimum wage legislation, strengthening collective bargaining rights, or creating incentives for employers to hire locally rather than relying on imported labor forces from abroad.

In order to evaluate the effectiveness of flexicurity policies it is important to consider both descriptive and explanatory models (Markey, 2020; Martin, 2022; Martin et al., 2021; McCrystal & Hardy, 2021; Mezihorak et al.; Morritt, 2022; Murphy & Turner, 2020). Descriptive models provide insight into how different countries have implemented these approaches—for example, Denmark's use of active labor market policies (ALMPs) which focus on providing unemployed individuals with skills-based training programs tailored specifically towards their needs—while explanatory models help us understand why certain strategies may work better than others in particular contexts. For instance, research suggests that ALMPs tend to be more successful when combined with other forms of social protection such as unemployment insurance or income support schemes.

There are some limitations associated with this approach which should not be overlooked (O'Keeffe & Papadopoulos, 2021; Oberfichtner et al., 2020; Opute & Koch, 2020; Ormaetxea, 2019; Ozkiziltan, 2019). For instance, critics argue that flexicurity policies often fail to take into account structural inequalities within societies —such as gender disparities or racial discrimination —which can disproportionately benefit certain groups over others. Additionally, there is evidence suggesting that these types of initiatives may not always result in improved employment outcomes due factors like inadequate funding levels or lack of coordination between government departments and other r organizations, etc.

Geographic mobility is an increasingly important issue in the world of work (Williamson et al., 2019; Wright; Wright & McLaughlin, 2021; Xie & Zhou, 2022; Yan, 2019; Yang et al.; Zbyszewska, 2021). As populations become more mobile, the implications for individuals, communities, and societies are far-reaching. In particular, youth mobility has been a focus of much research and debate in recent years. On one hand, it can be seen as a positive force that allows young people to gain new skills and experiences while also providing economic benefits to their home countries through remittances or other forms of investment. On the other hand, there are concerns about potential negative impacts such as increased inequality or exploitation of vulnerable workers by unscrupulous employers.

In order to better understand these issues, it is necessary to look at both descriptive models which provide an overview of existing trends as well as explanatory models which attempt to explain why certain patterns emerge in the first place (Tiraboschi, 2020; Tomassetti, 2021; Trif & Szabo; Truyols, 2019; Tu et al., 2022; Velluti, 2022; Vinichenko et al., 2020). For example, studies have shown that migration flows tend to follow certain paths—such as from rural areas into cities—and this could be due either structural factors (e.g., lack of job opportunities) or individual motivations (e.g., desire for higher wages). Additionally, researchers have identified various push/pull factors which influence decisions about where people choose to move including economic incentives, family ties, political instability, etc.

At the same time however we must also consider how different stakeholders view these issues differently —for instance governments may prioritize economic growth whereas NGOs might emphasize social justice objectives (Giannakopoulos & Laliotis, 2020; Giraud, 2020; Godino & Molina, 2022; Gooberman, 2022; Goods & Ellem; Goyer et al., 2022). This means that any policy interventions need to take into account multiple perspectives if they are going to achieve meaningful results. The next section focuses on the brain drain that the developing world is grappling with even as gap year students visit to engage in charity and leisure.

8.3. DEVELOPING COUNTRIES DEALING WITH A BRAIN DRAIN

Brain drains, also known as human capital flight, is a phenomenon in which highly skilled and educated individuals migrate from their home countries to other nations with more attractive economic opportunities (Hamberger, 2020; Harvey & Turnbull, 2020; Hendy, 2022; Herrero, 2022; Hilgert, 2019; Hirsch & Mueller, 2020). This has become an increasingly pressing issue for many developing countries that are struggling to retain their most talented citizens. In this section, we will explore the various arguments surrounding brain drain and examine how it affects both sending and receiving countries.

The primary argument in favor of brain drain is that it can benefit both sending and receiving countries by providing access to new skill sets and knowledge (Ahuja, 2020; Amosse et al., 2019; Archel et al., 2022; Ashwin et al., 2020; Avgar, 2020; Baines & Armstrong, 2019). For example, when highly-skilled professionals move abroad they often bring valuable expertise with them such as technological know-how or business acumen which can help stimulate economic growth in the host country. Additionally, these migrants may be able to transfer money back home through remittances which can provide much needed financial support for families living in poverty-stricken areas.

On the other hand, there are several criticisms of brain drain that must be taken into consideration when evaluating its overall impact on society. One major concern is that it leads to a "brain waste" effect where those who leave do not use their full potential due to lack of opportunity or resources available in the host country (Kapur & McHale, 2005). Furthermore, some argue that brain drain exacerbates inequality between rich and poor nations since those who have higher levels of education tend to migrate more frequently than those without (Docquier & Rapoport, 2012). Finally, there is evidence suggesting that migration does not always lead to positive outcomes for either party; research shows that while some migrants experience success after moving abroad others struggle with language barriers or cultural differences leading them into precarious situations (Bhagwati, 2004). As Figure 8.5 shows, the recent COVID-19 pandemic had a profound effect on brain drain.

High skilled labor migration is a phenomenon that has been gaining traction in recent years as more and more people move abroad for better job opportunities or higher wages (Goods & Ellem; Goyer et al., 2022; Graca, 2021; Gramano & Gaudio, 2019; Grodem & Hippe, 2019; Guillaume, 2022).

This type of migration can have both positive and negative effects on the countries involved depending on the context. It is pertinent to discuss some of the "pull" and "push" factors associated with high skilled labor migration by looking at contemporary examples from around the world.

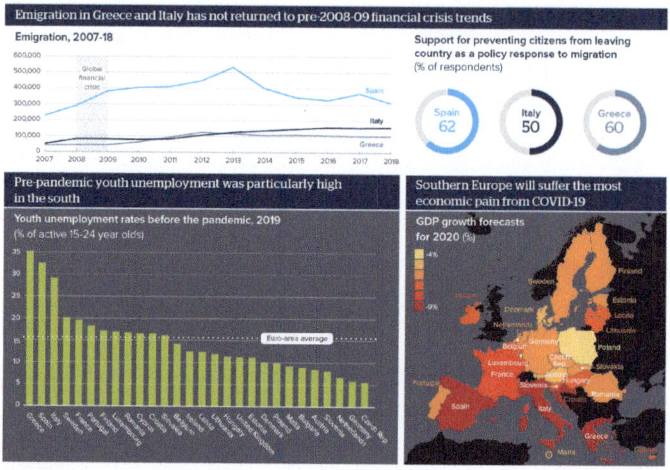

Figure 8.5. *COVID-19 worsens Southern Europe brain drain.*

Source: Oxford Analytica Daily Brief.

The most obvious pull factor for high skilled labor migrants is economic opportunity – they are often attracted to countries where there are better job prospects or higher wages than what they would find in their home country (Docquier & Rapoport, 2012). For example, many Indian IT professionals have moved to the United States due to its strong economy and abundance of tech jobs (Kapur & McHale, 2005). Similarly, many African doctors migrate to Europe or North America because these regions offer much higher salaries than what they could earn back home (OECD, 2018).

On the other hand, push factors refer to conditions that make it difficult for individuals to stay in their home country such as political instability or lack of access to resources like healthcare or education (Bhagwati, 2004). For instance, Syrian refugees fleeing civil war have had no choice but to leave their homes behind in search of safety elsewhere. Similarly, Venezuelans escaping an economic crisis have also been forced out of their homeland due poverty and food shortages.

In addition to these two main categories there are also other important considerations when discussing high skilled labor migration such as cultural differences between host countries and immigrants which can lead either successful integration into society or feelings of alienation among newcomers (Bhagwati, 2004). While some migrants may experience financial success in their new home, they may still feel disconnected from the culture and language of their host country. Others are so disillusioned by the experience that they opt to return home at the earliest opportunity.

The impact of brain drain on industrialized countries is generally positive as these nations benefit from an influx of highly skilled workers who can contribute to economic growth (OECD, 2018). For example, many tech companies in Silicon Valley have been able to hire talented engineers from India or China which has allowed them to stay competitive in a global market. On the other hand, developing countries are more likely to suffer negative consequences due to brain drain since they lose valuable human capital that could be used for development projects such as building infrastructure or providing healthcare services (Bhagwati, 2004). This is especially true for African nations where doctors and nurses often migrate abroad leaving behind a shortage of medical professionals at home.

While industrialized countries may benefit economically from an influx of talent, developing countries tend to suffer due to loss of valuable human capital needed for development projects (Ackers, 2020; Addison & Teixeira, 2019a, b; Adewumi, 2021; Agarwal et al., 2020; Ahuja, 2020). It is therefore important for governments around the world to take into account both push and pull factors when designing policies related immigration so that all parties involved can reap maximum benefits while minimizing potential harms caused by brain drain. In recent years, the political economy of expatriates has become an increasingly important topic for both academics and policy makers. As Figure 8.6 shows, this is a problem that can impact various countries with some possibilities of intersection.

This is due to the fact that high skilled labor migration can have a significant impact on both sending and receiving countries (Walters & Wadsworth, 2020; Warner, 2019; William & Cunningham, 2021; Williamson et al., 2019). On one hand, industrialized nations such as the United States or Canada may benefit from an influx of talented individuals who bring with them valuable skills and knowledge (Borjas, 2003). This can lead to increased economic growth through innovation, improved productivity levels, and higher wages for native workers. On the other hand, market fundamentalist perspectives on migrant labor tend to overlook the potential harms caused by brain drain in developing countries.

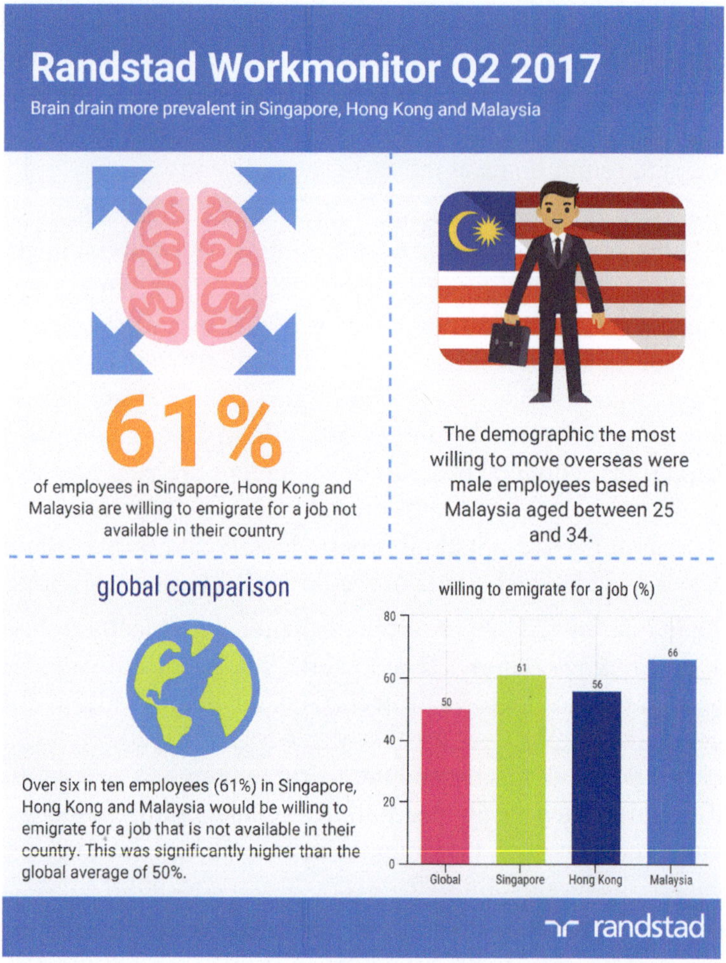

Figure 8.6. *Brain drains in Malaysia, Hong Kong, and Singapore.*

Source: Randstad Malaysia.

This is because these views focus solely on economic gains and ignore social costs such as loss of human capital needed for development projects (Kapur et al., 2005). Furthermore, they often fail to take into account the fact that many migrants are forced to leave their home countries due to poverty or political instability (Castles & Miller, 2009). As a result, policies based on this perspective may lead to further exploitation of vulnerable populations and exacerbate existing inequalities between sending and receiving nations.

In order to address these issues, it is important for governments around the world to consider both push and pull factors when designing immigration policies. For example, some countries have implemented programs which allow skilled workers from developing nation's access to higher education opportunities abroad while also providing incentives for them to return home after completing their studies (Gibney, 2010). Such initiatives can help ensure that expatriates contribute positively towards development in their home country while still allowing them access educational resources not available locally.

Migration has become an increasingly important issue in today's globalized world. While market fundamentalist perspectives may be useful in certain contexts, they cannot provide a comprehensive understanding of all aspects related immigration policy making (Svec et al., 2021; Tavora, 2019; Teipen & Mehl, 2021; Tesser & Serapioni, 2021; Thomas & Turnbull, 2021; Thornthwaite & Sheldon, 2019). It is therefore essential for governments around the world to take into account both economic benefits as well as social costs associated with migrant labor when formulating policies so that all parties involved can reap maximum benefits while minimizing potential harms caused by brain drain.

Marxist critiques of brain drain have become increasingly relevant in recent years as the phenomenon has grown in scope and complexity (Bischoff et al., 2021; Bogoeski, 2022; Bondy, 2022; Boumans, 2022; Bourguignon & Floquet, 2019; Bradley & Rowland, 2021). Marxists argue that migration is a result of global capitalism, which creates an unequal distribution of resources between countries (Gibney, 2010). This leads to a situation where people from poorer countries are forced to migrate due to lack of economic opportunities at home. Furthermore, they contend that migrant labor serves only to further entrench existing power structures by providing cheap labor for wealthy nations while depriving developing countries of valuable human capital (Foner, 2002).

In order to address these issues, it is essential for governments around the world to take into account both economic benefits as well as social costs associated with migrant labor when formulating policies so that all parties involved can reap maximum benefits while minimizing potential harms caused by brain drain (Jirjahn, 2022; Joyce et al.; Junior, 2022; Kaine, 2020; Katsabian, 2021; Kilic, 2021; Kolling & Schnabel, 2022). For instance, some countries have implemented initiatives such as "brain circulation" whereby expatriates are encouraged to return home after completing their studies and work commitments. Additionally, governments should strive towards creating an environment where immigrants feel welcome and respected so that they can fully integrate into society without fear of discrimination or persecution (Foner, 2002).

Moreover, international organizations must work together in order to ensure fair treatment and equitable access to resources for all migrants regardless their country origin or destination (Roche, n.d.; Roche & Gormley, 2020; Rosetti, 2019; Roy & Dubey, 2022; Roy, 2022; Roychowdhury, 2019; Rubery et al.). Only then will we be able to move beyond simplistic market-based approaches and towards more holistic solutions capable of addressing the complex challenges posed by contemporary migration patterns. Brain drain has been a major issue in the global economy for decades, and it is often seen as a neo-colonial and quasi-imperialist instrumentality. This phenomenon occurs when highly skilled individuals migrate from their home countries to other nations with better economic opportunities or higher wages. While this can be beneficial for the receiving country, it can also have negative consequences on the sending nation due to loss of human capital and potential brain gain (Kapur et al., 2005).

The effects of brain drain are particularly pronounced in developing countries where there is already limited access to resources such as education, healthcare, and employment opportunities (Foner, 2002). In these contexts, migration of educated professionals can lead to further disparities between rich and poor populations as well as increased inequality within society (Kapur et al., 2005). Moreover, some scholars argue that brain drain serves to perpetuate existing power dynamics by allowing wealthy nations to "poach" talent from poorer ones without providing any meaningful compensation or support (Foner, 2002; Kapur et al., 2005).

In order to mitigate these issues associated with brain drain, governments must take proactive steps towards creating an environment conducive for both immigrants and native citizens alike (Mailand, 2019; Markey, 2020; Martin, 2022; Martin et al., 2021; McCrystal & Hardy, 2021; Mezihorak et al.; Morritt, 2022). For instance, they should strive towards improving educational infrastructure so that more people have access to quality training programs which will enable them to stay competitive in today's job market. Additionally, policies should be implemented which encourage foreign investment while simultaneously protecting local industries from being taken over by multinational corporations. Furthermore, there should be ongoing engagement and support for those that choose to complete their studies abroad (Kapur et al., 2005). Meanwhile the developed nations are facing another entirely different problem of de-industrialization.

8.4. THE DE-INDUSTRIALIZATION OF ADVANCED NATIONS AND THE WORKFORCE

De-industrialization is a process of economic restructuring that has been occurring in many countries around the world since the 1970s (Howell, 2021; Hungler, 2022; Ilsoe & Soderqvist; Jarota, 2022; Jha & Singh, 2019; Jiang & Yao, 2020). It involves a shift away from manufacturing and industrial production, towards services and other non-manufacturing activities. This shift has had far-reaching implications for economies, societies, and individuals alike. In this section, we will explore what de-industrialization is, its causes and consequences, as well as some of the debates surrounding it.

At its core, de-industrialization refers to a decline in employment in manufacturing industries relative to other sectors such as services or agriculture (Schlachter, 2019; Schmidt & Muller, 2021; Schofield-Georgeson, 2022; Schofield-Georgeson & Rawling, 2020). This can be seen most clearly when looking at changes in gross domestic product (GDP) over time; if GDP growth is driven primarily by service sector activity rather than industry then this indicates an economy undergoing de-industrialization. The phenomenon has been observed across developed nations including the United States and Europe but also developing countries like India and China where rapid economic growth has led to increased demand for services rather than goods produced through traditional industrial processes.

The causes of de-industrialization are complex but generally involve technological advances which have made certain types of labor obsolete or less competitive with cheaper alternatives abroad; globalization which allows companies to move their operations overseas; government policies such as deregulation which reduce barriers to entry into new markets; shifts in consumer preferences away from manufactured products towards services; and structural changes within economies due to aging populations or changing demographics among others factors (Teipen & Mehl, 2021; Tesser & Serapioni, 2021; Thomas & Turnbull, 2021; Thornthwaite & Sheldon, 2019, 2021). The consequences of deindustrialization vary depending on context but typically include job losses for those employed in affected industries leading to higher levels of unemployment particularly among lower skilled workers who may not have access to alternative sources of income or training opportunities needed for reemployment elsewhere; reduced wages due to competition from cheaper foreign labor forces resulting in decreased purchasing power for consumers; increased inequality between regions with different levels of development leading potentially lead social unrest or political instability; environmental degradation caused by pollution associated with industrial production; and finally slower overall economic growth due largely declining productivity gains associated with fewer investments being made into research and development (R&D).

Academic studies have highlighted both positive aspects related to de-industrialization such as improved living standards through greater access to services like healthcare education, etc., while also noting potential negative impacts on local communities whose livelihoods depend heavily on traditional forms of industry (Seghezzi; Sheldon & Thornthwaite, 2020; Smith, 2019; Solaiman; Stanev, 2019; Stanford, 2021; Stapley, 2021). For example, one study found that while there were significant benefits associated with moving away from heavy industry, these were often concentrated geographically leaving behind areas still dependent upon them struggling economically. Similarly, another study noted how despite increased incomes overall poverty rates remained unchanged suggesting that any gains were not evenly distributed throughout society. These findings suggest that policy makers need to take into account regional differences when formulating strategies to address issues related to de-industrialization.

There are various theories attempting to explain why certain countries experience more pronounced effects than others, however none provide a comprehensive explanation of all cases (Behrens et al., 2020; Behrens & Pekarek, n.d.; Belizon, 2019; Bellace et al., 2021; Ben & Sage, 2022; Berry & McDaniel, 2022). One popular theory suggests that 'latecomers,' i.e., those who enter the global market later – tend to suffer more severe consequences because they lack established infrastructure networks necessary to compete effectively against already established players. Another argues the opposite, namely early adopters benefit most since they are able capitalize first mover advantage before competitors catch up. Both these arguments are limited in scope. However, given the complexity of the issues further research is required to better understand underlying dynamics involved in each particular case study situation.

It is clear to see why debate surrounding the topic remains ongoing today given wide ranging implications both positive and negative terms discussed above (Addison & Teixeira, 2019b; Adewumi, 2021; Agarwal et al., 2020; Ahuja, 2020; Amosse et al., 2019; Archel et al., 2022). While much progress has been made in understanding nature causes effects various descriptive explanatory models exist, limitations remain making it difficult to draw definitive conclusions about best way forward addressing challenges posed by the process of de-industrialization. It is expected that going forward future generations will face similar problems unless appropriate measures taken now ensure sustainable long-term solutions implemented as soon as possible to prevent further damage being done. Figure 8.7 highlights some trends in de-industrialization.

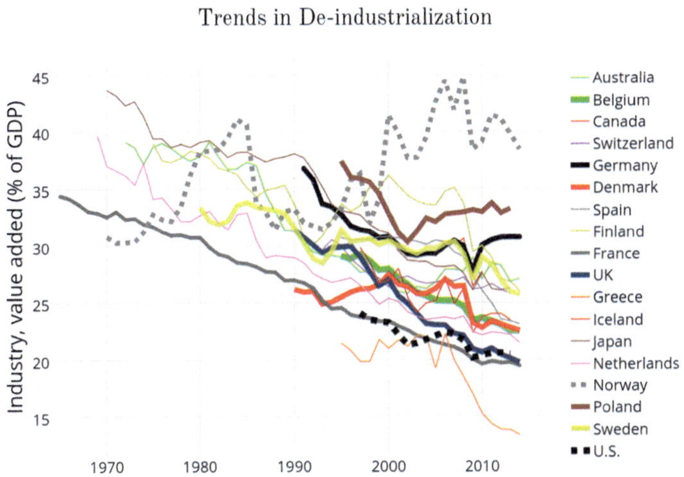

Figure 8.7. *Trends in European de-industrialization.*

Source: Plotly.

On one hand, there are those who argue that de-industrialization can lead to increased economic growth due to increased efficiency and productivity gains as well as improved access to global markets (Lawreniuk, 2023; Lee & Tapia, 2021; Leggett, 2019; Ligthart et al., 2022; Liu, 2023; Lize et al., 2022; Lloyd & Payne, 2021). This argument suggests that countries which have embraced de-industrialization have seen their economies grow faster than those which have not adopted such policies. For example, China's rapid industrial development over the past two decades has been largely attributed to its embrace of de-industrialization strategies. Similarly, India's economy has grown significantly since embracing similar policies in 1991.

On the other hand, there are also arguments suggesting that de-industrialization can lead to job losses and social unrest due to reduced employment opportunities in certain sectors or regions where industries were once located (Desai & Randeria, 2020; Devinatz, 2020, 2022; Di Carlo, 2020; Diessner et al., 2022; Dobbins et al., 2020). This argument suggests that while some countries may benefit from increased economic growth due to greater efficiency gains associated with de-industrialization processes; others may suffer from decreased employment opportunities leading them into poverty or even civil unrest if appropriate measures are not taken by governments or international organizations such as the World Bank or IMF (International Monetary Fund). Examples include Argentina during its 2001 financial crisis when unemployment rose dramatically following large scale factory closures resulting from government-imposed austerity measures; as well as Greece during its 2010 debt crisis when public sector jobs were cut drastically leading people on streets protesting against austerity measures implemented by European Union (EU) authorities at times.

In addition, there are also debates surrounding whether de-industrialization is necessarily a bad thing all times given potential benefits mentioned above (Schuessler et al., 2019; Schuhrke, 2019; Scrimger, 2020; Seghezzi; Sheldon & Thornthwaite, 2020; Smith, 2019). Some suggest companies able to take advantage of new technologies become a more competitive marketplace allowing them to increase profits margins reduce costs production since they are able to capitalize first mover advantage before competitors catch up. Both these arguments have limited scope however given complexity of the issues further research is required to better understand the underlying dynamics involved in each particular case study situation.

In order to better understand these issues, it is important to look at existing academic studies which have examined them in detail (Ozkiziltan, 2019, 2020; Peetz, 2021; Peetz et al., 2020; Peruzzo et al.; Pitteloud, 2022; Preminger & Bondy). For example, research conducted by economists such as David Autor and Daron Acemoglu suggests that while deindustrialization may bring short term gains in terms of economic growth, its long-term effects on employment levels can be more damaging than initially thought. Similarly, sociologists like Richard Sennett have argued that de-industrialization leads not only to job losses but also a decline in social capital due to reduced opportunities for meaningful work and community engagement among workers affected by factory closures or relocations overseas.

It is also worth noting that different models exist when attempting to explain why certain regions experience higher rates of de-industrialization than others (Colas-Neila & Fargas, 2019; Collins et al., 2020; Cooke et al., 2019; Croucher & Okland, 2021; D'Art, 2020; da Costa & Horn, 2021). For instance, some scholars suggest that globalization plays an important role here; with multinational corporations increasingly looking towards cheaper labor markets abroad rather than investing domestically – leading ultimately towards a hollowing out of local industry over time. Others however point out structural factors such as technological change or government policies which favor foreign investment over domestic production could also be responsible for driving down industrial activity within certain areas.

Finally, case studies examining particular instances where deindustrialization occurred provide useful insights into how best address challenges posed (Morritt, 2022; Murphy & Turner, 2020; Nespoli, 2019; Newman et al., 2019; Nga & Nga, 2021; Ngai, 2020; Nicklich & Helfen, 2019). One example would be city Detroit United States whose economy heavily reliant automotive manufacturing until mid-20th century when large number jobs lost result closure various car plants area. Despite efforts revive region since then still remains largely impoverished today highlighting potential dangers associated rapid changes industrial landscape without appropriate measures taken protect people's livelihoods future generations come.

Deindustrialization continues to remain a highly relevant subject in our contemporary world given the wide-ranging implications discussed above (Civinskas & Dvorak, 2019; Clayton, 2021; Clibborn, 2019, 2020, 2021; Colas-Neila & Fargas, 2019). While much progress has been made in understanding the nature and causes of its effects, various descriptive and explanatory models exist with their own limitations making it difficult to draw definitive conclusions about the best way forward when addressing the challenges posed going forward. Unless appropriate measures are taken now to ensure sustainable long-term solutions are implemented soon, future generations may face similar problems with further damage being done to both our environment and people's lives worldwide if current trends continue unchecked.

The impact of deindustrialization has reached countries like China which are considered the unmatched powerhouses of manufacturing and export today (*see* Figure 8.8). In this context, it is important to consider the potential of a new form of industrial relations as a way to cope with de-industrialization (Martin et al., 2021; McCrystal & Hardy, 2021; Mezihorak et al.; Morritt, 2022; Murphy & Turner, 2020; Nespoli, 2019). This could involve an approach that seeks to combine elements from both traditional and modern models in order to create a more balanced system which takes into account the needs of all stakeholders involved. Such an approach would need to be based on principles such as mutual respect, collaboration, and trust between employers and employees while also recognizing the importance of economic efficiency and productivity. It should also take into account various legal frameworks, ethical considerations, and social norms in order for it to be effective in practice.

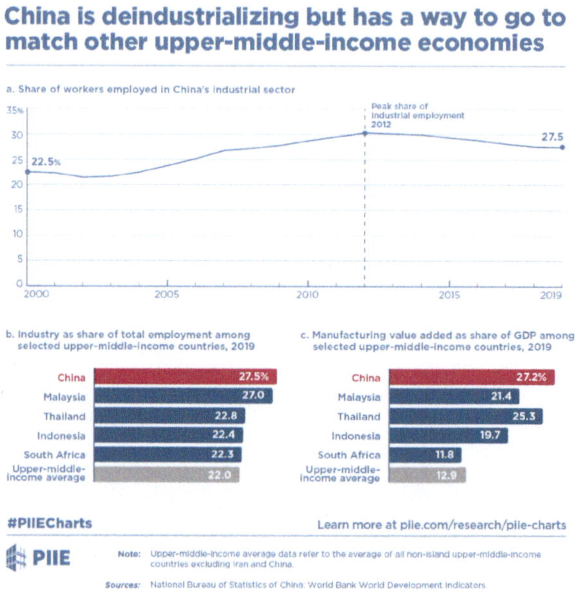

Figure 8.8. *Comparing China's de-industrialization with other middle-income countries.*

Source: PIIE.

To further explore this concept, we can look at some existing case studies which have been conducted over recent years (Drucza, 2019; Dupuis & Greer, 2022; Edwards & Hodder, 2022; Ellem, 2021; Ellem et al., 2020; Engblom & Lundberg, 2019). For example, research by academics such as Professor John Dunlop has highlighted how collective bargaining agreements (CBAs) can help improve working conditions for employees while still allowing companies to remain competitive within their respective markets (Dunlop et al., 2019). Similarly, other studies have shown how employee participation schemes can lead to increased job satisfaction among workers due to their feeling more valued by their employer (Kumar & Singh, 2018). These examples demonstrate how certain forms of industrial relations may offer viable solutions when addressing issues related to de-industrialization – however they are not without limitations either.

There is much debate surrounding what constitutes an appropriate model for dealing with deindustrialization – with many different theories being put forward each having its own merits but also drawbacks (Mahas-Demydas & Rudnytska, 2019; Mahmood & Banerjee, 2020; Mailand, 2019; Markey, 2020; Martin, 2022). While no single solution will work universally across all contexts given the complexity of the issue at hand; it is clear that any conceptual model developed must take into consideration multiple factors including economic efficiency, legal frameworks, and ethical considerations if it is truly going make a difference in helping prevent further damage. The final section in this final chapter will address the enduring problem of structural unemployment.

8.5. HOW ARE WE GOING TO DEAL WITH STRUCTURAL UNEMPLOYMENT?

Structural unemployment is a major issue in today's economy, and it has been the subject of much debate among economists (Leggett, 2019; Ligthart et al., 2022; Liu, 2023; Lize et al., 2022; Lloyd & Payne, 2021; Lukacova et al., 2022; Lyddon, 2021). Structural unemployment occurs when there are more job seekers than available jobs due to changes in technology, global competition, or other factors that make certain skills obsolete. In this closing section, we will discuss some of the key trends in structural unemployment and evaluate their implications for policy makers and employers.

One trend that has emerged over the past few decades is an increase in long-term structural unemployment (Giraud, 2020; Godino & Molina, 2022; Gooberman, 2022; Goods & Ellem; Goyer et al., 2022; Graca, 2021; Gramano & Gaudio, 2019). This type of unemployment occurs when workers remain unemployed for extended periods of time because they lack the necessary skills or experience to find new employment opportunities. According to research conducted by Harvard University economist Lawrence Katz, long-term structural unemployment rose from 4% in 1979 to 8% by 2007. This suggests that many workers have become "trapped" in low-paying jobs with little opportunity for advancement or wage growth due to technological advances and globalization which have made certain skills obsolete.

Another trend related to structural unemployment is a shift away from traditional manufacturing industries towards service sector jobs such as retail salespersons, food preparation workers, healthcare aides, etc., which tend to be lower paying than manufacturing positions but require fewer specialized skill sets (Fergus & Godfrey, 2021; Flynn & Schroder, 2021;

Foley & Williamson, 2021; Ford & Gillan, 2022; Ford & Ward, 2021). According to data from the Bureau of Labor Statistics (BLS), between 2000 and 2018 there was a net loss of 5 million manufacturing jobs while service sector employment increased by 10 million during this same period. This shift away from higher paying industrial work towards lower paying service sector positions has contributed significantly to rising levels of income inequality across developed countries like the United States where wages at all levels have stagnated since 1980 despite increases in productivity over this same period according to BLS data.

Another important factor contributing to increasing levels of structural unemployment is automation which has replaced human labor with machines on factory floors around the world leading directly or indirectly millions out of work worldwide according to Oxford Economics estimates (Thornthwaite & Sheldon, 2021; Tiraboschi, 2020; Tomassetti, 2021; Trif & Szabo; Truyols, 2019; Tu et al., 2022). Automation not only eliminates existing jobs but also creates new ones requiring different skill sets making it difficult for displaced workers who lack these new qualifications find suitable employment opportunities quickly enough before their savings run out leaving them no choice but accept whatever job they can get regardless of if its pay rate does not cover basic living expenses let alone provide any kind economic security.

Understanding current trends related structurally unemployed individuals provides valuable insights into how best address the problem in both the short term and longer term (Bhuta, 2022; Bischoff et al., 2021; Bogoeski, 2022; Bondy, 2022; Boumans, 2022; Bourguignon & Floquet, 2019). This can be done through ALMPs such as training programs targeted towards those affected most severely as well longer term through investments in education infrastructure to ensure future generations are better equipped to handle the changing nature of the modern workplace. Although the challenges posed by structurally unemployed populations are complex and multifaceted, recognizing the underlying causes helps to inform effective solutions to reduce the negative impacts associated with prolonged periods without gainful employment and hence improve the overall quality life for citizens and societies in general.

Neo-liberal perspectives on structural unemployment have become increasingly prominent in recent years (Clibborn, 2019, 2020, 2021; Colas-Neila & Fargas, 2019; Collins et al., 2020; Cooke et al., 2019). This is due to the fact that many of today's jobs require specific skills and qualifications, which are not always available to those who have been displaced from their previous positions. As a result, these individuals often find themselves unable to secure employment that pays enough for them to cover basic living expenses or provide any kind of economic security. This will become an increasingly important aspect of the post-COVID-19 recovery (*see* Figure 8.9).

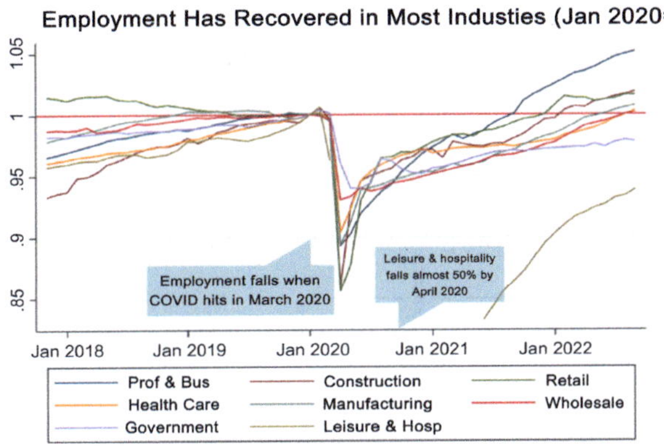

Figure 8.9. *Post-COVID-19 recoveries in various industries.*

Source: Roosevelt Institute.

In order to address this issue, it is important to understand the underlying causes of structural unemployment (Sheldon & Thornthwaite, 2020; Smith, 2019; Solaiman; Stanev, 2019; Stanford, 2021; Stapley, 2021). One key factor is technological advancement; as technology continues to evolve at an ever-increasing rate, certain job roles become obsolete while new ones emerge requiring different sets of skills and qualifications. For example, automation has replaced many manual labor jobs such as factory workers and assembly line operators with machines capable of performing tasks more efficiently than humans can. Similarly, advances in artificial intelligence (AI) have led some companies to replace customer service representatives with automated chatbots programmed with natural language processing algorithms designed specifically for customer interactions.

Another factor contributing towards structural unemployment is globalization; increased competition from foreign markets has caused businesses within domestic economies to downsize or close altogether resulting in large numbers of people being laid off without suitable alternative employment opportunities nearby (Devinatz, 2020, 2022; Di Carlo, 2020; Diessner et al., 2022; Dobbins et al., 2020, 2021). Furthermore, even when these individuals do manage to find work elsewhere, they may be required to possess additional qualifications which they previously did not need. Meanwhile those that support globalization ignore the plight of domestic workers who face competition from abroad.

To combat this problem, governments must implement ALMPs such as training programs targeted towards those affected most severely by the structurally unemployed population (Ramsay & Webster, 2019; Ravn & Oyum, 2020; Razak et al., 2022; Refslund & Arnholtz, 2022; Ritson, 2019a). These initiatives should focus on providing individuals access to resources necessary to develop relevant skill sets and equip them to better handle the changing nature of the modern workplace. Additionally, investments in education infrastructure ensure that future generations are better equipped to handle similar situations arising due rapid advancements in technology, also an essential part of a long-term solution. Another important philosophical and policy orientation that is associated with structural unemployment is the Washington Consensus.

The Washington Consensus is a set of economic policies that have been widely adopted by governments around the world since the 1980s (Gasparri et al., 2019; Gasparri & Tassinari, 2020; Gavin, 2022; Giannakopoulos & Laliotis, 2020; Giraud, 2020). It is based on neo-liberal principles, which emphasize free markets and limited government intervention in the economy. The consensus has come under increasing criticism in recent years due to its perceived failure to address structural unemployment and inequality. It is appropriate to provide an overview of the Washington Consensus, discuss emerging debates surrounding it, evaluate descriptive and explanatory models related to it, summarize existing case studies and their implications, as well as highlight relevant theories and their limitations.

The Washington Consensus was developed by economists at the IMF during negotiations with Latin American countries in 1989. Its main components include fiscal discipline; public expenditure prioritization; tax reform; liberalization of interest rates; competitive exchange rates; trade liberalization; foreign direct investment promotion; privatization of state enterprises; deregulation of labor markets and financial systems (Vulkan & Larsson, 2019; Walker, 2020; Walters & Wadsworth, 2020; Warner, 2019; William & Cunningham, 2021). These policies were intended to promote economic growth through increased competition among firms while reducing government spending on social services such as health care or education. However, critics argue that these policies have had negative consequences for many countries' economies due to their focus on short-term gains rather than long-term development strategies. In terms of descriptive models related to the Washington Consensus, there are several key arguments made by both proponents and opponents alike (Bray et al., 2020; Budd, 2020; Cabeza, 2019; Cam, 2021; Campolieti, 2020; Cesari et al., 2019; Chan, 2020a, b). Firstly, proponents argue that these policies can lead to greater efficiency within an economy due to increased competition between firms resulting from reduced regulation or lower taxes – this could potentially lead to higher levels of productivity overall if implemented correctly. On the other hand, opponents point out potential drawbacks associated with such measures including decreased job security, rising inequality, environmental degradation, etc. Furthermore, some scholars suggest that certain aspects of the consensus may be beneficial to developing nations when combined appropriately with ALMPs to ensure individuals access to the resources that are necessary to develop relevant skill sets and equip them to better handle the changing nature of the modern workplace.

Existing case studies also provide valuable insights into how different countries have responded to implementation of various elements of the consensus (Baturina et al., 2021; Beattie, 2019; Bechter et al., 2021; Bedkar & Prashad, 2020; Behrens et al., 2020; Behrens & Pekarek). For example, Chile experienced significant economic growth following the introduction neoliberal reforms in the early 1990s. However, this came at the cost of rising inequality and poverty levels amongst the population particularly those living in rural areas where access to the resources needed to take advantage of new opportunities are more difficult to obtain. Similarly, Argentina saw rapid expansion of the private sector but again this trend was accompanied by increased income disparities leading to widespread protests against austerity measures imposed by an agreement with the IMF in 2001. Meanwhile Okun's Law (*see* Figure 8.10) has attempted to explain unemployment and economic growth.

Okun's Law is an economic concept that states there is a direct relationship between the rate of unemployment and the rate of economic growth (Sanz et al., 2020; Schlachter, 2019; Schmidt & Muller, 2021; Schofield-Georgeson, 2022; Schofield-Georgeson & Rawling, 2020). It was first proposed by Arthur Okun, an American economist, in 1962. The law suggests that for every 1% increase in GDP, there will be a corresponding decrease in the unemployment rate of 2%. This means that if GDP increases by 5%, then the unemployment rate should drop by 10%.

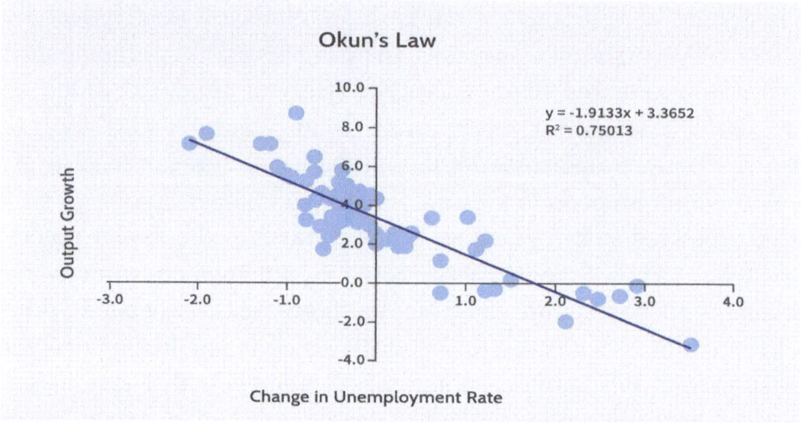

Figure 8.10. *Okun's law on output growth and unemployment.*

Source: Investopedia.

The assumptions behind Okun's Law are based on two main factors: labor market flexibility and aggregate demand (Baines & Armstrong, 2019; Baines & Cunningham, 2020; Bancarzewski & Hardy, 2021; Barklamb, 2021; Barry & Wilkinson, 2022). Labor market flexibility refers to how quickly workers can adjust their skills or move to different locations when job opportunities arise. Aggregate demand is determined by consumer spending, government spending, investment spending, and net exports. When these two factors are taken into account, it becomes easier to understand why changes in GDP have such a large impact on employment levels.

Despite its usefulness as an analytical tool for understanding macroeconomic trends, Okun's Law has some limitations which must be considered before using it as a policy guide (Novitz & Andrijasevic, 2020; Nowak, 2021; Nurlinah et al., 2021; O'Keeffe & Papadopoulos, 2021; Oberfichtner et al., 2020). For example, it does not take into account structural changes within economies such as technological advances or shifts in global trade patterns which could lead to long-term changes in employment levels even without any change in GDP growth rates. Additionally, since this law only looks at short-term fluctuations rather than long-term trends it may not accurately reflect underlying economic conditions over time periods longer than one year or so.

Okun's Law can help explain structural unemployment but cannot provide solutions for preventing or mitigating its effects on individuals and communities affected by high levels of joblessness due to changing economic conditions beyond their control (Ashwin et al., 2020; Avgar, 2020;

Baines & Armstrong, 2019; Baines & Cunningham, 2020; Bancarzewski & Hardy, 2021). To address this issue governments, need to implement policies designed specifically with structural unemployment prevention and mitigation goals in mind such as providing targeted training programs for those who have been displaced from their jobs due to automation or other technological advancements; increasing access to education; creating incentives for businesses investing locally; expanding public works projects, etc. These types of initiatives can help ensure that people remain employed despite rapid changes occurring within economies around them while also helping reduce inequality gaps caused by persistent disparities between certain groups within society who tend to suffer more from prolonged periods of joblessness than others do.

Although Okun's Law provides useful insights into macroeconomic trends related to employment levels, its limitations mean that policymakers must look beyond just this single metric when attempting to tackle issues like structural unemployment (Lukacova et al., 2022; Lyddon, 2021; Lyutov, 2022; MacKenzie & Lucio, 2019; Madimutsa; Mahas-Demydas & Rudnytska, 2019). By implementing targeted policies aimed at addressing specific causes of joblessness, governments can better equip citizens with the tools they need to succeed economically regardless of what type of environment they find themselves living in. Indeed, these criticisms have informed trade unions in responding to structural unemployment.

Trade unions have been at the forefront of responding to this challenge, advocating for policies that can help mitigate its effects on workers and their families (MacKenzie & Lucio, 2019; Madimutsa; Mahas-Demydas & Rudnytska, 2019; Mahmood & Banerjee, 2020; Mailand, 2019). One approach taken by trade unions has been to focus on investments in education and infrastructure that can ensure future generations are better equipped to handle the changing nature of the modern workplace. For example, research conducted by economists at Harvard University found that increased investment in public education was associated with higher wages for low-skilled workers over time (Krueger & Summers, 1988). Similarly, a study from Oxford University concluded that investing in infrastructure projects could create jobs for those who had previously been unemployed due to structural changes (Bryson et al., 2017). These findings suggest that targeted investments may be an effective way of addressing issues related to structural unemployment.

Another response proposed by trade unions has been critiques of Washington Consensus initiatives which emphasize market liberalization as a solution for economic growth (Rodrik, 1997). While there is evidence suggesting these policies can lead to short-term gains, they often fail to address underlying problems such as inequality or lack of access to resources needed for development (Stiglitz, 2002; Rodrik, 2003). As such, trade unionists argue that more comprehensive approaches should be taken when dealing with structurally unemployed populations across the globe. This includes providing individuals with access not only to employment opportunities but also resources necessary for developing relevant skill sets so they are better prepared for future challenges posed by advancing technology and globalization forces (ILO, 2018).

Finally, emerging debates surrounding neo-liberal perspectives on structurally unemployed populations have raised philosophical arguments about what implications prolonged periods without gainful employment might have on quality of life both citizens themselves as well as societies at large (Gillespie, 2016; Brown, 2019). In order to inform these discussions further research into existing case studies is needed so potential areas improvement can be identified. Such analysis could provide valuable insights into how best to tackle this complex problem. While there is no single solution capable of addressing all issues raised regarding structural unemployment critiques, any interventionist initiatives should focus on providing individuals access resources necessary to develop relevant skill sets for a changing modern workplace.

CHAPTER 8 SUMMARY

This final chapter of the book has created a picture of what the future of industrial relations might look like. For instance, working from home is no longer a peculiarity for workers with unique needs. Rather, it is one of the options that are open to all employees. This ties in with the trend towards having a younger and more mobile workforce. At the same time, the job's landscape is challenged by a brain drain among relatively poorer nations as well as the de-industrialization of the more advanced nations. Some of these trends have resurrected the age-old problem of structural unemployment. It is hoped that effective industrial relations will do much to overcome some of these challenges. This book has therefore been part of that journey towards better understanding how employees relate to their employers across the globe.

CHAPTER 9

Concluding Remarks

This book has sought to highlight some of the pertinent issues when trying to conceptualize and operationalize industrial relations. The first chapter introduced us to industrial relations. For example, it defined what an employment contract comprises and its implications in terms of the roles or responsibilities that are allotted to workers and their employers. The chapter highlighted other interested parties, such as the state and industrialists or the business sector, which need to operate in an environment without industrial conflict or strife. The second chapter set out a legal context for industrial relations. The chapter highlighted the critical role of social concerns about working conditions, trade unionism, politics, and the wider economy. In doing so, the chapter advocated for the use of communication and social dialog to resolve conflicts rather than waiting for them to escalate into a crisis.

The third chapter conceptualized industrial relations, starting with their history. It also explored some of the conflict resolution techniques that are typically utilized. The theme of communication emerged as an important component. We also considered the role of arbitration in preventing violence and industrial strife. The fourth chapter took up these considerations and expanded them as it explored the practice of industrial relations. For instance, the chapter showed how good governance translates into better industrial relations. However, the chapter also highlighted the importance of productivity and efficiency. We considered a case study of multinational corporations to evaluate how internationalized industrial relations can be turned into local realities of the workplace. The plight of migrant workers demonstrates that transnational or trans-border employment is not without its pitfalls. The fifth chapter charted the evolution and revolution of industrial relations. This started with the origins of the trade union movement before moving on to some of its modalities, including collective bargaining. The chapter showed how globalization and outsourcing impact the growth of trade unionism. The use of International Framework Agreements (IFAs) was presented as a potential solution to some of the disparities that exist in the implementation of industrial relations. The sixth chapter then critiqued the notion of industrial relations as far as it has not fully addressed some of the challenges in the workplace. These include racism, exclusion of those with disabilities, health, and safety concerns, child labor, and the exploitation of workers on temporary contracts.

The seventh chapter highlighted some frameworks for contemporary industrial relations. These included provisions for an aging population, responses to modern technology, reforming the trade union movement, and improving contracting arrangements. The final chapter in the book then highlights some current and future trends in industrial relations. These include greater reliance on working from home, mobility of the workforce, the "brain drain," deindustrialization, and structural unemployment. In doing so, the book laid the groundwork for further research into the improvement of industrial relations. I hope you have enjoyed reading this book and will follow the others in the series.

BIBLIOGRAPHY

1. Abd, R. S. S., & Mahmod, N., (2021). Ratification of international labor convention and the reformation of trade union recognition process in Malaysia [article]. *Pertanika Journal of Social Science and Humanities, 29*(1), 193–206. https://doi.org/10.47836/pjssh.29.1.11.
2. Abd, R. S. S., & Mahmood, N., (2019). An analysis of the good faith bargaining practice in the trade union recognition process: Reform of the Malaysian trade union legal framework [article]. *IIUM Law Journal, 27*(2), 501–524. <Go to ISI>://WOS:000504059800009.
3. Ackers, P., (2020). Industrial relations and the limits of the state: Can a left labor government resurrect comprehensive sectoral collective bargaining and restore trade union power? [article]. *Political Quarterly, 91*(1), 173–181. https://doi.org/10.1111/1467-923x.12788.
4. Addison, J. T., & Teixeira, P., (2019a). Strikes, employee workplace representation, unionism, and industrial relations quality in European establishments [article]. *Journal of Economic Behavior & Organization, 159*, 109–133. https://doi.org/10.1016/j.jebo.2019.01.006.
5. Addison, J. T., & Teixeira, P., (2019b). Workplace employee representation and industrial relations performance: New evidence from the 2013 European company survey [article]. *Jahrbucher Fur Nationalokonomie Und Statistik, 239*(1), 111–154. https://doi.org/10.1515/jbnst-2017-0146.
6. Adewumi, S. A., (2021). Employment casualization and trade union survival strategies in the beverage sector in Lagos, Nigeria [article]. *Journal of Public Affairs, 21*(3), 9, Article pa2256. https://doi.org/10.1002/pa.2256.

7. Agarwal, R., Shirke, A., & Panackal, N., (2020). Enablers of the collective bargaining in industrial relations: A study of India's industrial policies through ISM and MICMAC analysis [article]. *Indian Journal of Labor Economics, 63*(3), 781–798. https://doi.org/10.1007/s41027-020-00241-6.
8. Ahuja, R., (2020). 'Produce or perish.' The crisis of the late 1940s and the place of labor in post-colonial India [article]. *Modern Asian Studies, 54*(4), 1041–1112. https://doi.org/10.1017/s0026749x17001007.
9. Amosse, T., Askenazy, P., Chevalier, M., Erhel, C., Petit, H., & Reberioux, A., (2019). Industrial relations and adjustments to the crisis: A comparative micro-statistical analysis of France and Great Britain [article]. *International Labor Review, 158*(3), 463–487. <Go to ISI>://WOS:000490274700001.
10. Archel, P., Carrasco, F., Garcia-Benau, M. A., & Larrinaga, C., (2022). Intellectual engagements of accounting academics: The 'forecasted losses' intervention [article]. *Critical Perspectives on Accounting, 86*, 13, Article 102359. https://doi.org/10.1016/j.cpa.2021.102359.
11. Ashwin, S., Oka, C., Schuessler, E., Alexander, R., & Lohmeyer, N., (2020). Spillover effects across transnational industrial relations agreements: The potential and limits of collective action in global supply chains [article]. *ILR Review, 73*(4), 995–1020, Article 0019793919896570. https://doi.org/10.1177/0019793919896570.
12. Avgar, A., (2020). Integrating conflict: A proposed framework for the interdisciplinary study of workplace conflict and its management [article]. *ILR Review, 73*(2), 281–311, Article 0019793919885819. https://doi.org/10.1177/0019793919885819.
13. Baines, D., & Armstrong, P., (2019). Non-job work/unpaid caring: Gendered industrial relations in long-term care [article]. *Gender Work and Organization, 26*(7), 934–947. https://doi.org/10.1111/gwao.12293.
14. Baines, D., & Cunningham, I., (2020). 'How could management let this happen?' Gender, unpaid work, and industrial relations in the nonprofit social services sector [article]. *Economic and Industrial Democracy, 41*(2), 436–456. https://doi.org/10.1177/0143831x17715768.
15. Bancarzewski, M., & Hardy, J., (2021). Workers' resistance in special economic zones in Poland [article]. *Employee Relations, 43*(1), 193–207. https://doi.org/10.1108/er-08-2019-0310.

16. Barklamb, S., (2021). Wake-up call for a dysfunctional system: Employer perspectives on industrial relations in 2020 [review]. *Journal of Industrial Relations, 63*(3), 411–421, Article 00221856211012823. https://doi.org/10.1177/00221856211012823.

17. Barry, M., & Wilkinson, A., (2022). Employee voice, psychologization, and human resource management (HRM) [article]. *Human Resource Management Journal, 32*(3), 631–646. https://doi.org/10.1111/1748-8583.12415.

18. Baturina, D., Bezovan, G., & Matancevic, J., (2021). Social dialogue 2030. A study of the future of social dialogue in Croatia by using the Delphi-method [article]. *Bogoslovska Smotra-Ephemerides Theologicae Zagrabienses, 91*(4), 775–799. https://doi.org/10.53745/bs.91.4.7.

19. Beattie, D., (2019). Time, memory, and history in the labor documentary film [article]. *Studies in Documentary Film, 13*(2), 93–102. https://doi.org/10.1080/17503280.2019.1595918.

20. Bechter, B., Braakmann, N., & Brandl, B., (2021). Variable pay systems and/or collective wage bargaining? Complements or substitutes? [article]. *ILR Review, 74*(2), 443–469, Article 0019793919883882. https://doi.org/10.1177/0019793919883882.

21. Bedkar, P., & Prashad, V., (2020). India's liberalization project and the future of trade unions [article]. *Tempo Social, 32*(1), 29–51. https://doi.org/10.11606/0103-2070.ts.2020.164980.

22. Behrens, M., & Pekarek, A. Delivering the goods? German industrial relations institutions during the COVID-19 crisis [article; early access]. *Industrial Relations, 19*. https://doi.org/10.1111/irel.12319.

23. Behrens, M., Colvin, A. J. S., Dorigatti, L., & Pekarek, A. H., (2020). Systems for conflict resolution in comparative perspective [article]. *ILR Review, 73*(2), 312–344, Article 0019793919870800. https://doi.org/10.1177/0019793919870800.

24. Belizon, M. J., (2019). Employee voice in Spanish subsidiaries of multinational firms [article]. *European Journal of Industrial Relations, 25*(1), 75–90. https://doi.org/10.1177/0959680118776076.

25. Bellace, J., Minster, A., Scott, K., Kelly, E. L., Kochan, T. A., Sako, M., & Kaufman, B. E., (2021). Commentary on new theories in employment relations [article]. *ILR Review, 74*(3), 798–826. https://doi.org/10.1177/0019793921994081.

26. Ben, L., & Sage, A. M., (2022). Talking about non-union collective agreements: A union perspective [article]. *Journal of Industrial Relations, 64*(1), 147–159, Article 00221856211051396. https://doi.org/10.1177/00221856211051396.
27. Berry, C., & McDaniel, S., (2022). Post-crisis precarity: Understanding attitudes to work and industrial relations among young people in the UK [article]. *Economic and Industrial Democracy, 43*(1), 322–343, Article 0143831x19894380. https://doi.org/10.1177/0143831x19894380.
28. Bhuta, A., (2022). Imbalancing act: India's industrial relations code, 2020 [article]. *Indian Journal of Labor Economics, 65*(3), 821–830. https://doi.org/10.1007/s41027-022-00389-3.
29. Bischoff, C., Masondo, T., & Webster, E., (2021). Workers' participation at plant level: A South African case study [article]. *Economic and Industrial Democracy, 42*(2), 376–394. https://doi.org/10.1177/0143831x18772185.
30. Bogoeski, V., (2022). Continuities of exploitation: Seasonal migrant workers in German agriculture during the COVID-19 pandemic [article]. *Journal of Law and Society, 49*(4), 681–702. https://doi.org/10.1111/jols.12389.
31. Bondy, A. S., (2022). Conflictual complementarity: New labor actors in corporatist industrial relations [article]. *Work Employment and Society, 36*(4), 683–700, Article 0950017020981557. https://doi.org/10.1177/0950017020981557.
32. Boumans, S., (2022). Neoliberalization of industrial relations: The ideational development of Dutch employers' organizations between 1976 and 2019 [article]. *Economic and Industrial Democracy, 43*(4), 1610–1631, Article 0143831x211020086. https://doi.org/10.1177/0143831x211020086.
33. Bourguignon, R., & Floquet, M., (2019). When union strategy meets business strategy: The union voucher at Axa [article]. *Business History, 61*(2), 260–280. https://doi.org/10.1080/00076791.2017.1368491.
34. Bradley, K., & Rowland, S., (2021). A poor woman's lawyer. Feminism, the labor movement, and working-class women's access to the law in England, 1890–1935 [article]. *Womens History Review, 30*(4), 632–649. https://doi.org/10.1080/09612025.2020.1803544.
35. Bray, M., Macneil, J., & Spiess, L., (2019). Unions and collective bargaining in Australia in 2018 [article]. *Journal of Industrial Relations, 61*(3), 357–381. https://doi.org/10.1177/0022185619834320.

36. Bray, M., McCrystal, S., & Spiess, L., (2020). Why doesn't anyone talk about non-union collective agreements? [article]. *Journal of Industrial Relations, 62*(5), 784–807, Article 0022185619899419. https://doi.org/10.1177/0022185619899419.

37. Budd, J. W., (2020). The psychologization of employment relations, alternative models of the employment relationship, and the OB turn [Review]. *Human Resource Management Journal, 30*(1), 73–83. https://doi.org/10.1111/1748-8583.12274.

38. Cabeza, J., (2019). Representation, trade union activity and technologies [article]. *Onati Socio-Legal Series, 9*(1), 96–108. https://doi.org/10.35295/osls.iisl/0000-0000-0000-1014.

39. Cam, E., (2021). From social policy to labor economics and industrial relations in Turkey: A critical history of an academic discipline [article]. *Labor History, 62*(2), 186–204. https://doi.org/10.1080/0023656x.2021.1897092.

40. Campolieti, M., (2020). The distribution of union size: Canada, 1913–2014 [article]. *Physica a-Statistical Mechanics and Its Applications, 558*, 16, Article 125007. https://doi.org/10.1016/j.physa.2020.125007.

41. Cesari, M. S., Bonelli, J. M., Russak, M., & Eggers, J., (2019). Contributions of trade unionism to sustainable development: The case of the IPLIDO-UTHGRA [article]. *European Journal of Sustainable Development, 8*(5), 47–56. https://doi.org/10.14207/ejsd.2019.v8n5p47.

42. Chan, A., (2020a). The emergence of labor unions from within Hong Kong's protest movement [article]. *Asia-Pacific Journal-Japan Focus, 18*(24), 9, Article 5522. https://doi.org/10.22459/mic.06.02.2020.08.

43. Chan, A., (2020b). Vietnams and China's diverging industrial relations systems: Cases of path dependency [article]. *Journal of Contemporary Asia, 50*(3), 321–340. https://doi.org/10.1080/00472336.2019.1623907.

44. Chantziaras, A., Dedoulis, E., & Leventis, S., (2020). The impact of labor unionization on monitoring costs [article]. *European Management Journal, 38*(2), 288–307. https://doi.org/10.1016/j.emj.2019.09.004.

45. Chen, L. W., Su, Z. X., & Wang, G. H. What does democratic management do in Chinese workplaces? Evidence from matched employer-employee data [article; early access]. *Human Resource Management Journal,* 26. https://doi.org/10.1111/1748-8583.12471.

46. Chen, Y., Kim, Y. K., Liu, Z. Q., & Wang, G. F., (2023). Predictors of employees' strike attitudes in multinational corporations in China: A multilevel relational model [article]. *International Journal of Human Resource Management, 34*(1), 28–67. https://doi.org/10.1080/09585192.2021.1958247.

47. Cillo, R., & Pradella, L., (2019). Remaking the labor movement in Italy: The revival of strikes at fiat-Chrysler automobiles in 2015–17 [article]. *Globalizations, 16*(4), 457–471. https://doi.org/10.1080/14747731.2018.1558821.

48. Civinskas, R., & Dvorak, J., (2019). In search of employee perspective: Understanding how Lithuanian companies use employees' representatives in the adoption of company's decisions [article]. *Administrative Sciences, 9*(4), 21, Article 78. https://doi.org/10.3390/admsci9040078.

49. Clayton, D., (2021). Conflict and conciliation: Industrial relations in an industrializing Hong Kong, ca. 1946–1960 [article]. *Labor History, 62*(4), 470–488. https://doi.org/10.1080/0023656x.2021.1934424.

50. Clibborn, S., (2019). Australian industrial relations in 2018: Inequality, policy stagnation and a brewing storm [article]. *Journal of Industrial Relations, 61*(3), 318–325. https://doi.org/10.1177/0022185619848372.

51. Clibborn, S., (2020). Australian industrial relations in 2019: The year wage theft went mainstream [article]. *Journal of Industrial Relations, 62*(3), 331–340, Article 0022185620913889. https://doi.org/10.1177/0022185620913889.

52. Clibborn, S., (2021). Australian industrial relations in 2020: COVID-19, crisis, and opportunity [article]. *Journal of Industrial Relations, 63*(3), 291–302, Article 00221856211012813. https://doi.org/10.1177/00221856211012813.

53. Colas-Neila, E., & Fargas, J., (2019). Guaranteed minimum income: New spaces for trade union action [article]. *Onati Socio-Legal Series, 9*(1), 109–127. https://doi.org/10.35295/osls.iisl/0000-0000-0000-1015.

54. Collins, N., Ren, S., & Warner, M., (2020). The changing role of the state in industrial relations since Vietnam's reform [article]. *Asia Pacific Journal of Human Resources, 58*(3), 450–468. https://doi.org/10.1111/1744-7941.12223.

55. Cooke, F. L., Xu, J. P., & Bian, H. M., (2019). The prospect of decent

work, decent industrial relations and decent social relations in China: Towards a multi-level and multi-disciplinary approach [article]. *International Journal of Human Resource Management, 30*(1), 122–155. https://doi.org/10.1080/09585192.2018.1521461.

56. Croucher, R., & Okland, G. M., (2021). Women production workers' introduction into a Norwegian Shipyard 1965–1989 [article]. *Business History, 63*(5), 776–794. https://doi.org/10.1080/00076791.2019.1642327.
57. D'Art, D., (2020). Freedom of association and statutory union recognition: A constitutional impossibility? [article]. *Irish Jurist, 63*(63), 82–112. <Go to ISI>://WOS:000664258300005.
58. Da Costa, R. M., & Horn, C. H., (2021). The co-evolution of technology and employment relations: Institutions, innovation, and change [article]. *Structural Change and Economic Dynamics, 58*, 313–324. https://doi.org/10.1016/j.strueco.2021.06.003.
59. Dalla, S. M., (2021). The ageing workforce and industrial relations: A new role for the Italian social partners? [article]. *E-Journal of International and Comparative Labor Studies, 10, 11*(3–1), 83–92. <Go to ISI>://WOS:000834256700005.
60. Darlington, R., & Mustchin, S., (2019). The role of the TUC in significant industrial disputes: An historical critical overview [article]. *Labor History, 60*(6), 626–645. https://doi.org/10.1080/0023656x.2019.1624698.
61. Das, R., (2023). Paradigm development and diffusion in human resource management over 39 years of scholarship [article]. *Employee Responsibilities and Rights Journal, 35*(1), 3–28. https://doi.org/10.1007/s10672-022-09432-3.
62. Das, S. C., & Singh, S., (2021). Trade unionism and industrial relations in Indian organizations: A scientific exploration [article]. *Pacific Business Review International, 13*(7), 39–49. <Go to ISI>://WOS:000670229200005.
63. De Amorim, W. A. C., Fischer, A. L., & Trullen, J., (2019). A comparative study of trade union influence over HRM practices in Spanish and Brazilian firms: The role of industrial relations systems and their historical evolution [article]. *International Studies of Management & Organization, 49*(4), 372–388. https://doi.org/10.1080/00208825.2019.1646487.

64. De Luna, D. B., (2022). Management, the state, and union-weakening practices in Chile: A case study approach of the dual and ambivalent role of the state in a process of democratization [article]. *Economic and Industrial Democracy, 43*(3), 1143–1163, Article 0143831x20975477. https://doi.org/10.1177/0143831x20975477.
65. De Prins, P., Stuer, D., & Gielens, T., (2020). Revitalizing social dialogue in the workplace: The impact of a cooperative industrial relations climate and sustainable HR practices on reducing employee harm [article]. *International Journal of Human Resource Management, 31*(13), 1684–1704. https://doi.org/10.1080/09585192.2017.1423098.
66. De Vaate, V. B., (2021). Collective redress and workers' rights in the Netherlands [article]. *European Labor Law Journal, 12*(4), 455–474. https://doi.org/10.1177/20319525211056605.
67. Demougin, P., Gooberman, L., Hauptmeier, M., & Heery, E., (2019). Employer organizations transformed [article]. *Human Resource Management Journal, 29*(1), 1–16. https://doi.org/10.1111/1748-8583.12222.
68. Desai, D., & Randeria, S., (2020). Unfreezing unspent social special-purpose funds for the COVID-19 crisis: Critical reflections from India [article]. *World Development, 136*, 4, Article 105138. https://doi.org/10.1016/j.worlddev.2020.105138.
69. Devinatz, V. G., (2020). Interpreting the communist party USA's historical role in the US trade unions: Insights from the early institutionalist theory of industrial relations [article]. *International Critical Thought, 10*(1), 138–149. https://doi.org/10.1080/21598282.2020.1740100.
70. Devinatz, V. G., (2022). US labor institutionalism's rise and decline and the death of US industrial relations [article]. *Employee Responsibilities and Rights Journal, 34*(3), 319–333. https://doi.org/10.1007/s10672-021-09390-2.
71. Di Carlo, D., (2020). Understanding wage restraint in the German public sector: Does the pattern bargaining hypothesis really hold water? [article]. *Industrial Relations Journal, 51*(3), 185–208. https://doi.org/10.1111/irj.12288.
72. Diessner, S., Durazzi, N., & Hope, D., (2022). Skill-biased liberalization: Germany's transition to the knowledge economy [article]. *Politics & Society, 50*(1), 117–155, Article 00323292211006563. https://doi.org/10.1177/00323292211006563.

73. Dobbins, T., Cullinane, N., & Sheehan, B. Ireland's conundrum on union bargaining rights: Assessing the industrial relations amendment act 2015 [article; early access]. *Industrial Relations Journal,* 17. https://doi.org/10.1111/irj.12281.

74. Dobbins, T., Cullinane, N., & Sheehan, B., (2020). Ireland's conundrum on union bargaining rights: Assessing the industrial relations amendment act 2015 [article]. *Industrial Relations Journal, 51*(1, 2), 75–91. <Go to ISI>://WOS:000520610000004.

75. Dobbins, T., Hughes, E., & Dundon, T., (2021). 'Zones of contention' in industrial relations: Framing *pluralism* as praxis [article]. *Journal of Industrial Relations, 63*(2), 149–176, Article 0022185620957700. https://doi.org/10.1177/0022185620957700.

76. Dockes, E., (2019). New trade union strategies for new forms of employment [article]. *European Labor Law Journal, 10*(3), 219–228. https://doi.org/10.1177/2031952519870061.

77. Dorigatti, L., & Pedersini, R., (2021). Industrial relations and inequality: The many conditions of a crucial relationship [article]. *Transfer-European Review of Labor and Research, 27*(1), 11–27. https://doi.org/10.1177/10242589211007400.

78. Dorigatti, L., Been, W. M., Burroni, L., Keune, M., Larsen, T. P., & Mailand, M. Playing alone? Interest representation in the videogame industry in Denmark, Italy, and the Netherlands [article; early access]. *Economic and Industrial Democracy,* 23. https://doi.org/10.1177/0143831x221129651.

79. Dorrenbacher, C., Tuselmann, H., Meissner, H. R., & Cao, Q., (2021). What shapes industrial relations in foreign affiliates? Comparative case study results from Germany [article]. *Critical Perspectives on International Business, 17*(4), 481–501. https://doi.org/10.1108/cpoib-07-2020-0090.

80. Drucza, K., (2019). Nepal's social security reforms, State-building, and the role of trade unions [article]. *Journal of South Asian Development, 14*(1), 62–82. https://doi.org/10.1177/0973174119849776.

81. Dupuis, M., & Greer, I., (2022). Recentralizing industrial relations? Local unions and the politics of insourcing in three North American automakers [article]. *ILR Review, 75*(4), 918–942, Article 00197939211015191. https://doi.org/10.1177/00197939211015191.

82. Edwards, P., & Hodder, A., (2022). Conflict and control in the contemporary workplace: Structured antagonism revisited [article]. *Industrial Relations Journal, 53*(3), 220–240. https://doi.org/10.1111/irj.12363.

83. Ellem, B., (2021). Labor and megaprojects: Rethinking productivity and industrial relations policy [article]. *Economic and Labor Relations Review, 32*(3), 399–416, Article 1035304620984294. https://doi.org/10.1177/1035304620984294.

84. Ellem, B., Sandstrom, J., & Persson, C., (2020). Neoliberal trajectories in mining: Comparing Malmfalten and the Pilbara [article]. *European Journal of Industrial Relations, 26*(3), 297–312. https://doi.org/10.1177/0959680119847873.

85. Engblom, S., & Lundberg, M., (2019). Answers to the new trade union strategies for new forms of employment questionnaire [article]. *European Labor Law Journal, 10*(3), 271–280. https://doi.org/10.1177/2031952519866536.

86. Espinosa, E. N. B., (2021). Managing industrial discontent in Britain, 1927–1930: The industrial cooperation talks and the segregation of the national unemployed workers' movement [article]. *Labor History, 62*(5, 6), 742–761. https://doi.org/10.1080/0023656x.2021.1984405.

87. Eustace, A., (2021). A shock to the system: Sectoral bargaining under threat in Ireland [article]. *European Labor Law Journal, 12*(2), 211–225. https://doi.org/10.1177/20319525211000360.

88. Fang, M. Y., Fan, P., Nepal, S., & Chang, P. C., (2021). Dual-mediation paths linking corporate social responsibility to employee's job performance: A multilevel approach [article]. *Frontiers in Psychology, 11*, 9, Article 612565. https://doi.org/10.3389/fpsyg.2020.612565.

89. Fergus, E., & Godfrey, S., (2021). Effective representation: Whereto for workers on fruit and wine farms in South Africa? [article]. *International Journal of Comparative Labor Law and Industrial Relations, 37*(1), 1–34. <Go to ISI>://WOS:000623620600001.

90. Flynn, M., & Schroder, H., (2021). Age, work, and pensions in the United Kingdom and Hong Kong: An institutional perspective [article]. *Economic and Industrial Democracy, 42*(2), 248–268. https://doi.org/10.1177/0143831x18763542.

91. Foley, M., & Williamson, S., (2021). Women, work, and industrial relations in Australia in 2020 [article]. *Journal of Industrial*

Relations, 63(3), 321–337, Article 0022185621996407. https://doi.org/10.1177/0022185621996407.

92. Ford, M., & Gillan, M., (2022). Understanding global union repertoires of action [article]. *Industrial Relations Journal, 53*(6), 559–577. https://doi.org/10.1111/irj.12386.
93. Ford, M., & Ward, K., (2021). COVID-19 in Southeast Asia: Implications for workers and unions [article]. *Journal of Industrial Relations, 63*(3), 432–450, Article 00221856211000097. https://doi.org/10.1177/00221856211000097.
94. Forde, C. The potential of archival methods in industrial relations, sociology of work, management, and HRM research: A case study of the relationship between temporary employment agencies and the state in the UK during the 1980s [article; early access]. *Labor & Industry-a Journal of the Social and Economic Relations of Work,* 19. https://doi.org/10.1080/10301763.2022.2158436.
95. Forsyth, A., (2022). COVID-19: Advancing the industrial relations reform objectives of Australian employers? [article]. *Australian Business Law Review, 50*(3), 151–172. <Go to ISI>://WOS:000896977100002.
96. Foster, D., Masso, M., & Osila, L., (2021). Work accommodations and sustainable working: The role of social partners and industrial relations in the employment of disabled and older people in Estonia, Hungary, and Poland [article]. *European Journal of Industrial Relations, 27*(2), 149–165, Article 0959680120971896. https://doi.org/10.1177/0959680120971896.
97. Franceschini, I., (2020). At the roots of labor activism: Chinese and Cambodian garment workers in comparative perspective [article]. *Journal of Contemporary Asia, 50*(1), 144–167. https://doi.org/10.1080/00472336.2018.1555272.
98. Freedland, M., & Dhorajiwala, H., (2019). UK response to new trade union strategies for new forms of employment [article]. *European Labor Law Journal, 10*(3), 281–290. https://doi.org/10.1177/2031952519866537.
99. Fuchs, D., Tse, P. F. Y., & Feng, X. J., (2019). Labor research under coercive authoritarianism: Comparative reflections on fieldwork challenges in China [article]. *Economic and Industrial Democracy, 40*(1), 132–155. https://doi.org/10.1177/0143831x18780337.
100. Galik, A., Bak, M., Balandynowicz-Panfil, K., & Cirella, G. T., (2022). Evaluating labor market flexibility using the TOPSIS method:

Sustainable industrial relations [article]. *Sustainability, 14*(1), 20, Article 526. https://doi.org/10.3390/su14010526.

101. Gall, G., (2021). Contemporary employer victimization of lay union representatives in Britain: Issues, dynamics, and extent [article]. *Capital and Class, 45*(1), 45–70. https://doi.org/10.1177/0309816819852752.
102. Gardawski, J., & Towalski, R., (2020). The comparative analysis of the industrial relations systems in Europe [article]. *International Journal of Management and Economics, 56*(1), 42–62. https://doi.org/10.2478/ijme-2020-0003.
103. Gasparri, S., & Tassinari, A., (2020). 'Smart' industrial relations in the making? Insights from analysis of union responses to digitalization in Italy [article]. *Relations Industrielles-Industrial Relations, 75*(4), 796–817. <Go to ISI>://WOS:000599211900008.
104. Gasparri, S., (2021). Framing work and welfare: Insights from the growing relevance of company welfare in Italy [article]. *Journal of Industrial Relations, 63*(2), 235–262, Article 0022185620973685. https://doi.org/10.1177/0022185620973685.
105. Gasparri, S., Ikeler, P., & Fullin, G., (2019). Trade union strategy in fashion retail in Italy and the USA: Converging divergence between institutions and mobilization? [article]. *European Journal of Industrial Relations, 25*(4), 345–361. https://doi.org/10.1177/0959680118817681.
106. Gavin, M., (2022). Unions and collective bargaining in Australia in 2021 [article]. *Journal of Industrial Relations, 64*(3), 362–379, Article 00221856221100381. https://doi.org/10.1177/00221856221100381.
107. Giannakopoulos, N., & Laliotis, I., (2020). Industrial relations reform, firm-level bargaining, and nominal wage floors [article]. *Manchester School, 88*(1), 37–59. https://doi.org/10.1111/manc.12273.
108. Giraud, B., (2020). The changing face of union action put to the test by neo-liberal reforms in France [article]. *Tempo Social, 32*(1), 137–156. https://doi.org/10.11606/0103-2070.ts.2020.164063.
109. Godino, A., & Molina, O., (2022). The industrial relations chameleon: Collective bargaining in the facility management business [article]. *Employee Relations, 44*(7), 1–18. https://doi.org/10.1108/er-12-2020-0526.
110. Gooberman, L., (2022). 'Revolution in the coalfields': Industrial relations in wartime South Wales, 1939–45 [article]. *Labor History, 63*(1), 55–72. https://doi.org/10.1080/0023656x.2022.2056585.

111. Goods, C., & Ellem, B. Employer associations: Climate change, power, and politics [article; early access]. *Economic and Industrial Democracy,* 23, Article 0143831x221081551. https://doi.org/10.1177/0143831x221081551.

112. Goyer, M., Glatzer, M., & Del, R. R. V., (2022). The management of the Eurozone in crisis times: Actors, institutions, and the case of bailout packages [article]. *European Journal of Industrial Relations, 28*(1), 7–25, Article 09596801211011355. https://doi.org/10.1177/09596801211011355.

113. Graca, M., (2021). For a right to have rights. Street-based female sex workers? Claims in Portugal [article]. *Portuguese Journal of Social Science, 20*(1, 2), 27–43. https://doi.org/10.1386/pjss_00032_1.

114. Gramano, E., & Gaudio, G., (2019). 'New trade union strategies for new forms of employment': Focus on Italy [article]. *European Labor Law Journal, 10*(3), 240–253. https://doi.org/10.1177/2031952519870028.

115. Grodem, A. S., & Hippe, J. M., (2019). Networking, lobbying, and bargaining for pensions: Trade union power in the Norwegian pension reform [article]. *Journal of Public Policy, 39*(3), 465–481, Article Pii s0143814x18000144. https://doi.org/10.1017/s0143814x18000144.

116. Guillaume, C., (2022). Legal expertise: A critical resource for trade unionists? Insights into the confederation Francaise Democratique du Travail [article]. *Industrial Law Journal, 51*(1), 38–61. https://doi.org/10.1093/indlaw/dwaa025.

117. Guiso, A., (2020). The long goodbye. Politics and economy in the crisis of the entrepreneurial state [article]. *Journal of Modern Italian Studies, 25*(1), 77–94. https://doi.org/10.1080/1354571x.2020.1688978.

118. Gunnigle, P., Lavelle, J., & Monaghan, S., (2019). Multinational companies and human resource management in Ireland during recession: A retrospective from a highly globalized economy [article]. *Thunderbird International Business Review, 61*(3), 481–489. https://doi.org/10.1002/tie.21978.

119. Gunther, W., & Hopner, M., (2023). Why does Germany abstain from statutory bargaining extensions? Explaining the exceptional German erosion of collective wage bargaining [article]. *Economic and Industrial Democracy, 44*(1), 88–108, Article 0143831x211065783. https://doi.org/10.1177/0143831x211065783.

120. Haipeter, T., (2020). Financial market capitalism and labor in Germany.

Merits and limits of a sociological concept [article]. *German Politics, 29*(3), 382–403. https://doi.org/10.1080/09644008.2018.1528236.

121. Hakansta, C., Albin, M., Kreshpaj, B., Gunn, V., Hogstedt, C., Matilla-Santander, N., O'Campo, P., et al. Power resources and the battle against precarious employment: Trade union activities within a tripartite initiative tackling undeclared work in Sweden [article; early access]. *Economic and Industrial Democracy,* 28. https://doi.org/10.1177/0143831x221131835.
122. Hamberger, J., (2020). Reviving Australia's system of enterprise bargaining [review]. *Journal of Industrial Relations, 62*(3), 461–476, Article 0022185620911674. https://doi.org/10.1177/0022185620911674.
123. Harvey, G., & Turnbull, P., (2020). Ricardo flies Ryanair: Strategic human resource management and competitive advantage in a single European aviation market [article]. *Human Resource Management Journal, 30*(4), 553–565. https://doi.org/10.1111/1748-8583.12315.
124. Hendy, L. J., (2022). Reflections on the role of the trade union lawyer [article]. *International Journal of Comparative Labor Law and Industrial Relations, 38*(2), 91–102. <Go to ISI>://WOS:000814202600002.
125. Herrero, D., (2022). Disentangling the transformation of the German model: The role of firms' strategic decisions and structural change [article]. *Competition & Change, 26*(3, 4), 357–383, Article 10245294211015479. https://doi.org/10.1177/10245294211015479.
126. Hilgert, J., (2019). Article 23(4) trade union rights and the United Nations policy of devolution on labor relations [article]. *Labor History, 60*(5), 503–519. https://doi.org/10.1080/0023656x.2019.1573975.
127. Hirsch, B., & Mueller, S., (2020). Firm wage premia, industrial relations, and rent sharing in Germany [article]. *ILR Review, 73*(5), 1119–1146, Article 0019793920917105. https://doi.org/10.1177/0019793920917105.
128. Hoffrogge, R., (2019). Voluntarism, corporatism, and path dependency: The metalworkers' unions amalgamated engineering union and IG metal and their place in the history of British and German industrial relations [article]. *German History, 37*(3), 327–344. https://doi.org/10.1093/gerhis/ghz037.
129. Howell, C., (2019). Neoliberalism, capitalist growth models, and the state: An agenda for industrial relations theory [review].

Journal of Industrial Relations, 61(3), 457–474. https://doi.org/10.1177/0022185619834047.

130. Howell, C., (2021). Rethinking the role of the state in employment relations for a neoliberal era [article]. *ILR Review, 74*(3), 739–772, Article 0019793920904663. https://doi.org/10.1177/0019793920904663.
131. Hungler, S., (2022). Labor law reforms after the populist turn in Hungary [article]. *Review of Central and East European Law, 47*(1), 84–114. https://doi.org/10.1163/15730352-bja10063.
132. Ilsoe, A., & Soderqvist, C. F. Will there be a Nordic model in the platform economy? Evasive and integrative platform strategies in Denmark and Sweden [article; early access]. *Regulation & Governance,* 19. https://doi.org/10.1111/rego.12465.
133. Jarota, M., (2022). Issues of awards given as a part of social arbitration in a collective dispute. De lege lata and de lege ferenda remarks [article]. *Review of European and Comparative Law, 48*(1), 7–28. https://doi.org/10.31743/recl.12240.
134. Jha, J. K., & Singh, M., (2019). Exploring the mechanisms of influence of ethical leadership on employment relations [article]. *IIMB Management Review, 31*(4), 385–395. https://doi.org/10.1016/j.iimb.2019.07.010.
135. Jiang, Y. Z., & Yao, Y., (2020). Industrial relations climate and employee intention to quit: The roles of voice and silence [article]. *Social Behavior and Personality, 48*(8), 13, Article e9235. https://doi.org/10.2224/sbp.9235.
136. Jirjahn, U. Membership in employers' associations and collective bargaining coverage in Germany [article; early access]. *Economic and Industrial Democracy,* 29, Article 0143831x221092484. https://doi.org/10.1177/0143831x221092484.
137. Jirjahn, U., (2022). On the determinants of bargaining-free membership in German employers' associations [article]. *Industrial Relations Journal, 53*(6), 545–558. https://doi.org/10.1111/irj.12385.
138. Joycc, S., Stuart, M., & Forde, C. Theorizing labor unrest and trade unionism in the platform economy [article; early access]. *New Technology Work and Employment,* 20. https://doi.org/10.1111/ntwe.12252.
139. Junior, R. T., (2022). Demeaning face of politics and bureaucracy in labor movement in Kenya: A quest for an effective labor law

[article]. *Novum Jus, 16*(2), 341–365. https://doi.org/10.14718/NovumJus.2022.16.2.13.

140. Kaine, S., (2020). Australian industrial relations and COVID-19 [article]. *Journal of Australian Political Economy,* (85), 130–137. <Go to ISI>://WOS:000593122800017.
141. Katsabian, T., (2021). Collective action in the digital reality: The case of platform-based workers [article]. *Modern Law Review, 84*(5), 1005–1040. https://doi.org/10.1111/1468-2230.12635.
142. Kilic, S., (2021). Does COVID-19 as a long wave turning point mean the end of neoliberalism? [article]. *Critical Sociology, 47*(4, 5), 609–623, Article 0896920520980083. https://doi.org/10.1177/0896920520980083.
143. Kolling, A., & Schnabel, C., (2022). Owners, external managers, and industrial relations in German establishments [article]. *British Journal of Industrial Relations, 60*(2), 424–443. https://doi.org/10.1111/bjir.12623.
144. Kowalewska, E. T., (2020). Between civic and legal constitutionalism: Dynamics of Poland's constitution-making projects of the 1990s [article]. *Onati Socio-Legal Series, 10*(4), 903–931. https://doi.org/10.35295/osls.Iisl/0000-0000-0000-1142.
145. Kupec, V., Svec, M., & Madlenak, A., (2022). European model of personal data protection (GDPR) in the practice of employee representatives with regard to the communication process [article]. *Ad Alta-Journal of Interdisciplinary Research, 12*(2), 152–157. <Go to ISI>://WOS:000921624200025.
146. Lamare, J. R., & Budd, J. W., (2022). The relative importance of industrial relations ideas in politics: A quantitative analysis of political party manifestos across 54 countries [article]. *Industrial Relations, 61*(1), 22–49. https://doi.org/10.1111/irel.12296.
147. Lansbury, R. D., (2021). Workplace reform: A new social contract for Australia [article]. *Asia Pacific Journal of Human Resources, 59*(4), 541–553. https://doi.org/10.1111/1744-7941.12287.
148. Larsson, B., (2020). Cultural obstacles in transnational trade union cooperation in Europe [article]. *Nordic Journal of Working Life Studies, 10*(1), 3–18. <Go to ISI>://WOS:000539959800002.
149. Lawreniuk, S., (2023). Zombie resistance: Reanimated labor struggles and the legal geographies of authoritarian neoliberalism in Cambodia

[article]. *Transactions of the Institute of British Geographers, 48*(1), 39–55. https://doi.org/10.1111/tran.12564.

150. Lee, T. L., & Tapia, M., (2021). Confronting race and other social identity erasures: The case for critical industrial relations theory [article]. *ILR Review, 74*(3), 637–662, Article 0019793921992080. https://doi.org/10.1177/0019793921992080.
151. Leggett, C., (2019). Industrial relations in Australia and the concept of fairness [article]. *E-Journal of International and Comparative Labor Studies, 8*(2), 1–3. <Go to ISI>://WOS:000473781000001.
152. Ligthart, P. E. M., Poutsma, E., & Brewster, C., (2022). The development of financial participation in Europe [article]. *British Journal of Industrial Relations, 60*(3), 479–510. https://doi.org/10.1111/bjir.12629.
153. Liu, H. Y., (2023). The role of the state in influencing work conditions in China's internet industry: Policy, evidence, and implications for industrial relations [article]. *Journal of Industrial Relations, 65*(1), 3–21, Article 00221856211068488. https://doi.org/10.1177/00221856211068488.
154. Lize, W., Greer, I., & Umney, C., (2022). Artistic work intermediaries as industrial relations institutions: The case of musicians [article]. *Economic and Industrial Democracy, 43*(2), 793–809, Article 0143831x20945789. https://doi.org/10.1177/0143831x20945789.
155. Lloyd, C., & Payne, J., (2021). Hard times in latte land? Analyzing pay and working time in the cafe industry in France, Norway, and the UK [article]. *Economic and Industrial Democracy, 42*(3), 805–827. https://doi.org/10.1177/0143831x18809887.
156. Lukacova, K., Kovacova, L., & Kahanec, M., (2022). Industrial relations and unemployment benefit schemes in the Visegrad countries during the COVID-19 pandemic [article]. *Transfer-European Review of Labor and Research, 28*(2), 229–246. https://doi.org/10.1177/10242589221099804.
157. Lyddon, D., (2021). Strike ballots under the 2016 trade union act: Unions mobilize to counter the latest legal onslaught [article]. *Industrial Relations Journal, 52*(6), 479–501. https://doi.org/10.1111/irj.12349.
158. Lyutov, N. L., (2022). Defining the employment discrimination: International labor standards and the Russian approach Br [article]. *Vestnik of Saint Petersburg University-Law-Vestnik Sankt-Peterburgskogo Universiteta-Pravo, 13*(4), 1041–1057. https://doi.org/10.21638/spbu14.2022.413.

159. MacKenzie, R., & Lucio, M. M., (2019). Regulation, migration, and the implications for industrial relations [article]. *Journal of Industrial Relations, 61*(2), 176–197. https://doi.org/10.1177/0022185618814280.

160. Madimutsa, C. Industrial relations, social dialogue, and pacification of public sector unions in Zambia: Rethinking trade union strategies [article; early access]. *Journal of Asian and African Studies,* 17, Article 00219096221090640. https://doi.org/10.1177/00219096221090640.

161. Mahas-Demydas, Y., & Rudnytska, O., (2019). Legal status of the trade unions in the Russian Empire In 1905–1917 [article]. *Skhidnoievropeiskyi Istorychnyi Visnyk-East European Historical Bulletin,* (12), 64–73. https://doi.org/10.24919/2519-058x.12.177554.

162. Mahmood, Z., & Banerjee, S., (2020). The state in industrial relations: Neoliberal intervention or intervening in neoliberalism? [article]. *Indian Journal of Labor Economics, 63*(3), 575–596. https://doi.org/10.1007/s41027-020-00233-6.

163. Mailand, M., (2019). Proactive employers and teachers' working time regulation: Public sector industrial conflicts in Denmark and Norway [article]. *Economic and Industrial Democracy, 40*(3), 682–699. https://doi.org/10.1177/0143831x16657414.

164. Markey, R., (2020). The impact of the COVID-19 virus on industrial relations [article]. *Journal of Australian Political Economy,* (85), 147–154. <Go to ISI>://WOS:000593122800019.

165. Martin, C. J., (2022). Fiction works cultural ideas and the design of industrial relations systems in Britain and Denmark [article]. *Industrial Relations, 61*(1), 50–67. https://doi.org/10.1111/irel.12289.

166. Martin, C. J., Nijhuis, D. O., & Olsson, E., (2021). Cultural images of labor conflict and coordination literature and the evolution of industrial relations systems [article]. *Archives Europeennes De Sociologie, 62*(3), 381–419, Article Pii s0003975621000187. https://doi.org/10.1017/s0003975621000187.

167. McCrystal, S., & Hardy, T., (2021). Filling the void? A critical analysis of competition regulation of collective bargaining amongst non-employees [article]. *International Journal of Comparative Labor Law and Industrial Relations, 37*(4), 355–384. <Go to ISI>://WOS:000755040600002.

168. Mezihorak, P., Murgia, A., Borghi, P., & Mondon-Navazo, M. Representing solo self-employed workers: The strengthening of relations

between traditional and new collective actors in industrial relations [article; early access]. *Work Employment and Society,* 19, Article 09500170211061227. https://doi.org/10.1177/09500170211061227.

169. Morritt, B. T., (2022). Systems of male privilege: The industrial relations policies of the Ford Motor company in the 1940s [article]. *Enterprise & Society, 23*(4), 1019–1046, Article Pii s1467222721000082. https://doi.org/10.1017/eso.2021.8.
170. Murphy, C., & Turner, T., (2020). Tipping the scales for labor in Ireland? Collective bargaining and the industrial relations (amendment) Act 2015 [article]. *Industrial Law Journal, 49*(1), 113–134. https://doi.org/10.1093/indlaw/dwz019.
171. Nespoli, F., (2019). When labor goes populist: How Italian populist leaders framed the labor market and industrial relations on social media [article]. *E-Journal of International and Comparative Labor Studies, 8*(2), 4-+. <Go to ISI>://WOS:000473781000002.
172. Newman, A., Cooper, B., Holland, P., Miao, Q., & Teicher, J., (2019). How do industrial relations climate and union instrumentality enhance employee performance? The mediating effects of perceived job security and trust in management [article]. *Human Resource Management, 58*(1), 35–44. https://doi.org/10.1002/hrm.21921.
173. Nga, L. T. T., & Nga, H. T., (2021). Law on the role of grassroot unions in implementation of social responsibilities at enterprises in the era of integration in Vietnam [article]. *Journal of Law and Political Sciences, 31*, 75–92. <Go to ISI>://WOS:000729099300004.
174. Ngai, P., (2020). Reflecting on Hong Kong protests in 2019–2020 [article]. *Hau-Journal of Ethnographic Theory, 10*(2), 333–338. https://doi.org/10.1086/709529.
175. Nicklich, M., & Helfen, M., (2019). Trade union renewal and 'organizing from below' in Germany: Institutional constraints, strategic dilemmas, and organizational tensions [article]. *European Journal of Industrial Relations, 25*(1), 57–73. https://doi.org/10.1177/0959680117752000.
176. Novitz, T., & Andrijasevic, R., (2020). Reform of the posting of workers regime – an assessment of the practical impact on unfree labor relations [article]. *JCMS-Journal of Common Market Studies, 58*(5), 1325–1341. https://doi.org/10.1111/jcms.13033.
177. Nowak, J., (2021). From industrial relations research to global labor studies: Moving labor research beyond eurocentrism [article].

Globalizations, 18(8), 1335–1348. https://doi.org/10.1080/14747731.2021.1874210.

178. Nurlinah, Haryanto, Sukri, & Sunardi, (2021). Informal politics and local labor activism in Indonesia [article]. *Critical Asian Studies, 53*(4), 561–581. https://doi.org/10.1080/14672715.2021.1965896.
179. O'Keeffe, P., & Papadopoulos, A., (2021). The Australian government's business-friendly employment response to COVID-19: A critical discourse analysis [article]. *Economic and Labor Relations Review, 32*(3), 453–471, Article 1035304621997891. https://doi.org/10.1177/1035304621997891.
180. Oberfichtner, M., Schnabel, C., & Topfer, M., (2020). Do unions and works councils really dampen the gender pay gap? Discordant evidence from Germany [article]. *Economics Letters, 196*, 4, Article 109509. https://doi.org/10.1016/j.econlet.2020.109509.
181. Opute, J., & Koch, K., (2020). Labor involvement as a participatory mechanism in developing economies: Contrasting the European model [article]. *E-Journal of International and Comparative Labor Studies, 9*(1), 52–74. <Go to ISI>://WOS:000577415200004.
182. Ormaetxea, E. T., (2019). The role of the trade union within the framework of company restructuring processes: Current legislation and lex ferenda proposals [article]. *Onati Socio-Legal Series, 9*(1), 70–95. https://doi.org/10.35295/osls.iisl/0000-0000-0000-1013.
183. Ozkiziltan, D., (2019). Authoritarian neoliberalism in AKP's Turkey: An industrial relations perspective [article]. *Industrial Relations Journal, 50*(3), 218–239. https://doi.org/10.1111/irj.12248.
184. Ozkiziltan, D., (2020). Protection of capitalism as a regime of rationality: A historical institutionalist rereading of modern Turkey's industrial relations [article]. *Journal of Development Studies, 56*(4), 732–747. https://doi.org/10.1080/00220388.2019.1590552.
185. Peetz, D., (2021). Is industrial relations reform the road to recovery in monopsonistic labor markets? [article]. *Economic and Labor Relations Review, 32*(3), 417–436, Article 10353046211015786. https://doi.org/10.1177/10353046211015786.
186. Peetz, D., Colley, L., & Nolan, R., (2020). The shock doctrine and industrial relations [article]. *Journal of Australian Political Economy,* (85), 138–146. <Go to ISI>://WOS:000593122800018.
187. Peruzzo, F., Grimaldi, E., Arienzo, A., D'Onofrio, G., Franchi, C.,

& Sebastianelli, P. New public management reforms and industrial relations in the Italian education system. A cultural political economy approach [article; early access]. *Journal of Educational Administration and History,* 19. https://doi.org/10.1080/00220620.2022.2094350.

188. Pitteloud, S., (2022). 'American management' vs 'Swiss labor peace.' The closure of the Swiss firestone factory in 1978 [article]. *Business History, 64*(9), 1648–1665. https://doi.org/10.1080/00076791.2020.1726890.
189. Preminger, J., & Bondy, A. S. Conflicting imperatives? Ethnonationalism and neoliberalism in industrial relations [article; early access]. *ILR Review,* 28. https://doi.org/10.1177/00197939221145117.
190. Quinlan, M., & Maxwell-Stewart, H. Inequality, worker mobilization and lessons from history: Australia 1788–1900 [article; early access]. *Labor & Industry-a Journal of the Social and Economic Relations of Work,* 24. https://doi.org/10.1080/10301763.2022.2088648.
191. Radzi, M., Bidin, A., Musa, M. K., & Hamid, N. A., (2022). Protecting gig workers' interests in Malaysia through registered association under societies act 1966 [article]. *IIUM Law Journal, 30*, 157–179. <Go to ISI>://WOS:000783349600006.
192. Ramsay, I., & Webster, M., (2019). The origins and evolution of the statutory duties of trade union officers [article]. *Australian Business Law Review, 47*(1), 23–39. <Go to ISI>://WOS:000471777900003.
193. Ravn, J. E., & Oyum, L., (2020). Towards 'multi-collar' unionism: Cases of trespassing professionals in Norwegian industrial relations [article]. *Economic and Industrial Democracy, 41*(4), 887–909. https://doi.org/10.1177/0143831x17743794.
194. Razak, S. S. A., Mahmod, N., Yee, L. S., & Kian, T. S., (2022). Integrating corporate social responsibility in reforming trade union recognition process [article]. *Asian Academy of Management Journal, 27*(1), 237–252. https://doi.org/10.21315/aamj2022.27.1.10.
195. Refslund, B., & Arnholtz, J., (2022). Power resource theory revisited: The perils and promises for understanding contemporary labor politics [article]. *Economic and Industrial Democracy, 43*(4), 1958–1979, Article 0143831x211053379. https://doi.org/10.1177/0143831x211053379.
196. Ritson, N. H., (2019a). An American oil multinational in the UK: Its formal review of industrial relations strategy [review]. *Labor History, 60*(3), 235–249. https://doi.org/10.1080/0023656x.2019.1537021.

197. Ritson, N. H., (2019b). Productivity, craftwork, and flexibility: The Mobil agreements [article]. *Labor History, 60*(6), 666–684. https://doi.org/10.1080/0023656x.2019.1626816.

198. Riva, E., & Rizza, R., (2021). Who receives occupational welfare? The importance of skills across Europe's diverse industrial relations regimes [article]. *Transfer-European Review of Labor and Research, 27*(1), 97–112, Article 1024258920980635. https://doi.org/10.1177/1024258920980635.

199. Roche, W. K. How effective is private dispute resolution? Evidence from Ireland [article; early access]. *Industrial Law Journal,* 38. https://doi.org/10.1093/indlaw/dwac018.

200. Roche, W. K., & Gormley, T., (2020). The durability of coordinated bargaining: Crisis, recovery, and pay fixing in Ireland [article]. *Economic and Industrial Democracy, 41*(2), 481–505. https://doi.org/10.1177/0143831x17718067.

201. Rosetti, N., (2019). Do European trade unions foster social solidarity? Evidence from multilevel data in 18 countries [article]. *Industrial Relations Journal, 50*(1), 84–101. https://doi.org/10.1111/irj.12242.

202. Roy, G. K., & Dubey, A., (2022). A note on industrial relations code, 2020 [article]. *Indian Journal of Labor Economics, 65*(2), 533–543. https://doi.org/10.1007/s41027-022-00368-8.

203. Roy, N. C., (2022). Factors influencing industrial relations in the Indian tea industry: Study in the Darjeeling, Terai, and Dooars regions [article]. *International Journal of Indian Culture and Business Management, 25*(1), 72–85. https://doi.org/10.1504/ijicbm.2022.120920.

204. Roychowdhury, A., (2019). Application of job security laws, workers' bargaining power and employment outcomes in India [article]. *Economic and Labor Relations Review, 30*(1), 120–141. https://doi.org/10.1177/1035304619831245.

205. Rubery, J., Grimshaw, D., Mehaut, P., & Weinkopf, C. Dualization and part-time work in France, Germany, and the UK: Accounting for within and between country differences in precarious work [article; early access]. *European Journal of Industrial Relations,* 19. https://doi.org/10.1177/09596801221120468.

206. Sakharuk, I., (2021). The protection of the worker's right to freedom of association: The ECtHR case-law [article]. *Access to Justice in Eastern Europe,* (1), 166–185. https://doi.org/10.33327/AJEE-18-4.1-a000051.

207. Sanchez-Mosquera, M., (2022). Somewhat more than path dependence: The Spanish employers' peak organization and social dialogue in light of the crisis of the industrial relations system [article]. *Economic and Industrial Democracy, 43*(4), 1655–1675, Article 0143831x211024717. https://doi.org/10.1177/0143831x211024717.

208. Sanz, P., Welz, C., Caprile, M., & Contreras, R. R., (2020). Industrial democracy in Europe: A quantitative approach [article]. *Labor & Industry-a Journal of the Social and Economic Relations of Work, 30*(2), 101–132. https://doi.org/10.1080/10301763.2020.1774101.

209. Schlachter, M., (2019). Trade union representation for new forms of employment [article]. *European Labor Law Journal, 10*(3), 229–239. https://doi.org/10.1177/2031952519870018.

210. Schmidt, W., & Muller, A., (2021). Workplace universalism and the integration of migrant workers and refugees in Germany [article]. *Industrial Relations Journal, 52*(2), 145–160. https://doi.org/10.1111/irj.12320.

211. Schofield-Georgeson, E., & Rawling, M., (2020). Industrial legislation in Australia in 2019 [article]. *Journal of Industrial Relations, 62*(3), 425–445, Article 0022185620911682. https://doi.org/10.1177/0022185620911682.

212. Schofield-Georgeson, E., (2022). The emergence of coercive federal Australian labor law, 1901–2020 [article]. *Journal of Industrial Relations, 64*(1), 52–76, Article 00221856211003921. https://doi.org/10.1177/00221856211003921.

213. Schuessler, E., Frenkel, S. J., & Wright, C. F., (2019). Governance of labor standards in Australian and German garment supply chains: The impact of rana plaza [article]. *ILR Review, 72*(3), 552–579. https://doi.org/10.1177/0019793918771360.

214. Schuhrke, J., (2019). "Comradely brainwashing": International development, labor education, and industrial relations in the cold war [article]. *Labor-Studies in Working-Class History of the Americas, 16*(3), 39–67. https://doi.org/10.1215/15476715-7569788.

215. Scrimger, P. J., (2020). Unions, industrial relations, and market income inequality in Canada's provinces [article]. *Relations Industrielles-Industrial Relations, 75*(2), 321–350. <Go to ISI>://WOS:000538776900006.

216. Seghezzi, F. Negotiation of psycho-social risks of remote working.

An enterprise-level comparison in Italy and France [article; early access]. *European Journal of Industrial Relations,* 18. https://doi.org/10.1177/09596801221122998.

217. Sheldon, P., & Thornthwaite, L., (2020). Employer and employer association matters in Australia in 2019 [article]. *Journal of Industrial Relations, 62*(3), 403–424, Article 0022185620908908. https://doi.org/10.1177/0022185620908908.
218. Smith, P., (2019). Rookes v. Barnard and the trade union question in British politics [article]. *Industrial Relations Journal, 50*(5, 6), 431–449. https://doi.org/10.1111/irj.12269.
219. Solaiman, B. Lobbying in the UK: Towards robust regulation [article; early access]. *Parliamentary Affairs,* 28. https://doi.org/10.1093/pa/gsab051.
220. Stanev, S., (2019). The right not to join a trade union in the case law of the ECtHR [article]. *E-Journal of International and Comparative Labor Studies, 8*(2), 47–51. <Go to ISI>://WOS:000473781000003.
221. Stanford, J., (2021). International approaches to solving the 'free rider' problem in industrial relations [article]. *Labor & Industry-a Journal of the Social and Economic Relations of Work, 31*(3), 278–300. https://doi.org/10.1080/10301763.2021.1987052.
222. Stapley, L., (2021). Organizational creativity-birth of a journal [article]. *Organizational and Social Dynamics, 21*(1), 1–10. <Go to ISI>://WOS:000685217700002.
223. Stevis, D., (2022). Towards a relational environmental labor studies [review]. *Journal of Industrial Relations, 64*(4), 608–619. https://doi.org/10.1177/00221856221112828.
224. Svec, M., Madlenak, A., Bezakova, Z., & Horecky, J., (2021). Possibilities and limitations of communication of special purpose civic associations – the case of internal communication of a trade union active in a company influenced by the groundswell concept [article]. *Communication Today, 12*(2), 32–44. <Go to ISI>://WOS:000728762000004.
225. Tavora, I., (2019). Collective bargaining in Portugal in the aftermath of the crisis: Trends and prospects [article]. *Industrial Relations Journal, 50*(5, 6), 548–563. https://doi.org/10.1111/irj.12273.
226. Teipen, C., & Mehl, F., (2021). Global value chains and industrial relations in the global south: Social upgrading paths in different

industries [article]. *Journal of Labor and Society, 24*(1), 214–236. https://doi.org/10.1163/24714607-20212008.

227. Tesser, C. D., & Serapioni, M., (2021). Obstacles to SUS universalization: Tax expenditures, labor union demands and health insurance state subsidy [article]. *Ciencia & Saude Coletiva, 26*(6), 2323–2333. https://doi.org/10.1590/1413-81232021266.22602019.
228. Thomas, H., & Turnbull, P., (2021). From a 'moral commentator' to a 'determined actor'? How the international labor organization (ILO) orchestrates the field of international industrial relations [article]. *British Journal of Industrial Relations, 59*(3), 874–898. https://doi.org/10.1111/bjir.12578.
229. Thornthwaite, L., & Sheldon, P., (2019). Employer and employer association matters in Australia in 2018 [article]. *Journal of Industrial Relations, 61*(3), 382–401. https://doi.org/10.1177/0022185619834323.
230. Thornthwaite, L., & Sheldon, P., (2021). Employer and employer association matters in Australia in 2020 [article]. *Journal of Industrial Relations, 63*(3), 357–376, Article 00221856211000406. https://doi.org/10.1177/00221856211000406.
231. Tiraboschi, M., (2020). The COVID-19 emergency from an 'industrial relations law' perspective. Some critical notes on the Italian case [article]. *E-Journal of International and Comparative Labor Studies, 9*(3), 41–56. <Go to ISI>://WOS:000661877700003.
232. Tomassetti, P. Energy transition: A labor law retrospective [article; early access]. *Industrial Law Journal,* 34. https://doi.org/10.1093/indlaw/dwac008.
233. Tomassetti, P., (2021). Just transition and industrial relations: The Italian patterns [article]. *E-Journal of International and Comparative Labor Studies, 10*(1), 52–65. <Go to ISI>://WOS:000672668800005.
234. Trif, A., & Szabo, I. G. Where to find power resources under a hostile government? The prospects for trade union revitalization after the loss of institutional resources in Hungary and Romania [article; early access]. *European Journal of Industrial Relations,* 18. https://doi.org/10.1177/09596801221136959.
235. Truyols, M. S., (2019). Coordination vs regulation. State's functions in industrial relations: The cases of Norway and Spain [article]. *Onati Socio-Legal Series, 9*(1), 128–144. https://doi.org/10.35295/osls.iisl/0000-0000-0000-1016.

236. Tu, Y. Q., Liu, R. X., & Li, H. Z., (2022). The development of digital economy and the future of the trade union law of the people's republic of China [article]. *Journal of Chinese Human Resources Management, 13*(2), 76–85. https://doi.org/10.47297/wspchrmWSP2040–800507.20221302.
237. Velluti, S., (2022). The European social dialogue as a source of EU legal acts following EPSU: Collective bargaining and industrial relations get lost in translation [article]. *Common Market Law Review, 59*(3), 871–888. <Go to ISI>://WOS:000814075700009.
238. Vinichenko, M. V., Klementyev, D. S., Rybakova, M. V., Malyshev, M. A., & Malysheva, N. S., (2020). Mechanisms for protecting the labor rights of employees in the system of social partnership [article]. *Revista Inclusiones, 7*, 1-+. <Go to ISI>://WOS:000583771900001.
239. Vulkan, P., & Larsson, B., (2019). Patterns of transnational trade union cooperation in Europe: The effect of regimes, sectors, and resources [article]. *European Journal of Industrial Relations, 25*(2), 147–162. https://doi.org/10.1177/0959680118783551.
240. Walker, M., (2020). Successful social media resistance: Implications for employee voice [article]. *Labor & Industry-a Journal of the Social and Economic Relations of Work, 30*(2), 174–184. https://doi.org/10.1080/10301763.2020.1772701.
241. Walters, D., & Wadsworth, E., (2020). Participation in safety and health in European workplaces: Framing the capture of representation [article]. *European Journal of Industrial Relations, 26*(1), 75–90. https://doi.org/10.1177/0959680119835670.
242. Warner, S., (2019). (Re)politicizing 'the governmental': Resisting the industrial relations act 1971 [article]. *British Journal of Politics & International Relations, 21*(3), 541–558. https://doi.org/10.1177/1369148119845336.
243. William, L., & Cunningham, I., (2021). Evaluating the role of trade unions and civil society organizations in supporting graduate educated disabled workers [article]. *Economic and Industrial Democracy, 42*(3), 648–666. https://doi.org/10.1177/0143831x18799899.
244. Williamson, S., Foley, M., & Cartwright, N., (2019). Women, work, and industrial relations in Australia in 2018 [article]. *Journal of Industrial Relations, 61*(3), 342–356. https://doi.org/10.1177/0022185619834051.

245. Wright, C. F. Addressing problems for labor not problems of labor: The need for a paradigm shift in work and industrial relations policy [article; early access]. *Labor & Industry-a Journal of the Social and Economic Relations of Work,* 11. https://doi.org/10.1080/10301763.2022.2051230.

246. Wright, C. F., & McLaughlin, C., (2021). Trade union legitimacy and legitimation politics in Australia and New Zealand [article]. *Industrial Relations, 60*(3), 338–369. https://doi.org/10.1111/irel.12285.

247. Xie, P. X., & Zhou, L., (2022). Keeping dispute resolution internal: Exploring the role of the industrial relations climate, organizational embeddedness, and organizational turbulence [article]. *Economic and Industrial Democracy, 43*(2), 898–917, Article 0143831x20959713. https://doi.org/10.1177/0143831x20959713.

248. Yan, D., (2019). Unveiling the legal effect of collective agreements in China [article]. *Employee Relations, 42*(2), 366–380. https://doi.org/10.1108/er-06-2019-0238.

249. Yang, L. Q., Zhang, Q., Gong, H., & Cheng, Y. Y. Cross-level effects of union practices on extra-role behaviors: The mediating role of industrial relations climate, union commitment and union instrumentality [article; early access]. *International Journal of Manpower,* 19. https://doi.org/10.1108/ijm-10-2020-0467.

250. Zbyszewska, A., (2021). Working with and around voluntarism: Union engagement with environmental sustainability in the UK [article]. *E-Journal of International and Comparative Labor Studies, 10*(1), 66–80. <Go to ISI>://WOS:000672668800006.

INDEX

D

E